INTRODUCTION

TO THE

DEVOUT LIFE

INTRODUCTION
TO THE
DEVOUT LIFE

ST. FRANCIS DE SALES

TRANSLATED, WITH AN

INTRODUCTION AND NOTES,

BY JOHN K. RYAN

IMAGE

New York

Copyright © 1950, 1952, 1966 by John K. Ryan
Study Guide copyright © 2014 by Image Books,
an imprint of the Crown Publishing Group,
a division of Random House LLC

Originally published in different form in the United States
by Harper & Row, New York, in 1950.

The Library of Congress has cataloged the 1972 Image Books edition
as follows:

Francis de Sales, 1567–1622.
[Introduction á la vie dévote.   English]
Introduction to the devout life / translated, with an introduction and
notes, by John K. Ryan.
p.   cm.
Translation of: Introduction á la vie dévote.
Reprint. Originally published: New York: Harper & Row, 1966.
1. Meditations—Early works to 1800.   I. Ryan, John Kenneth,
1897–   . II. Title.
BX2179.F8I49   1989
248.4'82—dc20   89-29043
                                                              CIP

ISBN 978-0-385-03009-0

PRINTED IN THE UNITED STATES OF AMERICA

Cover illustration by Darren Booth
Cover design by Jessie Sayward Bright

44 43 42 41 40 39 38

CONTENTS

TRANSLATOR'S
INTRODUCTION

When Claude de Granier, bishop of Geneva
but with residence at Annecy in Savoy,
requested the Holy See for a coadjutor in
1599, he submitted the name of one of his
own priests, Francis de Sales, as his personal
choice for the position. Although at that time
he was only thirty-one years old, Francis de
Sales was already known in Rome. Two years
before, he had gone from Annecy to Geneva
at the request of Pope Clement VIII to
attempt the conversion of Théodore de Bèze,
Calvin's associate and biographer, who was
then in his seventy-eighth year and the last
survivor among the chief reformers.[1] As a
result of Bishop Granier's recommendation,
Pope Clement VIII called Francis de Sales
down to Rome for a personal interview and
before an assembly of Cardinals, with St.
Robert Bellarmine and Caesar Baronius

among those present, the pope questioned the future bishop. At the end of the examination he said to him: "Drink, my son, from your well-springs and from your living sources. May these waters issue forth so that everyone may drink his fill from them."[2]

It is not solely in the deeds that Francis de Sales performed during the remaining twenty-three years of his life or in his character as a canonized saint, nor only in the religious communities that he has inspired, that the hope and prophecy in the pope's words have been fulfilled. The writings that St. Francis left behind him—the treatise *On the Love of God*,[3] the *Controversies*, *Defense of the Standard of the Holy Cross*, sermons, letters,[4] various minor works, and the *Introduction to the Devout Life*—have been wellsprings from which countless men and women have drawn light and strength. This has been particularly true of the *Introduction to the Devout Life*. Great saints as well as lesser souls have learned from this book:

> *Hither as to their fountain other stars*
> *Repairing, in their golden urns draw light.*[5]

All of St. Francis de Sales' writings were produced to answer needs and demands that arose in the course of his life's work and all are illustrative of his singleness of purpose in doing the work for which God had destined him. Certain of his shorter works are pamphlets written to explain Catholic doctrine and answer objections to it. When he was attacked in writing for raising a cross on the highway leading from Annecy to Geneva, he answered by writing the *Defense of the Standard of the Holy Cross*. When those who sought his advice could not confer with him in person, he wrote letters to them. From such situations his most famous book emerged.

The direction of souls was always a principal activity in the life of St. Francis de Sales as a priest and bishop. He was ready at all times to spend himself in hearing confessions, giving personal instructions, preaching sermons, and writing letters, and it was out of such concern for the advancement and perfection of individual souls that the *Introduction* grew. It is true that his friend King Henry IV of France encouraged and urged on the saint in his work of instructing the people in their religion, but the king did not inspire or originate his plan to write the *Introduction to the Devout Life*, as is sometimes stated. Its beginnings are found rather in the letters on spiritual subjects written to such friends as Mme. de Chantal, the Abbess Rose Bourgeois, and his own sister, Mme. Brulart. But it is especially in the character and needs of another of his penitents, Mme. de Charmoisy, that the *Introduction* has its source.

Marie du Chastel, a maid of honor in the household of Catherine of Cleves, dowager Duchess of Guise, had married in 1600 at Paris a relative of Francis de Sales, Claude de Charmoisy, ambassador of the Duke of Savoy to the republic of Berne. After her marriage Mme. de Charmoisy resided in Savoy and, because of a lawsuit, found it necessary to spend the early part of 1607 in Annecy. It was at this time that her spiritual direction was undertaken by the saint, who continued his instructions by letter. Mme. de Charmoisy herself has left an account of the origin of the *Introduction*.

At the beginning, when I placed my soul in the hands of the said Servant of God, occasion arose for my return to court. As I was greatly apprehensive of this, I went to confer with the said Servant of God, declaring to him my apprehensions. He then said to me: "Have courage, my child; do not fear that on this account you will fall back. For if you are faithful to God, he will never fail you; even though he has to stop the sun and the moon, he will give you enough time to perform your exercises and all else that you must do." For this reason he determined to give me some instructions in writing upon this subject, and these I communicated to a Jesuit father, who found them so excellent and useful that he urged the blessed Servant of God to have them printed. This was the reason why he composed the *Introduction to the Devout Life*, into which book he inserted them.[6]

In a letter preserved at Annecy, St. Francis de Sales himself identifies the religious to whom Mme. de Charmoisy showed his letters. He was Père Jean Fourier, or Forier, a member of the Society of Jesus.

> She showed it to the Reverend Father Forier, then rector of the College of Chambéry, and now that at Avignon, whom she knew to be my great friend and to whom moreover I often rendered an account of my deeds. It was he who urged me so strongly to publish these writings that after I had hastily reviewed them and made some little adjustments, I sent them to the printer.[7]

St. Francis worked on the *Introduction* during 1607 and 1608 and gave it to the printer in August, 1608. As the "privilege du roy" is dated November 10, 1608, the earliest the book could have appeared is the end of the year 1608. However, the first edition bears the date 1609 on its title page, which reads:

> *Introduction A La Vie Devote, Par François de Sales, Evesque & Prelat de Geneve.* A Lyon, Chez Pierre Rigaud, en ruë Merciere au coing de ruë Ferrandiere, à l'Horloge. MDCIX. Avec approbation des Docteurs, & Privilege du Roy.

A second edition "en laquelle le tout a este reveu, corrigé et augmenté par l'Auteur," was called for in 1609, and a third in 1610. However, this second edition was defective, as St. Francis states in his foreword to the third. He had added new material to his book, but unfortunately three chapters that were in the original edition were inadvertently left out of the second. These were chapters 23, 28, and 29 in the second part of the first edition, which are chapters 25, 26, and 27 in the definitive edition. The popularity of the work is further seen in the fact that there were three printings of the second edition and many printings both of the third and of the fourth editions, which appeared in 1616. Moreover, unauthorized editions were put out. Of these the following are known: Douai, Bath. Bellere, 1610, 1611, and 1616; Bordeaux, Millange, 1613; and Paris, Thomas de le Ruelle, 1615.

Always a careful writer, St. Francis found time to revise an Italian version of his book and also to give the French original a thorough revision. He was disturbed by the typographical errors in the earlier editions, some, he said, chargeable to himself and some to the printer, and wished to leave behind him as accurate a copy of his work as he could. This final revision was made in Paris, where he spent the months from November, 1618 to September, 1619 as a member of an embassy sent from the court of Savoy to that of France. The title page of this last edition to pass through the author's hands reads:

Introduction à la Vie Devote par François de Sales, Evesque de Geneve. Derniere Edition, reveue, corrigée et augmentée par l'Autheur, durant ses Predications à Paris. A Paris, chez Joseph Cottereau, rüe sainct Jacques à la Prudence. M.DC.XIX. Avec Approbation des Docteurs.

It is this edition that serves as the text for the critical edition put forth by Dom B. Mackey and published in the third volume of the Annecy edition of the works of St. Francis de Sales.

When the *Introduction to the Devout Life* first appeared, it was recognized as a masterpiece of mystical and devotional literature, and for more than three and a half centuries there has been no dissent from this judgment. Its greatness lies in many things: in its originality, its completeness, its sincerity, its balance, its penetration, and its style. It is one of those rare productions of human genius which are completely successful in what they wish to do. As such it is beyond adverse criticism in any important way.

The originality of the *Introduction* lies not so much in its particular parts as in its entire conception. Perhaps it is true, as St. Francis says in his preface, that he does not say anything not already said by devotional writers, although he may be said to err in the way of modesty. But the principles and applications that are scattered throughout earlier authors are collected and systematized and synthesized in his work. It is because St. Francis de Sales saw the lack of a work such as his *Introduction* that he wrote it. That it is systematic and complete as well as original is seen by an examination of the table of contents.

The greatness of this work is shown in what may be called the symmetry of the saint's thought. Throughout the work delicate balance and just proportions are everywhere preserved. St. Francis avoids the extremes that lead to danger or are themselves dangerous. His purpose is to arouse in his reader a complete love of God and an absolute confidence in him. This life of devotion is as open to soldiers, shopkeepers, courtiers, statesmen and men of affairs, and women in their homes as it is to solitaries in the desert and nuns in their cells. To the diversity of men and women he presents ways and means to attain holiness of life that are perfectly adapted to their varying conditions of life. What he urges upon all men and women is hatred of sin, detachment from the things of the world, love of God, and constancy in prayer to him.

In the *Introduction* St. Francis de Sales gives one of the clearest statements in religious literature of the theory and practice of the purgative way, the illuminative way, and the unitive way, the three levels of thought and conduct that are required for a completely moral and religious life. To live such a life there must be first of all a catharsis, a cleansing of the soul from serious sin if it be found there. The man who has fallen into mortal sin and is unrepentant—who is guilty, say, of grave offenses against justice and charity or addicted to such sins as "cry to heaven for vengeance,"[8] or who has apostasized from the faith or does not fulfill its strict obligations—such a man lacks sanctifying grace and has suffered spiritual death. For him the first step toward the devout life must be on this road of purgation and it consists in genuine repentance for those grave sins and a firm purpose of amendment. There is a second purgation, one of all affection for such sins, and the cleansing process goes on to venial sins, that is, slight offenses against God, and to evil inclinations. St. Francis describes this complete catharsis and persuades the reader of its necessity. Then he proceeds to show him the means to achieve it in a series of ten carefully thought out meditations, along with advice as to the need of a prudent spiritual director, instructions on how to make a general confession, and finally a powerful set of resolutions to be made after the general confession. St. Francis helps the reader to see himself for what he is, for what he ought to be, and for what he can be if he cooperates with the grace that God will give to him.

Discussion of the purgative way makes up the first part of the *Introduction* and the remaining parts of the work are concerned chiefly with the illuminative and unitive ways. Everything in the ninety-five chapters in these four parts is designed to enlighten the soul as to moral and spiritual realities and to bring it into closer union with God. Only mortal sin—by which the whole man sins, as has been said,[9] and by which he therefore wholly rejects God and his grace and mercy—can keep a soul from God. But for souls that are free from mortal sin, truly friends with God, and sharers in his divine life of charity, there are varying degrees of knowledge and love. In order to aid its readers to grow in knowledge of God and his purposes and to choose more freely and fully what God wills, the *Introduction* tells us of the nature, kinds, and necessity of prayer, examination of conscience, assistance at holy Mass and participation in spiritual exercises, hearing and reading the word of God, sacramental confession, and holy Communion. Counsels are given for the practice of the various virtues, especially those required for our particular state of life, and on how to recognize and meet temptations that inevitably come because of our character and duties. As he tells us of such things we realize how St. Francis himself is filled with love of God and of his fellow men. It may be seen as well that he is always guided by the truest kind of prudence, for he is a realist and knows how easy it is for us to forget the joy and ardor of the first days of our spiritual life, to let our resolutions fade from memory, and to give up our devout practices. Hence he calls for an annual renewal of our initial resolutions, shows us how to examine our state of soul toward God, ourselves, and our neighbor, and gives reasons for this renewal and for perseverance in good works.

Like other great spiritual writers and like all the teaching and practice of the Church, St. Francis shows us that the three ways are not completely separate stages on life's highway. It is not merely that a man travels once and for all along the purgative way, then starts out upon the illuminative way, and having finished it enters the unitive way. "The life of man on earth is a warfare,"[10] and part of this lifelong struggle is against the constant danger of moral and spiritual lapse and collapse, against the lingering effects of past misdeeds, and against the solicitations of the flesh, the allurements of the world, and the snares of the devil. Our minds will never be sufficiently clear of sin and temptation; still less will they ever have sufficient knowledge of the full character and necessity of the moral and intellectual virtues and of God and his holy will.[11] "This is the will of God, your sanctification,"[12] says St. Paul. Can we, St. Francis de Sales would ask, ever know enough about "the depth of the wisdom of the knowledge of God" and about "how incomprehensible are his judgements and how unsearchable his ways?"[13] Throughout his life a man must be on the purgative, the illuminative, and the unitive ways. Only if he perseveres will he come to the end of the purgative way and to the fulfillment of the illuminative and unitive ways. Hence St. Francis de Sales closes his great book with these words:

> Look up to heaven, and do not forfeit it for earth. Look down into hell, and do not cast yourself into it for the sake of fleeting things. Look

upon Jesus Christ, and do not renounce him for all the world. And when the labors of a devout life seem hard to you sing with St. Francis of Assisi:

> Such are the joys that lure my sight,
> All pains grow sweet, all labors light.

Live, Jesus! to whom, with the Father and the Holy Spirit, be all honor and glory, now and throughout the endless ages of eternity. Amen.

The beauty and the persuasive power of St. Francis' book are as apparent in translation as they are in the original. The warmth and charm of his character, his complete integrity, and his intensity of thought and feeling reveal themselves not only in what he writes but in how he writes. Clarity of thought reveals itself in clarity of language and fullness of thought in fullness of expression. Familiarity with his subject makes the saint see countless parallels between it and what he has observed and read. Here the critic may perhaps find a fault. St. Francis is a master at making comparisons that light up and enliven the subject at hand. Some of these analogies sound strange to our ears: they are chiefly drawn from Pliny and Dioscorides, who sometimes attributed to plants and animals powers and activities that a better natural history discounts or denies. Yet even in this there is a charm that would be lost if strict fact replaced the fancies of an earlier day.

So great and immediate was the success of the *Introduction to the Devout Life* that even during the author's lifetime translations of it were made into the principal European languages. The first English translation appeared in 1613. One Latin translation appeared about 1612 and another was published at Cologne in 1614. A Spanish translation was published in 1618, and a Flemish one some time earlier. St. Francis himself in a letter written in 1610 mentions a translation into Italian, and later he assisted Padre Antoniotti, S.J., with his translation, which was published at Turin in 1621. When the first German translation was made is not known, but in 1627 there is mention that one was in use. By 1656 the work had been translated into seventeen languages. Since then, countless editions of the work have appeared in many languages and dialects including Basque, modern Greek, Armenian, and Chinese.

The history of the English translation of the *Introduction to the Devout Life* bears further testimony to the need and value of the work. The first translation was made by "I.Y.," who has been identified as John Yakesley and as John Yaworth. Its title page reads:

> An Introduction to a Devout Life. Composed in Frenche by the R. Father in God, Francis Sales, Bishop of Geneva, and translated into English by I. Y. Rouen, Hamilton, 1613.

The translation won a popularity as immediate as that of the original work. A second edition was put forth at Rouen in 1613, and a third in 1614. Other editions were published: at London in 1616, at Paris in 1637, at Lyons without date, and at Dublin in 1673. I.Y. used the third (1610) edition of the *Introduction* for his translation and hence it is not complete. As translators are often tempted to do, he took certain liberties with the original text. Thus he sought to improve upon St. Francis by changing Philothea into Philotheus.

Because of the shortcomings of the I.Y. translation, a new edition was put out thirty-five years later by a group of English priests of Tourney College in Paris. The reasons for this edition are given in the preface:

> It has been formerly translated by a revered person of our country; but he in his great humility exposing it to the reviewing of others, it fell into the hands of some, who, enlarging the author's style by many unnecessary paraphrases, have in divers places confounded his sense

and made the book less portable. In this edition we hope we have remedied both these inconveniences. The first by following the true sense of the author, and his own expressions, as near to the life, as the two languages will meet. The second by printing it in somewhat a less character than formerly.

The title page reads:

A new edition of the Introduction to a Devout Life of B. Francis de Sales . . . Together with a Summary of his life, and a collection of his choicest maximes . . . Set forth by the English Priests of Tourney College at Paris. Paris, 1648.

This edition was reprinted in London in 1675, 1726, and 1741.

It is this version that has been most widely read in English-speaking countries. It has been printed countless times in various places, with changes in spelling, punctuation, and other details. Moreover, it served as a basis for Bishop Richard Challoner's revision, first published in London in 1762 and subsequently often reprinted. Since then further translations have been published by W. J. B. Richards (London, 1848), Thomas Barnes (London, 1906), Allan Ross (London, 1924), and Michael Day (London, 1961).

In addition to the numerous printings of the English translations of the *Introduction*, there is other evidence of the widespread acceptance of the work and its subsequent influence. Marie de Médicis presented a copy in a jeweled binding to King James I of England, the son of Mary, Queen of Scots. William Laud, Anglican Archbishop of Canterbury, executed by the Parliamentary authorities in 1645, expressed his approval of the book. By far the most striking testimony to the *Introduction*'s power is found in the proclamation issued by King Charles I on May 14, 1637, ordering that all copies in England be seized and burned. The connection of the Stuart family with the book does not end in this way. James II, the last Catholic king of England and the son of Charles I, gave order to a London printer in 1685 to prepare a special edition of the *Introduction* for use by the royal family and in the chapel royal. His own son, the Old Pretender, in turn possessed and annotated a copy that is still preserved in the Visitation Convent in Paris.

How widely the earlier editions of the translation were received among non-Catholics it is impossible to say. Nevertheless, by the end of the seventeenth century William Nicholls, rector of the parish of Selsey in Sussex, saw an opportunity to prepare a special edition for Protestant readers. The title page of his work reads:

> An Introduction, To A Devout Life. By Francis Sales, Bishop and Prince of Geneva. Translated and Reformed from the Errors of the Popish Edition. To which is perfixed [*sic*] a Discourse, of the Rise and Progress of the Spiritual Books in the Romish Church. By William Nicholls, D.D. London, Printed by E. Holt, for Tho. Bennet at the Half-Moon in St. Paul's Church-Yard; and J. Sprint at the Bell in Little-Britain, 1701.

Nicholls had a good deal of admiration for the *Introduction* but took great liberties with it. In general, references to the Holy Sacrifice of the Mass, sacramental confession, invocation of the saints, Catholic prayers and devotions, and stories taken from the lives and legends of the saints were excised. A few chapters are omitted and certain changes are made in the text, some of them minor but others quite serious.[14]

This translation was first published by Harper in 1950 and subsequently by Doubleday as an Image Book. It was revised and published as one of the Harper Torchbooks, a paperback series, in 1966. It has been further revised for this new edition as an Image Book. It is based on the text of the original French work as established by Dom B. Mackey in the Annecy edition. An attempt has been made to give a complete and accurate English rendition of the *Introduction to the Devout Life*. There has been no wish to depart from the thought of St. Francis de Sales in any detail or to improve upon him in any manner. It is the translator's hope to share to some small extent in the great aim that St. Francis de Sales had in writing his mystical and devotional masterpiece: that its readers may "put this little book to good use and receive great blessings from it."

—*John K. Ryan*
The School of Philosophy
The Catholic University of America

PRINCIPAL DATES
in the life of
ST. FRANCIS DE SALES

1567   Born on August 21 in the Château de Sales, at Thorens in Savoy.

1580–88 Student of the humanities and philosophy at the Jesuit College of Clérmont in Paris from 1580 or 1581 to 1588.

1586   The spiritual crisis of his life: the temptation to despair.

1588–92 Student of law and theology at the University of Padua, where he receives the doctorate in law, in September, 1591.

1592   Returns to Savoy, is admitted as an advocate before the senate of Chambéry, and is given the title of Seigneur de Villaroget.

1593   Made provost of the cathedral chapter of Geneva on March 7, and ordained priest on December 18 at Annecy.

1594–98 Apostolate of Chablais. Writes the *Controversies* and the *Defense of the Standard of the Holy Cross.*

1595 Armed attack made on his life on January 8.

1597 Visits Geneva at the request of Pope Clement VIII and tries to convert Théodore de Bèze.

1599 Is called to Rome by Pope Clement VIII and is appointed coadjutor to the bishop of Geneva.

1601 Death of his father.

1602 Visits Paris upon a religious and diplomatic mission. Is consecrated bishop of Geneva on December 8.

1604 Preaches Lenten sermons at Dijon, meets the future St. Jeanne Françoise de Chantal, and later becomes her spiritual director.

1607 Begins writing the *Treatise of the Love of God* and also a rule for the proposed Institute of the Visitation.

1609 Publication of the *Introduction to the Devout Life.*

1610 Death of his mother. Foundation of the Institute of the Visitation.

1616 Refuses to leave Annecy when it is besieged.

1618–19 Final visit to Paris, November, 1618, to September, 1619.

1619 Publication of the definitive edition of the *Introduction to the Devout Life.*

1622 Dies at Lyons on December 28.

1661 Declared blessed by Pope Alexander VII on December 28.

1665 Declared a saint by Pope Alexander VII on April 19, with his feast on January 29.

1877 Declared a doctor of the universal Church by Pope Pius IX on July 7.

1923 Encyclical *Rerum Omnium* of Pope Pius XI in commemoration of the tercentenary of St. Francis de Sales' death.

DEDICATORY PRAYER

Ah, sweet Jesus, my Lord, my Savior, and my God, behold me here prostrate before your Majesty[1] as I pledge and consecrate this work to your glory. By your blessing give life to its words so that the souls for whom it has been written may receive from it the sacred inspirations I desire for them, in particular that of imploring your infinite mercy in my behalf to the end that while I point out to others the way of devotion in this world I myself may not be rejected[2] and eternally condemned in the other, but that with them I may forever sing as a canticle of triumph words that with my whole heart I utter in witness of fidelity amid the hazards of this mortal life:

Live, Jesus! Live, Jesus![3]

Yes, Lord Jesus, live and reign in our hearts forever and ever. Amen.

NOTICE TO THE READER

THIRD EDITION

This little book issued from my hands in the year 1608. In its second edition it was enlarged by several chapters, but three of those in the first edition were left out by mistake. Since then it has frequently been reprinted without my sanction, and with the printings errors have been multiplied. It is now put forth corrected again and containing all its chapters, but still without references because the learned do not need them and the others do not bother about them. When I use the words of Scripture it is not always to explain them but rather to explain my own meaning by them as being more agreeable and venerable. If God answers my prayers, you will put this little book to good use and receive great blessings from it.

SECOND EDITION

My dear reader, a second edition gives you this little book revised, corrected, and enlarged by several chapters and some important matter. I have not wished to enrich it with any references, as some have desired me to do, because the learned do not need such things and the others do not bother about them. When I make use of the words of Scripture it is not always to explain them but rather to explain my own meaning by them, since they are more venerable and pleasing to devout souls. I have given further explanatory matter in the preface. May our Lord be with you.

THE
AUTHOR'S
PREFACE

My dear reader, I ask you to read this preface both for your benefit and for mine.

Glycera, a bouquet maker, was so skillful at changing flowers in order and arrangement and out of the same ones made so many different kinds of bouquets that the painter Pausias, who wished to portray her different arrangements, was unable to do so.[1] He could not vary his paintings in as many ways as Glycera did her bouquets. In like manner the Holy Spirit disposes and orders in many different ways the devout instructions he gives us by the tongues and pens of his servants. Although the doctrine is always the same, statements of it differ greatly according to the various ways in which their books are composed. I neither can nor will, nor indeed should I, write in this *Introduction* anything but what has already been published by our predecessors on the same subject. The flowers I present to you, my reader, are the same; the bouquet I have made out of them differs from others because it has been fashioned in a different order and way.

Almost all those who have hitherto written about devotion have been concerned with instructing persons wholly withdrawn from the world or have at least taught a kind of devotion that leads to such complete retirement. My purpose is to instruct those who live in town, within families, or at court, and by their state of life are obliged to live an ordinary life as to outward appearances. Frequently, on the pretext of some supposed impossibility, they will not even think of undertaking a devout life. It is their opinion that just as no animal dares to taste the seed of the herb called *palma Christi*,[2] so no one should aspire to the palm of Christian piety as long as he is living under the pressure of worldly affairs. I shall show to such men that just as the mother of pearl fish lives in the sea without taking in a single drop of salt water,[3] just as near the Chelodonian islands springs of fresh water may be found in the depths of the sea,[4] and just as the firefly passes through flames without burning its wings,[5] so also a strong, resolute soul can live in the world without being infected by any of its moods, find sweet springs of piety amid its salty waves, and fly through the flames of earthly lusts without burning the wings of its holy desires for a devout life. True, this is a difficult task, and therefore I wish that many souls would strive to accomplish it with greater ardor than has hitherto been shown. Weak as I am, I shall try by this treatise to provide some assistance to those who with a generous heart undertake so worthy a project.

It is not by my own choice or inclination that this *Introduction* is now made public. A truly devout soul,[6] who had some time earlier received from God the grace of aspiring to a devout life, desired my particular assistance for that purpose. As I was under many obligations to her and had long before perceived in her a genuine disposition to piety, I applied myself very diligently to her instruction. Having conducted her through all the exercises suitable to her purpose and state of life, I left certain written notes for her use. Later she showed them to an important, learned, and devout religious[7] who believed that many others might profit from them and urged me to publish them. It was not hard for him to persuade me to do so since his friendship had great influence on my will and his judgment great authority over my own.

To make the whole work more useful and acceptable I have now revised the different parts, connected them together, and added many pieces of counsel and instruction adapted to my purpose. I have done all this with almost no leisure time at my disposal. Hence you will find here nothing precise, but merely a collection of bits of good advice stated in plain, intelligible words. At least that is what I have tried to do. With regard to literary embellishments, I have not even thought of them as I have had plenty of other things to do.

I address my words to Philothea since I wish to direct what was first written for one person alone to the general benefit of many souls; hence I use a name that can refer to all who aspire to devotion. Philothea signifies a soul loving, or in love with, God.

Throughout this entire book I keep in mind a soul who out of desire for devotion aspires to the love of God. I have therefore divided this *Introduction* into five parts. In the first part, by warning against certain things that need correction and by certain exercises I try to change Philothea's simple desire into a solid resolution. After a general confession she at length makes this in the form of a firm protestation, followed by Holy Communion, in which she gives herself up to her Savior and happily enters into his holy love. This done, in order to lead her further on I show her the two great means by which she can unite herself to his Divine Majesty. These are use of the sacraments, by which God comes to us, and holy prayer, by which he attracts us to himself. I devote the second part to this. In the third part I show her how she ought to practice the various virtues most needed for her progress, and I pause only to give advice on certain particular subjects she could hardly have received from others or learned for herself. In the fourth part I call her attention to some of the snares of her enemies and show her how she must avoid them and press forward. In the fifth and last part I have her retire apart for awhile in order to refresh herself, get back her breath, and recover strength so that she may afterwards more successfully gain ground and advance in the devout life.

Our age is very captious. I foresee that many people will say that it is only members of religious communities and persons dedicated to devotion who should give special direction in piety, that such things require more leisure than a bishop in charge of a diocese as large as mine can have, and that such an undertaking is too distracting for a mind that should be employed in matters of importance. For my own part, dear reader, together with the great St. Dionysius[8] I tell you that it is primarily the duty of bishops to lead souls to perfection, since their order is as supreme among men as that of the seraphim among angels. Hence their leisure cannot be better employed than in such work. The ancient bishops and fathers of the Church were at least as careful about their duties as we are, yet, as we see from their letters, they did not refuse to take charge of the particular conduct of several souls who had turned to them for assistance. In this they imitated the apostles who, while working with special and particular affection to gather in all men, picked out certain extraordinary ears of grain. Who does not know that Timothy, Titus, Philemon, Onesimus, St. Tecla, and Appia were the dear children of the great St. Paul, just as St. Mark and St. Petronilla were of St. Peter—St. Petronilla, I say, who, as Baronius[9] and Galonius[10] learnedly prove, was not St. Peter's physical but solely his spiritual daughter? And did not St. John write one of his canonical epistles to the devout Lady Electa?[11]

It is a burden, I admit, to give particular direction to souls, but it is a burden bringing comfort like that felt by harvesters and workers in the vineyard, for they are never happier than when busiest and having the heaviest work. It is labor that refreshes and revives the heart by the sweet delight it arouses in those engaged in it, just as cinnamon refreshes those who carry it about in Arabia Felix. It is said that when a tigress finds one of her whelps left in her path by a hunter who wishes to trick her while he carries off the rest of the litter, then no matter how heavy it is she puts it on her back and yet does not feel encumbered.[12] On the contrary, she is more active as she runs back to the safety of her den for natural love lightens her burden. How much more willingly will a fatherly heart take charge of a soul in which he finds a desire for holy perfection and carry it in his breast as a mother does her little child without being wearied by so precious a burden! But his must be truly a father's heart. For this reason the apostles and apostolic men call their disciples not only their children but still more tenderly their little children.

It is true, my dear reader, that I write about the devout life although I myself am not devout. Yet it is certainly not without a desire of becoming so and it is such affection that encourages me to instruct you. As a great man of letters has said, "To study is a good way to learn; to hear is a still better way; to teach is the best of all."[13] "It often happens," says St. Augustine[14] in a letter to Florentina, "that the office of giving gives us the merit to receive," and the office of teaching serves as foundation for learning.

Alexander ordered that a portrait of the beautiful Campaspe, who was very dear to him, should be painted by the hand of the great Apelles. Since Apelles was obliged to look directly at Campaspe for long periods, he simultaneously traced her features on the tablet and impressed his love for them on his own heart. At length he fell so passionately in love that Alexander saw it, took pity on him, and gave her to him in marriage, thus for Apelles' sake depriving himself of the woman dearest to him in all the world. "In this deed," says Pliny, "he showed his greatness of mind as much as he could have by the most famous victory."[15] My reader, my friend, it is my belief that it is God's will that I, a bishop, should paint on men's hearts not only the ordinary virtues but also God's dearest and most beloved devotion. I willingly undertake to do this both to obey him and to do my duty and also in the hope that by engraving devotion on the minds of others my own mind will be filled with a holy love for it. If God's Majesty ever sees me passionately in love with devotion, he will give her to me in an eternal marriage. When the beautiful, chaste Rebecca watered Isaac's camels she was destined to be his wife and on his behalf she received golden earrings and bracelets.[16] Thus through God's infinite goodness I urge on to myself that when I lead his beloved flock to the healthful waters of devotion he will make my soul his spouse and put in my ears the golden words of his holy love and in my arms strength to practice them well. In this last lies the essence of true devotion. I humbly beseech his Divine Majesty to grant this to me and to all the children of his Church—the Church to which I forever submit my writings, my deeds, my words, my acts of will, and my thoughts.

Annecy, the Feast of St. Mary Magdalen, 1609

THE FIRST PART
OF THE INTRODUCTION

Instructions and Exercises Needed to
Lead the Soul from Its First Desire for
the Devout Life Until Brought to a
Full Resolution to Embrace It

1. DESCRIPTION OF TRUE DEVOTION

You wish to live a life of devotion, dearest Philothea, because you are a Christian and know that it is a virtue most pleasing to God's Majesty. Since little faults committed in the beginning of a project grow infinitely greater in its course and finally are almost irreparable,[1] above all else you must know what the virtue of devotion is. There is only one true devotion but there are many that are false and empty. If you are unable to recognize which kind is true, you can easily be deceived and led astray by following one that is offensive and superstitious.

In his pictures Arelius painted all faces after the manner and appearance of the women he loved,[2] and so too everyone paints devotion according to his own passions and fancies. A man given to fasting thinks himself very devout if he fasts, although his heart may be filled with hatred. Much concerned with sobriety, he doesn't dare to wet his tongue with wine or even water but won't hesitate to drink deep of his neighbor's blood by detraction and calumny. Another man thinks himself devout because he daily recites a vast number of prayers, but after saying them he utters the most disagreeable, arrogant, and harmful words at home and among the neighbors. Another gladly takes a coin out of his purse and gives it to the poor, but he cannot extract kindness from his heart and forgive his enemics. Another forgives his enemies but never pays his creditors unless compelled to do so by force of law. All these men are usually considered to be devout, but they are by no means such. Saul's servants searched for David in his house but Michol had put a statue on his bed, covered it with David's clothes, and thus led them to think that it was David himself lying there sick and sleeping.[3] In the same manner, many persons clothe themselves with certain outward actions connected with holy devotion and the world believes that they are truly devout and spiritual whereas they are in fact nothing but copies and phantoms of devotion.

Genuine, living devotion, Philothea, presupposes love of God, and hence it is simply true love of God. Yet it is not always love as such. Inasmuch as divine love adorns the soul, it is called grace, which makes us pleasing to his Divine Majesty. Inasmuch as it strengthens us to do good, it is called charity. When it has reached a degree of perfection at which it not only makes us do good but also do this carefully, frequently, and promptly, it is called devotion. Ostriches never fly; hens fly in a clumsy fashion, near the ground, and only once in a while, but eagles, doves, and swallows fly aloft, swiftly and frequently. In like manner, sinners in no way fly up towards God, but make their whole course here upon the earth and for the earth. Good people who have not as yet attained to devotion fly toward God by their good works but do so infrequently, slowly, and awkwardly. Devout souls ascend to him more frequently, promptly, and with lofty flights. In short, devotion is simply that spiritual agility and vivacity by which charity works in us or by aid of which we work quickly and lovingly. Just as it is the function of charity to enable us to observe all God's commandments in general and without exception, so it is the part of devotion to enable us to observe them more quickly and diligently. Hence a man who does not observe all God's commandments cannot be held to be either good or devout. To be good he must have charity, and to be devout, in addition to charity he must have great ardor and readiness in performing charitable actions.

Since devotion consists in a certain degree of eminent charity, it not only makes us prompt, active, and faithful in observance of God's commands, but in addition it arouses us to do quickly and lovingly as many good works as possible, both those commanded and those merely counselled or inspired. A man just recovered from illness walks only as far as he must and then slowly and with difficulty; so also a sinner just healed of his iniquity walks as far as God commands him, but he walks slowly and with difficulty until such time as he has attained to devotion. Then like a man in sound health he not only walks but runs and leaps forward "on the way of God's commandments."[4] Furthermore, he moves and runs in the paths of his heavenly counsels and inspirations. To conclude, charity and devotion differ no more from one another than does flame from the fire. Charity is spiritual fire and when it bursts into flames, it is called devotion. Hence devotion adds nothing to the fire of charity except the flame that makes charity prompt, active, and diligent[5] not only to observe God's commandments but also to fulfill his heavenly counsels and inspirations.

2. THE PROPRIETY AND EXCELLENCE OF DEVOTION

The men who discouraged the Israelites from going into the Promised Land told them that it was a country that "devoured its inhabitants." In other words, they said that the air was so malignant it was impossible to live there for long and its natives such monsters that they ate men like locusts.[1] It is in this manner, my dear Philothea, that the world vilifies holy devotion as much as it can. It pictures devout persons as having discontented, gloomy, sullen faces and claims that devotion brings on depression and unbearable moods. But just as Joshua and Caleb held both that the Promised Land was good and beautiful and that its possession would be sweet and agreeable[2] so too the Holy Spirit by the mouths of all the saints and our Lord by his own mouth[3] assure us that a devout life is a life that is sweet, happy, and lovable.

The world sees devout people as they pray, fast, endure injuries, take care of the sick, give alms to the poor, keep vigils, restrain anger, suppress their passions, give up sensual pleasures, and perform other actions painful and rigorous in themselves and by their very nature. But the world does not see the heartfelt inward devotion that renders all such actions pleasant, sweet, and easy. Look at the bees amid the banks of thyme. They find there a very bitter juice but when they suck it out they change it into honey because they have the ability to do so. O worldly men! it is true that devout souls encounter great bitterness in their works of mortification but by performing them they change them into something most sweet and delicious. Because the martyrs were devout men and women fire, flame, wheel, and sword seemed to be flowers and perfume to them. If devotion can sweeten the most cruel torments and even death itself, what must it do for virtuous actions?

Sugar sweetens green fruit and in ripe fruit corrects whatever is crude and unwholesome. Now devotion is true spiritual sugar for it removes bitterness from mortification and anything harmful from our consolations. From the poor it takes away discontent, care from the rich, grief from the oppressed, pride from the exalted, melancholy from the solitary, and dissipation from those who live in society. It serves with equal benefit as fire in winter and dew in summer. It knows how to use prosperity and how to endure want. It makes honor and contempt alike useful to us. It accepts pleasure and pain with a heart that is nearly always the same, and it fills us with a marvelous sweetness.

Consider Jacob's ladder,[4] for it is a true picture of the devout life. The two sides between which we climb upward and to which the rungs are fastened represent prayer, which calls down God's love, and the sacraments, which confer it. The rungs are the various degrees of charity by which we advance from virtue to virtue, either descending by deeds of help and support for our neighbor or by contemplation ascending to a loving union with God. I ask you to regard attentively those who are on this ladder. They are either men with angelic hearts or angels in human bodies. They are not young, although they seem to be so because they are full of vigor and spiritual agility. They have wings to soar aloft to God in holy prayer and they also have feet to walk among men in a holy and lovable way of life. Their faces are beautiful and joyous because they accept all things meekly and mildly. Their legs, arms, and heads are uncovered because in their thoughts, affections, and deeds they have no purpose or motive but that of pleasing God. The rest of their body is clothed but only by a decent light robe, because they use the world and worldly things but do so in a most pure and proper way, taking of them only what is necessary for their condition. Such are devout persons.

Believe me, my dear Philothea, devotion is the delight of delights and queen of the virtues since it is the perfection of charity. If charity is milk, devotion is its cream; if it is a plant, devotion is its blossom; if it is a precious stone, devotion is its luster; if it is a rich ointment, devotion is its odor, yes, the odor of sweetness which comforts men and rejoices angels.

3. DEVOTION IS POSSIBLE IN EVERY VOCATION AND PROFESSION

When he created things God commanded plants to bring forth their fruits, each one according to its kind,[1] and in like manner he commands

Christians, the living plants of his Church,[2] to bring forth the fruits of devotion, each according to his position and vocation. Devotion must be exercised in different ways by the gentleman, the worker, the servant, the prince, the widow, the young girl, and the married woman. Not only is this true, but the practice of devotion must also be adapted to the strength, activities, and duties of each particular person. I ask you, Philothea, is it fitting for a bishop to want to live a solitary life like a Carthusian? Or for married men to want to own no more property than a Capuchin, for a skilled workman to spend the whole day in church like a religious, for a religious to be constantly subject to every sort of call in his neighbor's service, as a bishop is? Would not such devotion be laughable, confused, impossible to carry out? Still this is a very common fault, and therefore the world, which does not distinguish between real devotion and the indiscretion of those who merely think themselves devout, murmurs at devotion itself and blames it, even though devotion cannot prevent such disorders.

No, Philothea, true devotion does us no harm whatsoever, but instead perfects all things. When it goes contrary to a man's lawful vocation, it is undoubtedly false. "The bee," Aristotle says, "extracts honey out of flowers without hurting them"[3] and leaves them as whole and fresh as it finds them. True devotion does better still. It not only does no injury to one's vocation or occupation, but on the contrary adorns and beautifies it. All kinds of precious stones take on greater luster when dipped into honey, each according to its color. So also every vocation becomes more agreeable when united with devotion. Care of one's family is rendered more peaceable, love of husband and wife more sincere, service of one's prince more faithful, and every type of employment more pleasant and agreeable.

It is an error, or rather a heresy, to wish to banish the devout life from the regiment of soldiers, the mechanic's shop, the court of princes, or the home of married people. It is true, Philothea, that purely contemplative, monastic, and religious devotion cannot be exercised in such states of life. However, besides those three kinds of devotion there are several others adapted to bring perfection to those living in the secular state. Examples in the Old Testament are Abraham, Isaac, and Jacob, David, Job, and Tobias, and Sarah, Rebecca, and Judith, and under the New Covenant, St. Joseph,[4] Lydia,[5] and St. Crispin[6] lived lives of perfect devotion in their workshops, and St. Anne,[7] St. Martha,[8] St. Monica[9] and Aquila and Priscilla[10] in their families, Cornelius,[11] St. Sebastian,[12] and St. Maurice[13] in the army, and Constantine,[14] Helena,[15] St. Louis,[16] Blessed Amadeus[17] and St. Edward[18] on their thrones did the same. There have even been many cases of people who lost perfection in solitude, which for all that is most desirable for perfection, and have kept it in the midst of crowds, which seem to offer little help to perfection. "Lot," St. Gregory says, "who was so chaste in the city defiled himself in the wilderness."[19] Wherever we may be, we can and should aspire to a perfect life.

4. NEED OF A GUIDE FOR BEGINNING DEVOTION AND MAKING PROGRESS IN IT

When commanded to go to Rages young Tobias answered, "I do not know the way," and his father replied, "Go then and find some man to lead you."[1] I say the same thing to you, Philothea. Do you seriously wish to travel the road to devotion? If so, look for a good man to guide and lead you. This is the most important of all words of advice. As the devout Avila says, "Although you seek God's will, you will never find it with such certainty as on the path of that humble obedience so highly praised and practiced by all devout writers."[2]

When the Blessed Mother Teresa saw the Lady Catherine of Cardona perform certain rigorous acts of penance, she had a great desire to imitate her. This was contrary to the advice of her confessor who forbade her to do so, and as she was tempted to disobey him, God said to her, "My daughter, you are on a good and safe road. Do you look at the penance that she does? I put higher value on your obedience."[3] Hence she loved this virtue so much that in addition to that owed to her superiors she made a vow of very special obedience to a certain excellent man and bound herself to follow his direction and example, and by doing so received very great consolations. Both before and after her in order to become better subjects of God many other devout souls have in like manner submitted their will to that of his servants. In her *Dialogues*[4] St. Catherine of Siena gives the highest praise to such obedience. A devout princess, St. Elizabeth, submitted herself with full obedience to the learned Master Conrad. The advice the great St. Louis gave to his son was this: "Go to confession frequently, and choose as your confessor an able and experienced man who can safely teach you the things that you must do."[5]

"A faithful friend," Holy Scripture says, "is a strong defence, and he who has found one has found a treasure. A faithful friend is the medicine of life and immortality, and those who fear the Lord find him."[6] As you see, these divine words chiefly refer to immortality, and for this we must above all else have this faithful friend who by advice and counsel guides our actions and thus protects us from the snares and deceits of the wicked one. For us he will be a treasure of wisdom in affliction, sorrow, and failure. He will serve as a medicine to ease and comfort our hearts when afflicted by spiritual sickness. He will guard us from evil and make our good still better. Should any infirmity come upon us, he will assist us and keep it from being unto death.

Who shall find such a friend? The Wise Man answers "Those who fear the Lord,"[7] that is, humble souls who sincerely desire to make spiritual progress. Since it is important for you, Philothea, to have a guide as you travel on this holy road to devotion, you must most insistently beseech God to provide you with one after his own heart. Have no misgivings in this regard for he who sent down an angel from heaven, as he did to young Tobias, will give you a good and faithful guide.

For you such a director ought always to be an angel. That is, when you have found him, do not look on him as a mere man; do not place confidence merely in him or in human learning but rather in God for he will befriend you and speak to you by means of this man. God will put into his heart and mouth whatever is requisite for your welfare. Hence you must listen to him as to an angel who comes down from heaven to lead you to it. Open your heart to him with all sincerity and fidelity; tell him clearly and without deception or dissimulation about what is good in you and what is bad. By such means the good will be examined and approved and what is bad will be corrected and repaired. You will be consoled and strengthened in your afflictions and moderated and regulated in your consolations. You must have unlimited confidence in him, mingled with holy reverence, so that reverence will neither lessen confidence nor confidence hinder reverence. Confide in him with a daughter's respect for her father; respect him with a son's confidence in his mother. In short, such friendship must be strong and sweet, completely holy, completely sacred, completely divine, completely spiritual.

For this purpose choose one out of a thousand, as Avila says.[8] For my part, I say one out of ten thousand, for there are fewer men than we realize who are capable of this task. He must be full of charity, knowledge, and prudence, and if any one of these three qualities is lacking there is danger. I tell you again, ask God for him, and having once found him, bless his Divine Majesty, stand firm, and do not look for another, but go forward with simplicity, humility, and confidence for you will make a most prosperous journey.

5. WE MUST FIRST BEGIN BY PURIFYING THE SOUL

"The flowers have appeared in our land, the time of pruning the vines has come,"[1] says the Sacred Spouse. What other flowers do we have in our hearts, Philothea, except good desires? As soon as they appear we must take a pruning knife in order to remove from our conscience all dead and worthless works. Before an alien girl was permitted to marry an Israelite she had to put aside her clothing as a captive, pare her nails, and shave off her hair.² So also a soul that hopes for the honor of being made spouse of the Son of God must "put off the old man, and put on the new"³ by forsaking sin and removing and cutting away whatever obstructs union with God. For us the beginning of good health is to be purged of our sinful tendencies.

In a single instant St. Paul was cleansed with a complete purgation,⁴ and so too were St. Catherine of Genoa,⁵ St. Mary Magdalen, St. Pelagia,⁶ and certain others. However such purgation is as miraculous and extraordinary in the order of grace as resurrection from the dead is in the order of nature and therefore we should not look for it. The usual purgation and healing, whether of body or of soul, takes place only little by little and by passing from one advance to another with difficulty and patience. Although the angels on Jacob's ladder had wings, they did not fly but went up and down in order and step by step. The soul that rises from sin to devotion has been compared to the dawning day,⁷ which at its approach does not drive out the darkness instantaneously but only little by little. A slow cure, as the maxim says, is always surest. Diseases of the soul as well as those of the body come posting on horseback but leave slowly and on foot.

In this enterprise we must have courage and patience, Philothea. What a pity it is to see souls who perceive themselves still subject to many imperfections after striving to be devout for a while and then begin to be dissatisfied, disturbed, and discouraged and almost let their hearts give in to a temptation to give up everything and go back to their old way of life. On the other hand, are not those souls also in extreme danger who by an opposite temptation think themselves cleansed of every imperfection on the very first day of their purgation, regard themselves as perfect before they have scarcely begun, and try to fly without wings? Philothea, they are in great peril of a relapse on being too soon out of the physician's care. Do not get up before the light has come, says the prophet, but "rise after you have sat down."[8] He himself practiced this lesson; although already washed and cleansed, he asked to be washed and cleansed still more and more.[9]

The work of purging the soul neither can nor should end except with our life itself. We must not be disturbed at our imperfections, since for us perfection consists in fighting against them. How can we fight against them unless we see them, or overcome them unless we face them? Our victory does not consist in being unconscious of them but in not consenting to them, and not to consent to them is to be displeased with them. To practice humility it is absolutely necessary for us at times to suffer wounds in this spiritual warfare, but we are never vanquished unless we lose our life or our courage. Imperfections and venial sins cannot deprive us of spiritual life; it is lost only by mortal sin. Therefore it only remains for us not to lose courage. Save me, O Lord, from cowardice and discouragement, David says.[10] Fortunately for us, in this war we are always victorious provided that we are willing to fight.

6. THE FIRST PURGATION, NAMELY, THAT OF MORTAL SIN

The first purgation we must make is that of sin and the way to make it is by the holy sacrament of penance. Look for the best confessor you can, and then get some of the little books written to help our conscience make a good confession, such as Granada,[1] Bruno,[2] Arias,[3] or Auger.[4] Read them carefully and note point by point in what way you have done wrong from the time you reached the use of reason down to the present hour. If you do not trust your memory, write down what you have noted. After you have prepared and gathered together your sinful states of conscience, detest and reject them by the greatest acts of contrition and sorrow your soul can conceive. At the same time, keep in mind these four things: that by sin you have lost God's grace, given up your place in paradise, chosen the eternal pains of hell, and rejected God's eternal love.

Note carefully, Philothea, that I speak of a general confession covering your whole life. I readily grant that this is not always absolutely necessary, but I consider it exceedingly useful in this opening period and therefore I earnestly advise it. It frequently happens that the routine confessions of those who lead the common, ordinary sort of life are filled with grave faults. Often they make little or even no preparation and do not have sufficient contrition. Too often it happens that they go to confession with a tacit intention of returning to sin, since they are unwilling to avoid its occasions or use the means necessary for amendment of life. In addition a general confession summons us to know ourselves, arouses wholesome sorrow for our past life, makes us marvel at the mercy of God who has so patiently waited for us, brings peace to our hearts, calms our minds, excites us to good resolutions, provides our spiritual director with an opportunity to advise us more properly as to our condition, and opens our hearts to reveal ourselves with confidence in subsequent confessions.

Since I speak here of a general renewal of your heart and complete conversion of your soul to God by undertaking a devout life, it seems to me, Philothea, that I am right in advising you to make a general confession.

7. THE SECOND PURGATION, NAMELY, OF AFFECTION FOR SIN

Although all the Israelites left Egypt in effect, not all of them left it in affection, and hence in the wilderness many of them regretted their lack of the onions and fleshpots of Egypt.[1] In like manner, there are penitents who leave sin in effect, but do not leave it in affection. They resolve never to sin again, but it is with a certain reluctance that they give up or abstain from the fatal delights of sin. Their heart renounces and shuns sin but looks back at it just as Lot's wife looked back at Sodom.[2]

They abstain from sin like sick men abstaining from melons. They don't eat them solely because the doctor warns them that they'll die if they do, but they begrudge giving them up, talk about them, would eat them if they could, want to smell them at least, and envy those who can eat them. In such a way weak, lazy penitents abstain regretfully for a while from sin. They would like very much to commit sins if they could do so without being damned. They speak about sin with a certain petulance and with liking for it and think those who commit sins are at peace with themselves. A man who had resolved to take vengeance on another will change his mind in the confessional but a little later you will find him among his friends talking delightedly about his quarrel and saying, "If it wasn't for the fear of God, I would do this or that," "In this matter of forgiving people the divine law is a hard thing," and "I wish to God it would let a man revenge himself." We all see that although this unfortunate man has been set free from sin he is still entangled by affection for it. Although he is out of Egypt in effect he is still there in appetite and in his longing for the garlic and onions on which he once glutted himself. He is like a woman who detests her illicit love affairs but still likes to be courted and pursued. Alas, all such people are in great peril!

Philothea, since you wish to live a devout life you must not only cease to sin but you must also purify your heart of all affection for sin. In addition to the danger of falling again, such base affections so lastingly weaken and weigh down your spirits that it will be impossible to do good works promptly, diligently, and frequently, and it is in this that the very essence of devotion consists. In my opinion souls that have recovered from the state of sin but still retain such affections and weaknesses are like girls who are pale in color and although not really sick act as if they are sick. They eat without appetite, sleep without getting any rest, laugh without joy, and drag themselves about rather than walk. In like manner such souls do good but with such spiritual weariness that it robs their good deeds of all grace and the deeds themselves are few in number and small in effect.

8. THE MEANS FOR MAKING THIS SECOND PURGATION

The highest motive for advancing to this second purgation is a strong, living conviction of the great evils sin brings upon us. In this way we arrive at a deep, intense contrition. No matter how slight contrition may be, provided only that it is genuine, and especially when it is joined to the power of the sacraments, it cleanses us sufficiently from sin. So too when it is great and intense it cleanses us from every affection for sin. A slight, weak hatred or grudge results in an aversion to the person we dislike and leads us to avoid his company. If it is a mortal, violent hatred we not only shun and detest him but we even loathe and find unendurable the conversation of his relatives, parents, and friends. We cannot even stand his picture or anything belonging to him. In like manner, when a penitent hates sin with only a weak but still genuine contrition he truly resolves never to sin again, but when he hates it with a strong, active contrition he not only detests sin but also the affections, connections, and occasions that lead to it. Philothea, we must increase our contrition and repentance as much as possible, and extend it to everything having the least relation to sin. At her conversion Mary Magdalen so effectively lost taste for her sins and the pleasure once taken in them that she never again thought about them. David affirms abhorrence not only of sin but also of all the ways and paths that lead to it.[1] In this point consists the soul's rejuvenation, which the same prophet compares to the renewal of the eagle.[2]

To attain such a conviction and contrition you must faithfully practice the following meditations. By the help of God's grace they will be very helpful in rooting out of your heart both sin and the chief affections for it. I have composed them for this purpose. Use them in the order in which I have placed them, taking only one each day, if possible in the morning, which is the best time for spiritual exercises, and think of them during the rest of the day. If you are not as yet accustomed to meditating, read what is said on this subject in the second part.

9. THE FIRST MEDITATION—ON OUR CREATION

PREPARATION

1. Place yourself in the presence of God.
2. Beseech him to inspire you.

CONSIDERATIONS

1. Consider that a certain number of years ago you were not yet in the world and that your present being was truly nothing. My soul, where were we at that time? The world had already existed for a long time, but of us there was as yet nothing.
2. God has drawn you out of that nothingness to make you what you now are and he has done so solely out of his own goodness and without need of you.
3. Consider the nature God has given to you. It is the highest in this visible world; it is capable of eternal life and of being perfectly united to his Divine Majesty.

AFFECTIONS AND RESOLUTIONS

1. Humble yourself profoundly before God, and like the Psalmist say with all your heart: "Lord, before you I am truly nothing. How were you mindful of me so as to create me?"[1] Alas, my soul, you were engulfed in that ancient nothing and you would still be there if God had not drawn you out of it. What could you have done in that nothingness?
2. Return thanks to God. My great and good Creator, how great is my

debt to you since you were moved to draw me out of nothing and by your mercy to make me what I am! What can I ever do to bless your holy name in a worthy manner and to render thanks to your immense mercy?

3. Rebuke yourself. Alas, my Creator, instead of uniting myself to you in love and service I have become a total rebel by my disorderly affections, separated myself from you, strayed far from you in order to embrace sin, and shown no more honor to your goodness than if you were not my Creator.

4. Abase yourself before God. My soul, "know that the Lord is your God. He has made you, and you have not made yourself."[2] O God, I am "the work of your hands."[3]

5. From now on, then, I will no longer be self-complacent, since of myself I am nothing. O dust and ashes,[4] or rather you who are truly nothing, why do you glory in yourself? To humble myself I resolve to do such and such things, to suffer such and such humiliations. I desire to change my life and henceforward to follow my Creator and to find honor in the state of being he has given me, employing it entirely in obedience to his will by such means as will be taught me and about which I will ask my spiritual director.

CONCLUSION

1. Give thanks to God. "Bless your God, O my soul, and let all my being praise his holy name,"[5] for his goodness has drawn me out of nothing and his mercy has created me.

2. Offer. O my God, with all my heart I offer you the being you have given me. I dedicate and consecrate it to you.

3. Pray. O God, strengthen me in these affections and resolutions. O Holy Virgin, recommend them to the mercy of your Son together with all those for whom I am bound to pray; and so on.

   Our Father, Hail Mary.

   After completing your prayer go back over it for a moment and out of the considerations you have made gather a little devotional bouquet to refresh you during the rest of the day.

10. THE SECOND MEDITATION—ON THE END FOR WHICH WE WERE CREATED

PREPARATION
1. Place yourself in the presence of God.
2. Beseech him to inspire you.

CONSIDERATIONS
1. God has placed you in this world not because he needs you in any way—you are altogether useless to him—but only to exercise his goodness in you by giving you his grace and glory. For this purpose he has given you intellect to know him, memory to be mindful of him, will to love him, imagination to picture to yourself his benefits, eyes to see his wonderful works, tongue to praise him, and so on with the other faculties.
2. Since you have been placed in this world for this purpose, all actions contrary to it must be rejected and avoided and those not serving this end should be despised as empty and useless.
3. Consider the unhappiness of worldly people who never think of all this but live as if they believe themselves created only to build houses, plant trees, pile up wealth, and do frivolous things.

AFFECTIONS AND RESOLUTIONS
1. Humble yourself and rebuke your soul for its misery, which up to now has been so great that it has seldom or never reflected on all this. Alas, you will say, what did I think about, O my God, when I did not think of you? What did I remember when I forgot you? What did I love when I did not love you? Alas, I should have fed

upon the truth but I glutted myself with vanity, and served the world which was made only to serve me.

2. Detest your past life. Vain thoughts and useless plans, I renounce you. Hateful and foolish memories, I abjure you. False and treacherous friendships, wasted, wretched deeds, useless self-indulgence, and onerous pleasures, I reject you.

3. Turn to God. My God and my Savior, you shall henceforward be the sole object of my thoughts. I will no longer turn my mind to thoughts that displease you. Every day of my life my memory will be filled with your great mercy that has been so sweetly shown to me. You shall be the joy of my heart and the sweetness of my affections. The trifling, foolish things which I have hitherto devoted myself to, the vain uses to which I have put my days, and the affections that have filled my heart shall from now on be looked on with horror. For this intention I will use such and such remedies.

CONCLUSION

1. Thank God, who has made you for so exalted an end. Lord, you have made me to the end that I forever may enjoy your immeasurable glory. When shall I be worthy of it, when shall I bless you as I ought?

2. Offer. My beloved Creator, I offer you these affections and resolutions with all my heart and soul.

3. Pray. I beseech you, O God, to look with favor on my desires and purposes and give your holy blessing to my soul to the end that it may be able to accomplish them through the merits of the Blood your blessed Son shed upon the Cross, etc.

Make a little spiritual bouquet.

11. THE THIRD MEDITATION—ON GOD'S BENEFACTIONS

PREPARATION

1. Place yourself in the presence of God.
2. Beseech him to inspire you.

CONSIDERATIONS

1. Consider the corporeal benefits that God has bestowed on you: the body itself, goods provided for its maintenance, health, lawful comforts, friends, aids, and helps. Consider all this in contrast to so many other persons more deserving than yourself but destitute of such blessings. Some are disabled in body, health, or members; others are left helpless under opprobrium, insult, and infamy. Still others are ground down by poverty. God has not decreed that you be so miserable.

2. Consider your gifts of mind. How many men there are in the world who are dull of mind, mad, or insane. Why are not you among their number? It is because God has favored you. How many there are who have been brought up harshly and in gross ignorance while God's providence has brought you up in freedom and dignity!

3. Consider your spiritual favors. Philothea, you are a child of the Church. From your childhood God has taught you to know him. How often he has given his sacraments to you! How often you have received his inspirations, interior lights, and admonitions for your amendment! How often has he forgiven your faults! How often has he delivered you from those occasions of damnation to which you have been exposed! Were not all those past years a time of leisure and opportunity to improve your soul's good? By noting each particular thing you perceive in some small way how gentle and gracious God has been to you.

AFFECTIONS AND RESOLUTIONS

1. Marvel at God's goodness. How good my God has been in my behalf! How good indeed! Lord, how rich is your heart in mercy[1] and how generous in good will! My soul, let us always recall the many graces he has shown to us.

2. Marvel at your own ingratitude. What am I, O Lord, that you are mindful of me?[2] And how great is my unworthiness! Alas, I have trodden your blessings underfoot. I have abused your graces and have perverted them into dishonor and contempt of your sovereign goodness. I have opposed the depths of my ingratitude to the depths of your grace and favor.

3. Arouse yourself to make this acknowledgement. Up, then, O my heart, resolve to be no longer faithless, ungrateful, and disloyal to this great benefactor. And how "shall my soul be henceforth wholly subject to God"[3] who has wrought so many wonders and graces in me and for me?

4. Philothea, keep your body safe from such and such pleasures and consecrate it to the service of God who has done so much for it. Set your soul to know and acknowledge him by such exercises as are needed for that purpose. Use diligently all the Church's means to save yourself and to love God. Yes, O my God, I will be assiduous in prayer and at the sacraments. I will listen to your holy word and put your inspirations and counsels into practice.

CONCLUSION

1. Thank God for the knowledge he has now given you of your duties and for all benefits already received.

2. Offer him your heart together with all your resolutions.

3. Pray that he may give you strength to practice them faithfully through the merits of his Son's death. Implore the intercession of the Virgin and the saints.

Our Father, etc.

Make a little spiritual bouquet.

12. THE FOURTH MEDITATION—ON SIN

PREPARATION

1. Place yourself in the presence of God.
2. Beseech him to inspire you.

CONSIDERATIONS

1. Recall to mind how long it is since you began to sin and note how greatly sins have multiplied in your heart since that first beginning and how every day you have increased them against God, yourself, and your neighbor by deed, word, desire, and thought.
2. Consider your evil inclinations and how often you have given way to them. By these two points you will discover that your sins are more numerous than the hairs of your head, yes, more than the sands of the sea.[1]
3. Consider particularly the sin of ingratitude to God, a general sin that reaches out to all the rest and makes them infinitely more enormous. Note then how many benefits God has granted you and how you have misused all of them against their giver. Note especially how many of his inspirations you have despised and how many good movements you have rendered useless. Even more than all the rest remember how many times you have received the sacraments—and where are their fruits? What has become of those precious jewels with which your beloved Spouse adorned you? All of them have been buried beneath your iniquities. With what preparation did you receive them? Think about such ingratitude. So often God has run

after you to save you, and you have always fled before him in order to destroy yourself.

1. Be in the utmost consternation at your misery. O my God! do I dare to stand before your eyes? Alas, I am only the corruption of the world and a sink of ingratitude and iniquity. Is it possible that I have been faithless that I have left neither a single sense nor one of my mental faculties uncorrupted, unviolated, and undefiled, and that not so much as a single day of my life has passed when I have not done most evil deeds? Should I thus repay the benefits brought to me by my Creator and by my Redeemer's Blood?

2. Ask pardon and, like the prodigal son, like Magdalen, like a woman who has defiled her marriage bed with adulterous deeds of every kind, cast yourself at the feet of the Lord. Have mercy, Lord, upon this sinful creature. Alas, O living fountain of compassion, have pity on this miserable wretch.

3. Resolve to live a better life. No, Lord, nevermore, with the help of your grace, no, nevermore will I abandon myself to sin. Alas, I have loved it too much. I detest it and I embrace you, the Father of mercy. In you I wish to live and die.

4. To wipe out my past sins I will bravely accuse myself of them, and I will not leave one of them without driving it out.

5. I will do all that I can to root out completely what is planted in my heart, particularly such and such things that have most troubled me.

6. To do this I will unfailingly embrace the means that I have been counselled to adopt, knowing that I have never done enough to repair such grievous faults.

CONCLUSION

1. Return thanks to God who has waited for you until this hour and has given you these good affections.
2. Offer your heart to him so that you can put them into effect.
3. Pray that he will strengthen you, etc.

13. THE FIFTH MEDITATION—ON DEATH

PREPARATION

1. Place yourself in the presence of God.
2. Beg him for his grace.
3. Imagine yourself to be lying on your deathbed, extremely ill and without any hope of recovery.

CONSIDERATIONS

1. Consider how uncertain is the day of your death. My soul, one day you will leave this body. When will it be? In winter or in summer? In the city or in the country? By day or at night? Suddenly or after due preparation? From sickness or by accident? Will you have time to make your confession or not? Will you be assisted by your confessor and spiritual director? Unfortunately, we know nothing whatsoever about all this. Only one thing is certain: we will die and sooner than we think.

2. Consider that for you the world will then come to an end because for you it will no longer be. Before your eyes it will be hurled over and over. Yes, at that moment all the pleasure, frivolity, worldly joy, and useless affection will appear before you like phantoms and misty clouds. Ah, my wretched soul, for what toys and idle fancies have I offended God! You will see that you have forsaken him for nothing at all. On the contrary, devotion and good works will then

seem sweet and desirable. Why did I not follow that lovely, pleasant path? Sins that once seemed so small will then appear as huge as mountains but your devotion very little.

3. Consider the long, languishing goodbye that your soul will give to this base world. It will bid farewell to wealth, to empty things and useless associations, to pleasures and pastimes, to friends and neighbors, to parents, children, husband, wife, in a word, to every creature, and at last to its own body, which it will leave behind, pale, ghastly, wasted, hideous, and loathsome.

4. Consider with what haste they will carry away that body and bury it in the earth, and this done, the world will scarcely think about you or keep your memory, any more than you have thought of others. "May God grant him peace," they will say, and that is all. O Death, how powerful thou art! How pitiless thou art!

5. Consider how the soul after leaving the body goes its way, either to the right or to the left. Alas, where will your soul go? Which way will it take? It will be none other than the one begun in this world.

AFFECTIONS AND RESOLUTIONS

1. Pray to God and cast yourself into his arms. Lord, take me under your protection on that dreadful day. Only make that last hour happy and favorable to me and rather let all the other days of my life be sad and sorrowful.

2. Despise this world. O world, since I do not know the hour when I must leave you, I will no longer set my heart on you. My dear friends, my dear relations, let me no longer love you except with a holy friendship that can last eternally. Why should I unite myself to you in such wise as to be forced to give up and break our union?

3. I wish to prepare myself for that hour and to take all needed care to make a blessed departure. With all my power I wish to insure a proper state of conscience and to correct such and such defects.

CONCLUSION

1. Return thanks to God for these resolutions which he has given you. Offer them to his Majesty. Beseech him again to grant you a happy death through the merits of his Son's death. Implore the assistance of the Virgin Mary and the saints.
2. *Our Father, Hail Mary.*
3. Make a bouquet of myrrh.

14. THE SIXTH MEDITATION—ON JUDGMENT

PREPARATION

1. Place yourself before God.
2. Beseech him to inspire you.

CONSIDERATIONS

1. At the end, after the time God has allotted for the duration of this world and after many signs and portents at which men will "wither away through fear"[1] and apprehension, fire like a raging torrent will burn and reduce to ashes the whole face of the earth. Nothing that we see here will escape it.
2. After this deluge of flame and thunderbolts all men will rise from the earth except those who have already risen, and at the voice of the angel they will appear in the valley of Josaphat.[2] But, alas, what differences there will be! Some will be glorious and resplendent in body, others will appear in hideous, frightful bodies.
3. Consider the majesty with which the sovereign Judge will appear, surrounded by all the angels and saints. Before him will be borne his cross, shining more brilliantly than the sun, a standard of mercy to the good and of punishment to the wicked.
4. By his awful command, which will be swiftly carried out, this sovereign Judge will separate the good from the bad and place the one at

his right hand and the other at his left. It will be an everlasting separation and after it these two groups will never again be together.

5.   When this separation has been made and all consciences laid bare we will clearly see the malice of the wicked and the contempt they have shown for God, and we will also see the repentance of the good and the effect of the graces they received from God. Nothing will lie hidden. O God, what horror for the evil, what comfort for the good!

6.   Consider that last sentence passed on the wicked: "Depart from me, you cursed, into everlasting fire which was prepared for the devil and his companions."[3] Weigh well those heavy words. "Depart," he says. It is a word of eternal abandonment that God utters to those unhappy souls and by it he banishes them forever from his face. He calls them cursed. O my soul, what a curse, what a general curse this is since it includes every kind of evil! It is an irrevocable curse for it includes both time and eternity. He adds, "into everlasting fire." Behold, O my heart, that vast eternity! O eternal eternity of pain, how dreadful thou art!

7.   Consider the contrary sentence passed on the good. "Come," says the Judge. Ah, this is the sweet word of salvation by which God draws us to himself and receives us into the bosom of his goodness. "You blessed of my Father." O welcome blessing, which includes all blessings! "Possess the kingdom prepared for you from the foundation of the world."[4] O God, what a grace this is, for this kingdom shall never have an end!

AFFECTIONS AND RESOLUTIONS

1.   Tremble, O my soul, at the remembrance of these things. O God, who can give me surety for that day when "the pillars of heaven"[5] will tremble with fear?

2.   Detest your sins for they alone can ruin you on that dreadful day.

3.   Ah, I will judge myself now so that I may not be judged![6] I will

examine my conscience and condemn, accuse, and amend myself so that the Judge will not condemn me on that dreadful day. I will confess my sins and accept all necessary advice, etc.

CONCLUSION

1. Thank God, who has given you means to safeguard yourself on that day and time to do penance.
2. Offer him your heart in order to do penance.
3. *Our Father, Hail Mary.*
   Prepare a bouquet.

15. THE SEVENTH MEDITATION—ON HELL

PREPARATION

1. Place yourself in the presence of God.
2. Humble yourself and ask his assistance.
3. Picture to yourself a gloomy city burning with sulphur and foul-smelling pitch and filled with people who cannot escape from it.

CONSIDERATIONS

1. The damned are in the depths of hell as though trapped in a doomed city where they suffer unspeakable torments in every sense and every member. Just as they used all their senses and members to commit sin, so in every member and in every sense they endure the punishments due to sin. Because of base and evil looks the eyes will endure the horrid sight of devils and hell. Because they took delight in vicious conversations the ears will hear nothing but wailing, lamentation, and despairing cries. So too for the other senses.
2. Beyond all such torments there is one still greater—the privation and loss of God's glory from which they are forever barred. If Absalom found privation of the loving face of David, his father,

more grievous than exile,[1] O God, what grief it is to be forever excluded from the sight of your sweet and gracious countenance!

3. Most of all consider the eternity of these sufferings, for it alone makes hell unbearable. Alas, if a flea in our ear or the heat of a slight fever makes a brief night long and tedious, how terrible will be eternal night with all its torments! Out of this eternity are born eternal despair and infinite rage and blasphemy.

AFFECTIONS AND RESOLUTIONS

1. Strike terror into your soul by the words of Isaias: "O my soul, how can you dwell with this everlasting burning and in this devouring fire?"[2] How can you think of parting from God forever?

2. Confess that you have deserved hell and at many times! But henceforth I will follow the contrary path. Why should I go down into that infinite pit?

3. I will make such and such efforts to avoid sin, for it alone can bring me to that eternal death.

Give thanks; offer; pray.

16. THE EIGHTH MEDITATION—ON PARADISE

PREPARATION

1. Place yourself in the presence of God.
2. Make an invocation.

CONSIDERATIONS

1. Consider a calm, beautiful night and think how good it is to see the sky with its countless varied stars. Next add its beauty to that of a fine day in such wise that the brilliant sun does not prevent a clear view of the stars or moon. Then say boldly that all this beauty put together is of no value when compared to the excellence of God's

paradise. Oh how lovely, how desirable is that place, how precious is that city!

2. Consider the nobility, beauty, and number of the citizens and inhabitants of that fortunate land—those millions upon millions of angels, cherubim, and seraphim, those bands of apostles, martyrs, confessors, virgins, and holy women. It is a countless throng. How fortunate is that company! If the least among them is more beautiful to see than the whole world, what will it be to see all of them together! O my God, how fortunate they are! They forever sing their sweet canticle of eternal love; they forever enjoy constant happiness. They give one another ineffable contentment and live in the consolation of a happy and indissoluble union.

3. Finally, how good it is for them to consider God who forever favors them with his beloved presence and by it infuses into their hearts the deepest delights! How good it is to be united forever with the source of all good! They are like happy birds that fly and sing perpetually in that divine air which surrounds them on every side with incredible pleasures. There each one does his utmost and without envy sings his Creator's praise. Be blessed forever, O sweet and sovereign Creator and Savior, you who are so good to us and so generously share with us your glory! With an everlasting blessing God blesses all his saints. Be blessed forever, he says, my beloved creatures, for you have served me and you will praise me eternally with so great a love and zeal.

AFFECTIONS AND RESOLUTIONS

1. Marvel at this heavenly fatherland and praise it. How beautiful you are, my dear Jerusalem, and how happy are your inhabitants.

2. Reproach your heart for its lack of courage up to now and for straying far from the path to this glorious dwelling. Why have I wandered so far from my sovereign happiness? Wretch that I am, for trifling, bitter pleasures I have a thousand thousand times forsaken

these eternal and infinite delights. How could I think of despising such deniable rewards for such empty and contemptible desires?

3. Fervently aspire to this most delightful abode. My good and sovereign Lord, since it has pleased you to direct my steps into your ways, nevermore will I turn away from them. Let us go forward, my dear soul, to that infinite repose, let us travel on to that blessed land which is promised to us. What are we doing in Egypt?

4. I will therefore put away everything that might lead me astray or delay me on this journey.

5. I will do such and such things as may conduct me thither.

      Give thanks; offer; pray.

17. THE NINTH MEDITATION—THE ELECTION AND CHOICE OF HEAVEN

PREPARATION

1. Place yourself in the presence of God.
2. Humble yourself before him and pray that he may inspire you.

CONSIDERATIONS

Imagine yourself to be in an open field, alone with your guardian angel, like young Tobias on his way to Rages. Imagine that he shows high heaven open before you with all its joys as pictured in the meditation you have made, and that he then shows you hell lying open beneath you with all the torments described in the meditation on hell. Situated thus in imagination and kneeling before your guardian angel:

1. Consider that it is strictly true that you stand between heaven and hell and that each of them lies open to receive you according to the choice you make.

2. Consider that the choice of one or the other of them that we make in this world will last eternally in the world to come.

3. Also, that although each of them is open to receive you in keeping with your choice, yet God, who is prepared to give you hell by his justice or heaven by his mercy, desires with an incomparable desire that you choose heaven. With all his power your guardian angel also urges you to do this and in God's name offers you a thousand graces and a thousand helps to assist you to obtain it.

4. From the heights of heaven Jesus Christ mercifully looks down upon you and graciously invites you there. He says, "Come, dear soul, and find everlasting rest in my bountiful arms where I have prepared undying delight for you in the abundance of my love." With your inward eyes behold the Blessed Virgin who maternally bids you: "Courage, my child, do not spurn my Son's desires or the many sighs that I have cast forth for you as I yearn with him for your eternal salvation." Behold the saints who exhort you and the millions of blessed souls who sweetly invite you and wish only to see your heart one day joined with theirs in praising and loving God forever. They assure you that the way to heaven is not as difficult as the world makes it out to be. "Be of good heart, dear brother," they say. "He who carefully considers the way of devotion by which we ascended hither will see that we acquired these delights by pleasures incomparably sweeter than those of the world."

ELECTION

1. Hell, I detest you now and forevermore. I detest your torments and your pains. I detest your accursed and wretched eternity. Above all, I detest the eternal blasphemies and maledictions that you eternally vomit forth against my God. I turn my heart and my soul toward you, O wondrous heaven, everlasting glory, and endless happiness, and choose my abiding place forever within your beauteous and

sacred mansions and among your holy, longed-for tabernacles. O my God, I bless your mercy and I accept the offer you are pleased to give to me. O Jesus, my Savior, I accept your everlasting love and I hail the place and lodging you have purchased for me in this blessed Jerusalem. Beyond any other reason I do so in order to love and bless you forever and ever.

2. Accept the help that the Virgin and the saints offer you. Promise that you will press forward on your way to join them. Reach out your hand to your guardian angel so that he may lead you on. Encourage your soul to make this choice.

18. THE TENTH MEDITATION—THE ELECTION AND CHOICE THE SOUL MAKES OF A DEVOUT LIFE

PREPARATION

1. Place yourself in the presence of God.
2. Humble yourself before him and implore his help.

CONSIDERATIONS

1. Again imagine yourself to be in an open field alone with your guardian angel and that you see the devil seated high upon a huge throne, attended by many infernal spirits and surrounded by a great throng of worldly people who with uncovered heads hail him as their lord and pay him homage, some by one sin and some by another. Note the faces of all the unfortunate courtiers of that abominable king. See how some of them are furious with hatred, envy, and anger, others are consumed with care and burdened down by worries as they think and strive to heap up wealth. See how others are bent upon vain pursuits that bring empty and unsatisfying pleasure and how others are defiled, ruined, and putrefied by their brutish lusts. See

how they are without rest, order, and decency. See how they despise one another and make only a false show of love. In a word, you see there a commonwealth lying in ruins and tyrannized over by this accursed king. All this will move you to compassion.

2. On the right side you see Jesus Christ crucified. With heartfelt love he prays for these poor tormented people so that they may be set free from such tyranny, and he calls them to himself. Around him you see a great throng of devout souls together with their guardian angels. Contemplate the beauty of this devout kingdom. How beautiful it is to see this throng of virgins, both men and women, all whiter than lilies, and this gathering of widows filled with sacred mortification and humility! See the crowded ranks of the married who live so calmly together in mutual respect, which cannot be had without great charity. See how these devout souls wed care of the exterior house to that of the interior, that is, the love of their earthly spouse with that of the heavenly Spouse. Consider them all as a group and see how all of them in a holy, sweet, and lovely manner attend on our Lord, and how they long to place him in the center of their hearts. They are joyful, but with a gracious, loving, and well-ordered joy. They love one another, but with a most pure and sacred love. Among these devout people those who suffer afflictions are not over-concerned about their sufferings and never lose courage. To conclude, look upon the eyes of the Savior who comforts them, and see how all of them together aspire to him.

3. You have already left Satan with his sad and wretched throng by way of the good affections that you have conceived. Still you have not yet joined Jesus the King, nor have you enrolled in his blessed company of devout souls, but you have always been between the two.

4. The Blessed Virgin, together with St. Joseph, St. Louis, St. Monica,

and a hundred thousand others in the ranks of those living in the world invite you and encourage you.

5. The crucified King calls you by name, "Come, my well-beloved, come, that I may crown you."[1]

ELECTION

1. O world! O abominable troop! No, never shall you see me beneath your banner! I have forever abandoned your mad, fruitless ways. King of pride, accursed king, infernal spirit, I renounce you and all your empty pomps! I detest you and all your works.

2. I turn to you, my own Jesus, King of happiness and eternal glory, and I embrace you with all the strength of my soul. I adore you with my whole heart. I choose you to be my King now and forever. By this inviolable act of fidelity I pay you irrevocable homage. I submit myself to your holy laws and ordinances.

3. O holy Virgin, my beloved Lady, I choose you for my guide. I put myself under your direction and offer you particular respect and special reverence. My guardian angel, present me to this sacred assembly. Do not forsake me until I have been enrolled in this blessed company. With them I say and I will say forever in testimony to my choice: Live, Jesus! Live, Jesus!

19. HOW TO MAKE A GENERAL CONFESSION

The following meditations, my dear Philothea, are necessary in order to carry out our purpose. When you have finished them, then proceed with a humble and confident mind to make your general confession. I ask you, don't let fears of any sort disturb you. The scorpion that bites us is poisonous at the moment it strikes, but when reduced to oil it is an effective remedy against its own sting.[1] Sin is shameful only when we commit it; when it has been converted by confession and repentance it becomes honorable and salutary. Contrition and confession are so beautiful and have so good an odor that they wipe away the ugliness of sin and purify its stench. Simon the leper called Magdalen a sinner but our Lord denied that she was one and spoke rather of the perfumes she poured out and of her great charity.[2] If we are truly humble, Philothea, our sins will be infinitely offensive to us since God is offended by them, while to accuse ourselves of our sins becomes sweet and pleasant since God is thereby honored. It is a kind of relief for us to inform our physician rightly as to the nature of a disease that torments us. When you kneel before your spiritual director, imagine that you are on Mount Calvary at the feet of Jesus Christ crucified and that his Precious Blood drops down on every side to cleanse away your iniquities. Although it is not the actual Blood of the Savior, what flows so abundantly over penitents in the confessional is the merit of his Blood. Open wide your heart so that you can cast out your sins in confession. As fast as they issue from it the precious merits of Christ's Passion enter there and fill it with blessings.

Be sure to state everything with candor and sincerity and in this way put your conscience completely at rest. This done, listen to the advice and commands of God's minister and say within your heart, "Speak, Lord, for your servant hears."[3] Yes, Philothea, it is God whom you hear for he has said to his vice-regents, "He who hears you hears me."[4] After your confession make the following protestation. Since it can serve as a conclusion to all your contrition, you should previously have meditated and reflected on it. Read it over carefully and with as much conviction as you can.

20. AN AUTHENTIC DECLARATION TO IMPRESS ON THE SOUL ITS RESOLUTION TO SERVE GOD AND TO CONCLUDE THE ACTS OF PENANCE[1]

I, the undersigned, standing in the presence of the eternal God and of the whole heavenly court, having considered the immense mercy of his divine goodness toward me, a most unworthy and wretched creature, whom he has created out of nothing, preserved, supported, delivered from so many dangers, and loaded with so many benefits, and considering above all the incomprehensible sweetness and mercy with which this most good God has so graciously borne with me in my iniquities, so frequently and so lovingly inspired and urged me to amendment, and so patiently waited for my repentance and conversion until this—year of my life, notwithstanding all the ingratitude, disloyalty, and infidelity by which I have so shamelessly offended him while delaying my conversion and despising his grace; having moreover reflected that on the day of my holy baptism I was so fortunately and holily vowed and dedicated to God to be his child, and that contrary to the profession then made in my name I have so greatly and so often, so execrably and so detestably profaned and violated my soul, applying and employing it against his Divine Majesty; having now at length returned to myself, prostrate in heart and spirit before the throne of divine justice, I acknowledge, avow, and confess myself lawfully attainted and convicted of treason against his Divine Majesty and guilty of the death and passion of Jesus Christ because of the sins I have committed, for which sins he died and suffered the torments of the cross, so that consequently I deserve to be cast away and condemned forever.

Turning toward the throne of the infinite mercy of this same eternal God, and having detested with my whole heart and with my whole strength the iniquitous deeds of my past life, I humbly ask and implore grace, and pardon, and mercy, together with complete absolution from my crime, by virtue of the death and passion of the same Lord and Redeemer of my soul. Relying on this as on the sole foundation of my hope, I again avow and renew the sacred profession of fidelity made in my behalf at my baptism, thus renouncing the devil, the world, and the flesh and detesting their wretched suggestions, vanities, and lusts for the whole time of my present life and for all eternity. Turning to my most gracious and merciful God, I desire, purpose, determine, and irrevocably resolve to serve and love him now and forever. To this end I give and consecrate to him my mind with all its faculties, my soul with all its powers, my heart with all its affections, and my body with all its senses. I protest that I will nevermore abuse any part of my being against his divine will and sovereign Majesty, to which I sacrifice and immolate myself in spirit so as to be forever his loyal, obedient, and faithful creature, without any will ever to revoke this resolution or to repent myself of it. But if, alas, through temptation by the enemy or human frailty I should chance to transgress in any point or fail to adhere to this my resolution and dedication, I protest from this moment and am determined, with the assistance of the Holy Spirit, to rise as soon as I perceive my fall and return again to God's mercy without any sloth or delay whatsoever.

This is my will, my intention, and my inviolable and irrevocable resolution, which I declare and confirm without reservation or exception in God's same sacred presence, before the eyes of the Church triumphant and in the sight of the Church militant, my mother, who hears this my declaration in the person of him who, as her representative, hears me in this action. May it please you, O my God, eternal, almighty, and all-good, Father, Son, and Holy Spirit, to confirm me in this resolution and to accept in the odor of sweetness this inward sacrifice of my heart. And as it has pleased you to grant me the inspiration and the will to do this, so also grant me the strength and the grace needed to perform it. O my God, you are my God,[2] the God of my heart,[3] the God of my soul, and the God of my spirit. As such I acknowledge and adore you now and forevermore. Live, Jesus!

21. CONCLUSION DRAWN FROM THIS FIRST PURGATION

After this protestation has been made attend carefully and open your heart's ears in order to hear in spirit the words of absolution which the same Savior of your soul, seated on the throne of his mercy on high in heaven will pronounce before all the angels and saints at the same instant as the priest in his name absolves you here below on earth. Then all this company of the blessed will rejoice in your happiness. With incomparable joy they will sing a spiritual canticle and all of them will give the kiss of peace and fellowship to your heart, now restored to grace and sanctity.

By God's mercy, Philothea, how wonderful is this contract whereby you have made a blissful treaty with his Divine Majesty! When you give yourself to him you win both him and yourself for eternal life. Hence nothing further remains but to take pen in hand and with a sincere heart sign your act of protestation. Then approach the altar where God in turn will sign and seal your absolution and the promise he makes to you of his paradise. In his sacrament he will put himself as a seal and sacred signet upon your heart, now made new again.[1] In this way, Philothea, your soul will be purged from sin and from all affection for sin.

Yet such affections easily spring up again in the soul because of our infirmity and concupiscence, which may be mortified but will never die as long as we live here upon earth. I will therefore give you certain instructions which, if carefully observed, will preserve you so effectively from mortal sin and all affection for it that it will never again find a place in your heart. In order that these same instructions may contribute to a still more perfect purification, before I give them to you I will say something about that absolute purity to which I wish to lead you.

22. WE MUST PURIFY OURSELVES OF AFFECTION FOR VENIAL SIN

As the day breaks we see more clearly in a mirror spots and stains on our faces; so also as the inward light of the Holy Spirit brightens our consciences we more clearly and distinctly see the sins, inclinations, and imperfections that can keep us from attaining to true devotion. The same light that enables us to see such defects and blemishes inflames us with desire to cleanse and purify ourselves of them.

You will find, my dear Philothea, that in addition to mortal sins and affections for mortal sins, from which you have been purified by the foregoing exercises already described, there still remain in your soul various inclinations and affections for venial sins. I do not say that you will find venial sins there, but I say that you will discover affections and inclinations to them. The second fact is very different from the other. We can never be completely free of venial sins, at least so as to continue for long in such purity, yet we can avoid all affection for venial sins. Surely it is one thing to tell a lie now and then as a joke in something of no importance and another thing to like lying and to have an affection for that kind of sin.

We must purge the soul of every affection to venial sin. That is to say, we must not voluntarily nourish a desire to continue and persevere in venial sin of any kind. It would be an extremely base thing to wish deliberately to retain in our heart anything so displeasing to God as a will to offend him. No matter how small it is, a venial sin offends God, although it does not offend him so much that he wills to damn or destroy us. But since venial sin offends him, any will and affection we have for venial sin is simply a resolution to be willing to offend his Divine Majesty. Is it in fact possible for a generous soul not only to be willing to offend God but even to have an affection for offending him?

Philothea, such affections are directly contrary to devotion, just as affections for mortal sin are directly contrary to charity. They weaken the powers of our spirit, stand in the way of God's consolations, and open the door to temptation. Although they do not kill the soul, they make it extremely ill. "Dying flies destroy, spoil, and damage the sweetness of the ointment," says the Wise Man,[1] meaning that the flies that do not stay in the ointment but eat some of it as they pass spoil only what they take and leave the rest untouched, while those that die in the ointment deprive it of all value and make it disgusting to us. In like manner venial sins that enter into a devout soul but do not stay there long do it no great damage, but if those same sins remain in the soul because of some affection it has for them, they undoubtedly cause it to lose "the sweetness of its ointment," that is, holy devotion.

Spiders do not kill bees but spoil and corrupt their honey and tangle the honeycombs with their webs so that the bees cannot do their work. This must be understood of times when the spiders stay among them. In like manner, venial sins do not kill the soul but spoil its devotion and so entangle its powers in bad habits and inclinations that it can no longer exert the prompt charity that constitutes devotion. This must also be understood of times when venial sin continues to dwell in our soul by an affection we have for it. Philothea, it is not a matter of any great moment to tell a little lie or to fall into some slight irregularity in words, actions, looks, dress, jokes, games, or dances, provided that as soon as these spiritual spiders have entered our conscience we chase them away and banish them, as flies do real spiders. If we let them remain in our hearts, and not only that, if we permit our

desires to retain and multiply them, we shall soon find our honey ruined and the hive that is our conscience corrupted and ruined. I ask
once more, what likelihood is there that a generous soul should be
pleased to displease God, or like being disagreeable to him, or really
will what it knows would offend him?

23. WE MUST PURIFY OURSELVES OF AFFECTION FOR USELESS AND DANGEROUS THINGS

Sports, banquets, parties, fine clothes, and stage comedies are all things
that, considered in themselves, are by no means evil. They are indifferent acts and therefore they can be either good or bad. At the same time
such things are always dangerous and to have an affection for them is
still more dangerous. Hence, Philothea, I hold that although it is licit to
engage in sports, dance, wear fine clothes, attend harmless comedies,
and enjoy banquets, to have a strong liking for such things is not only
opposed to devotion but also extremely harmful and dangerous. It is
not evil to do such things but it is evil to be attached to them. It is a pity
to sow such vain and foolish affections in our heart's soil. They usurp
the place of worthwhile interests and hinder the sap of our soul from
being used for good inclinations.

The ancient Nazarenes abstained not only from anything that
might inebriate them but also from both sweet grapes and bitter.[1] This
was not because such grapes could intoxicate them but because there
was danger that eating sour grapes would arouse an appetite for fresh
grapes and eating fresh grapes would arouse an appetite to drink must[2]
and wine. I do not hold that we can never use these dangerous things,
but I say that we can never set our affections on them without damage
to devotion. When stags have put on too much weight they scatter and
hide in thickets; they know that fat slows them up so that they cannot

run if they are pursued. So also when man's heart is burdened with these useless, superfluous, and dangerous affections, it certainly cannot run quickly, lightly, and easily after God, the true end of the devout life. Children amuse themselves by eagerly running after butterflies and because they are children no one finds fault with them. But is it not ridiculous, or rather lamentable, to see mature men set their hearts and affections on such worthless trifles as the things I have named, things that are not only useless but put us in peril of becoming irregular and undisciplined in our pursuit of them? For such reasons, my dear Philothea, I say that we must purge ourselves of these affections. Although such acts are not always opposed to devotion, the affections are always damaging to it.

24. WE MUST PURGE OURSELVES OF OUR EVIL INCLINATIONS

We have certain natural inclinations, Philothea, that do not spring from particular sins and are not properly sins, either mortal or venial; they are called imperfections and the acts issuing from them are called defects and failings. For example, according to St. Jerome,[1] St. Paula was so much inclined to sadness and grief that after her children and husband died she was in danger of dying of grief. This was an imperfection but not a sin, since it was against her liking and will. Some people are naturally cheerful, while others are gloomy; some contradict others, while others are inclined to indignation; some are prone to anger and some to love. In short, there are few people in whom we may not observe some such imperfections. Now although they are peculiar and natural to each of us, by care and a contrary affection we can correct and restrain them and even completely purify and free ourselves of them. Philothea, I insist that we must do this. Just as a way has been found to change bitter almond trees into sweet by piercing them at the bottom to let out the juice,[2] why may not we let out our perverse inclinations and thus become better? There is no nature so good that it cannot be perverted to evil by vicious habits; there is none so perverse that it cannot, first by God's grace and secondly by our own labor and care, be brought under control and overcome. I am now going to give you certain instructions and propose certain exercises by which you can purge your soul of dangerous affections, imperfections, and all liking for venial sins and safeguard your conscience more and more against all mortal sin. May God grant you the grace to practice them well.

THE SECOND PART OF THE INTRODUCTION

Various Instructions for Elevating the Soul to God by Prayer and the Sacraments

1. THE NECESSITY OF PRAYER

1. Since prayer places our intellect in the brilliance of God's light and exposes our will to the warmth of his heavenly love, nothing else so effectively purifies our intellect of ignorance and our will of depraved affections. It is a stream of holy water that flows forth and makes the plants of our good desires grow green and flourish and quenches the passions within our hearts.

2. I especially counsel you to practice mental prayer, the prayer of the heart, and particularly that which centers on the life and passion of our Lord. By often turning your eyes on him in meditation, your whole soul will be filled with him. You will learn his ways and form your actions after the pattern

of his. He is "the light of the world,"[1] and therefore it is in him and by him and for him that we must be instructed and enlightened. He is the tree of desire in whose shade we must be refreshed.[2] He is that living "fountain of Jacob"[3] in which we can wash ourselves clean of all our stains. Finally, just as little children learn to speak by listening to their mothers and lisping words with them, so also by keeping close to our Savior in meditation and observing his words, actions, and affections we learn by his grace to speak, act, and will like him.

We must pause here, Philothea, and I assure you that we cannot go to God the Father except through this gate.[4] Just as the glass in a mirror could never catch our gaze unless there was tin or lead behind it, so also in this world by our own efforts we could not successfully contemplate the godhead unless it had been united to the sacred humanity of our Savior. His life and death are the most fitting, sweet, wonderful, and profitable subject that we can choose for our ordinary meditations. It is not without purpose that our Savior calls himself "the bread that came down from heaven."[5] Just as bread is eaten with all kinds of food, so also the Savior should be meditated on, considered, and sought for in all our prayers and actions. His life and death have been analyzed and arranged according to various points for purposes of meditation by many authors. Those whom I recommend to you are St. Bonaventure,[6] Bellintani,[7] Bruno,[8] Capilia,[9] Granada,[10] and Du Pont.[11]

3. Set aside an hour every day before dinner, if possible early in the morning, when your mind is less distracted and fresher after the night's rest. Don't extend it for more than an hour unless your spiritual director expressly tells you to do so.

4. If you can perform this exercise in church and find sufficient quiet there, that will be the easiest and most convenient place for you since no one—father or mother, husband or wife, or anyone else—can very well keep you from spending an hour in church. On the other hand because of obligations to others you perhaps could not be sure of a free hour at home.

5. Begin all your prayers, whether mental or vocal, in the presence of God. Keep to this rule without any exception and you will quickly see how helpful it will be.

6. If you follow my advice, Philothea, you will say your *Pater, Ave Maria,* and *Credo* in Latin, but you should also learn to understand well the words in your own language so that while saying them in the common language of the Church you can also appreciate the wonderful and beautiful meaning of those holy prayers. They must be said with strict attention of mind and with affections aroused by the meaning of the words. Do not hurry along and say many things but try to speak from your heart. A single *Our Father* said with feeling has greater value than many said quickly and hurriedly.

7. The rosary is a very useful form of prayer, provided you know how to say it properly. To do this, get one of the little books that teach us the way to recite it. It is also a good thing to say the litanies of our Lord, our Lady, and the saints and other vocal prayers that may be found in approved manuals and books of hours. However, if you have the gift of mental prayer, you should always give it first place. Afterwards if you cannot say your vocal prayers because of your many duties or for some other reason, don't be disturbed on that account. Be satisfied with saying either before or after your meditation the Lord's prayer, the Angelic Salutation, and the Apostles' Creed.

8. During vocal prayer if you find your heart drawn and invited to interior or mental prayer, don't refuse to take it up. Let your mind turn very gently in that direction and don't be concerned at not finishing the vocal prayers you intended to say. The mental prayer you substitute for them is more pleasing to God and more profitable for your soul. I make an exception for the Divine Office,[12] if you are obliged to say it, as in that case you must fulfill your obligation.

9. If it should happen through pressure of business or for some other reason that your whole morning has passed by without this exercise of mental prayer—you must not let this happen if it is possible to

prevent it—try to repair this loss after dinner. This should be done some hours after your meal, since if it were right away and before digestion had advanced, you would be drowsy and your health might be injured. But if you cannot do this at any time during the day, you must repair the loss by multiplying ejaculatory prayers and reading books of devotion, together with some act of penance which may prevent the bad consequences of this defect. Along with this, make a firm resolution to return to your custom on the next day.

2. A SHORT METHOD OF MEDITATION, AND FIRST OF THE PRESENCE OF GOD, WHICH IS THE FIRST POINT OF THE PREPARATION

It may be that you do not know how to pray mentally, Philothea, for unfortunately this is something that few people in our time know how to do. For this reason I will give you a short, simple method to use until you are more fully instructed by reading some of the many good books written on the subject, and above all by practice. I will first explain the preparatory part. This consists in two points: (1) place yourself in the presence of God, and (2) invoke his assistance. To help you place yourself in God's presence, I propose four principal means that you can use for this beginning.

The first consists of a lively, attentive realization of God's absolute presence, that is, that God is in all things and all places. There is no place or thing in this world where he is not truly present. Just as wherever birds fly they always encounter the air, so also wherever we go or wherever we are we find God present. Everyone knows this truth but everyone does not try to bring it home to himself. Blind men do not see a prince who is present among them, and therefore do not show him the respect they do after being told of his presence. However, because they do not actually see him they easily forget his presence, and having forgotten it, they still more easily lose the respect and reverence owed to him. Unfortunately, Philothea, we do not see God who is present with us. Although faith assures us of his presence, yet because we do not see him with our eyes we often forget about him and behave as if God were far distant from us. We really know that he is present in all things, but because we do not reflect on that fact we act as if we did not know it. This is why before praying we must always arouse our souls to explicit thought and consideration of God's presence. Such was David's mental state when he cried out: "If I go up to the heavens, O my God, you are there; if I descend into hell, you are there."[1] Hence we should use the words of Jacob, for when he saw the sacred ladder he said: "How awesome is this place! Truly the Lord is in this place, and I did not know it."[2] The meaning is that he did not reflect on God's presence, for he could not have been ignorant of the fact that God is in everything and every place. Therefore, when you prepare to pray you must say with your whole heart and in your heart, "O my heart, my heart, God is truly here!"

The second way to place yourself in God's holy presence is to remember that he is not only in the place where you are but also that he is present in a most particular manner in your heart and in the very center of your spirit. He enlivens and animates it by his divine presence, for he is there as the heart of your heart and the spirit of your spirit. Just as the soul is diffused throughout the entire body and is therefore present in every part of the body but resides in a special manner in the heart, so also God is present in all things but always resides in a special manner in our spirit. For this reason David calls him "the God of his heart,"[3] and St. Paul says that "we live, and move, and are in God."[4] Therefore in consideration of this truth excite in your heart great reverence toward God who is so intimately present in it.

A third way is to consider how our Savior in his humanity gazes down from heaven on all mankind and particularly on Christians, who are his children, and most especially on those who are at prayer, whose actions and conduct he observes. This is by no means a mere figment of the imagination but the very truth. Although we do not see him, it remains true that from on high he beholds us. At the time of his martyrdom, St. Stephen saw him in this way.[5] Hence we may truly say with the Spouse, "Here, he stands behind our wall, gazing through the windows, looking through the lattices."[6]

A fourth method consists in use of simple imagination when we represent to ourselves the Savior in his sacred humanity as if he were near us, just as we sometimes imagine a friend to be present and say, "I imagine that I see such a one who is doing this or that," or "I seem to see him" or something similar. If the most Blessed Sacrament of the Altar is present, then Christ's presence is real and not purely imaginary. The species and appearances of bread are like a tapestry behind which our Lord is really present[7] and sees and observes us, although we do not see him in his own form.

Hence you will employ one of these four means of placing yourself in the presence of God before prayer. Do not use them all at once, but only one at a time and that briefly and simply.

3. THE INVOCATION, THE SECOND POINT OF PREPARATION

The invocation is made in the following way. Knowing that it stands in God's presence, your soul prostrates itself before him with the most profound reverence. It acknowledges that it is most unworthy to appear before such sovereign Majesty, but since it knows that this same supreme goodness wills that it should be so, it implores his grace in order to serve and adore him properly in this meditation. If you so wish you can use some short, ardent words, such as those of David: "O God, cast me not out from your presence and your holy Spirit take not from me."[1] "Let your face shine upon your servant,"[2] and "I will consider the wonders of your law."[3] "Give me discernment and I will keep it with my whole heart."[4] "I am your servant; give me discernment,"[5] and similar words. It will also be helpful to invoke your guardian angel as well as the holy saints who had part in the mystery on which you meditate. For example, when meditating on the death of our Lord, you can invoke our Lady, St. John, Mary Magdalen, and the good thief, begging that the affections and interior movements they then conceived may be shared with you. When meditating on your own death you can invoke your guardian angel, who will then be with you, to inspire you with suitable considerations. So also for the other mysteries.

4. THE SUBJECT OF THE MYSTERY, THE THIRD POINT OF PREPARATION

In addition to these two ordinary points in the preparation there is a third, which is not common to every kind of meditation. Some call this third point the composition of place and others the interior lesson. This is simply to picture in imagination the entire mystery you wish to meditate on as if it really took place here before us. For example, if you wish to meditate on our Lord on the Cross, imagine that you are on Mount Calvary and that there you see and hear all that was done or said on the day of his passion. Or if you wish, for it is all one, imagine that in the very place where you are our Lord is crucified in the manner described by the holy evangelists. It is the same when you meditate on death, as I have noted in the meditation on it, and so also on hell or on any similar mystery in which visible and sensible objects form part of the subject. As to other mysteries, such as God's greatness, the excellency of the virtues, or the end for which we have been created, such things are invisible and there is no question of using our imagination in this way. It is true that we may use some similitude or comparison to assist us in our consideration of them but this involves some difficulty. My intention is to explain this so simply that your mind will not be too much concerned about making use of such devices.

By such imaginative means we restrict our mind to the mystery on which we meditate so that it will not wander about, just as we cage a bird or put a leash on a hawk so he can rest on our hand. Perhaps someone will tell you that it is better to represent such mysteries by the simple thoughts of faith and completely intellectual and spiritual conceptions, or else to consider them as taking place within your own soul. This method is too subtle for beginners. Until God raises you up higher, Philothea, I advise you to remain in the low valley I have shown you.

5. CONSIDERATIONS, THE SECOND PART OF MEDITATION

After the imagination has done its part there follows the act of the intellect and this we term meditation. This is simply to make one or more considerations in order to raise our affections to God and the things of God. Hence meditation differs from study and other thoughts and considerations done not to acquire virtue or love of God but for other ends and intentions, such as to become learned, to write, or to reason. Having restricted our mind within the limits of the subject we wish to meditate on, as I have said, whether by imagination if the subject is one of sense perception or by a simple proposal of it if it is not sensible, then begin by forming considerations of it on the pattern of meditations that I have given to you. If your mind finds enough appeal, light, and fruit in any of them, remain with that point and do not go on any further. Imitate the bees, who do not leave a flower as long as they can extract any honey out of it. But if you do not come on anything that appeals to you after you have examined and tried it for a while, then go on to another, but proceed calmly and simply in this matter and do not rush yourself.

6. AFFECTIONS AND RESOLUTIONS,
THE THIRD PART OF MEDITATION

Meditation produces devout movements in the will, the affective part of our soul, such as love of God and neighbor, desire for heaven and glory, zeal for the salvation of souls, imitation of the life of our Lord, compassion, awe, joy, fear of God's displeasure, judgment, and hell, hatred of sin, confidence in God's goodness and mercy, and deep sorrow for the sins of our past life. In such affections our mind should open up as much as possible. If you wish to be assisted in this, open up the first volume of the *Meditations* by Dom Andrea Capiglia[1] and consult its preface where he shows the way to expand such affections. Father Arias[2] does the same thing more fully in his *Treatise on Prayer*.

However, you must not dwell so long on these general reflections, Philothea, as to change them into special and particular resolutions for your own correction and improvement. For example, the first word our Lord spoke on the cross will undoubtedly excite in your soul a holy longing to imitate him, namely, a desire to pardon your enemies and to love them. I point out that this will be only a little thing unless you add a special resolution like this: Well, then, from now on I will not be offended by the disagreeable words a man or woman—e.g., some man or woman who is my neighbor, a manservant, or maid—says to me, or by scornful treatment suffered from some one or other. On the contrary, I will say and do such and such a thing in order to win him over and appease him. Thus also with regard to other such matters. In this way, Philothea, you will correct your faults in a short time, whereas by affections alone it would be a slow, difficult task.

7. CONCLUSION AND SPIRITUAL BOUQUET

Finally, we must conclude our meditation with three acts, and they must be made with the greatest possible humility. The first is the act of thanksgiving, by which we return thanks to God for the affections and resolutions he has given us and for his goodness and mercy, which we have found in the mystery meditated on. The second is the act of offering, by which we offer to God his own goodness and mercy, his Son's death, Blood, and virtues, and in union with them our own affections and resolutions. The third act is that of supplication, by which we beseech God and implore him to share with us the graces and virtues of his Son and to bless our affections and resolutions so that we may faithfully fulfill them. We then pray for the Church, our pastors, relatives, friends, and others, using for that purpose the intercession of our Lady, the angels, and the saints. Lastly, as I have already noted, we must say the *Pater Noster*, and the *Ave Maria*, which are the general and necessary prayers of all the faithful.

In addition to all this, as I have already told you, you must gather a little devotional bouquet. I explain my meaning. People who have been walking about in a beautiful garden do not like to leave without gathering in their hands four or five flowers to smell and keep for the rest of the day. In the same way, when our soul has carefully considered by meditation a certain mystery we should select one, two, or three points that we liked best and that are most adapted to our improvement, think frequently about them, and smell them spiritually during the rest of the day. This is done in the place where we meditated, either remaining there alone or walking by ourselves for some time.

8. CERTAIN USEFUL INSTRUCTIONS
ON THE SUBJECT OF MEDITATION

Most of all, Philothea, after you rise from meditation you must remember the resolutions and decisions you have made and carefully put them into effect on that very day. This is the great fruit of meditation and without it meditation is often not only useless but even harmful. Virtues meditated on but not practiced sometimes inflate our minds and courage and we think that we are really such as we have thought and resolved to be. Certainly this is true if our resolutions are lively and solid; they are not such but even vain and dangerous if we do not practice them. By all means, therefore, we must try to practice them and to seek occasions, small or great, to do so. For example, if I have resolved to win over by mildness the hearts of those who offend me, I will look this very day for an opportunity to meet them and greet them in a friendly way. If I cannot meet them, at least I will speak of them and pray to God in their behalf.

After finishing your mental prayer, watch against disturbing your heart lest you spill the balm that it has received through prayer. I mean that if possible you must keep silence for a little while and gently transfer your heart from prayer to other duties. Preserve as long as you can the feelings and affections you have conceived. A man who has been given a precious liquid in a porcelain vase to carry home walks carefully, does not look from side to side, but looks now straight ahead for fear of stumbling against a stone or making a false step and now at the vase to see that it doesn't spill. You must do the same thing after you finish your meditation. Don't let anything distract you but simply look straight ahead. In other words, if you meet anyone with whom you have to talk, nothing can be done about it and you must adapt yourself to the situation. However, you must keep watch on your heart, so that as little of the liquor of holy prayer as possible is spilt out.

You must even accustom yourself to know how to pass from prayer

to all the various duties your vocation and state of life rightly and lawfully require of you, even though they appear far different from the affections you received in prayer. I mean that the lawyer must be able to
pass from prayer to pleading cases, the merchant to commerce, and the
married woman to her duties as wife and her household tasks with so
much ease and tranquillity that their minds are not disturbed. Since
both prayer and your other duties are in conformity with God's will,
you must pass from one to the other with a devout and humble mind.

It may sometimes happen that immediately after the preparation you
will feel that your affections are drawn wholly towards God. In this case,
Philothea, you must give them free rein and not follow the method I have
shown you. Ordinarily, consideration must precede affections and resolutions. However, when the Holy Spirit gives you the affections before
the consideration, you must not look for the consideration since it is used
only to arouse the affections. In a word, whenever affections present
themselves you must accept them and make room for them whether they
come before or after the considerations. Although I have put the affections after all the considerations, I have done so merely to distinguish
more clearly between the parts of prayer. In fact, it is a general rule never
to restrain the affections but to let them have a free course when they
present themselves. I say this not only with regard to the other affections
but also in respect to acts of thanksgiving, offering, and prayer, which
may likewise be made during the considerations. They must not be restrained any more than the other affections, although later it is necessary
to resume and repeat them as a conclusion to the meditation. As for the
resolutions, they must always be made after the affections and at the end
of the whole meditation before the conclusion, since in them we represent to ourselves particular, familiar objects. Hence if we placed them
among the affections they would expose us to distractions.

While we are forming our affections and resolutions, it is good to
employ colloquies and to speak sometimes to our Lord, sometimes to angels and to persons represented in the mysteries, to saints, ourselves, our

own hearts, sinners, and even to insensible creatures, as we see David doing in the Psalms and other saints in their prayers and meditations.

9. THE DRYNESS SOMETIMES EXPERIENCED IN MEDITATION

If it should happen that you find no joy or comfort in meditation, Philothea, I urge you not to be disturbed but to open your heart's door to words of vocal prayer. Express sorrow for yourself to our Lord, confess your unworthiness, ask him to help you, kiss his image if you have it near you, and repeat Jacob's words, "Lord, I will not let you go until you bless me,"[1] or those of the Canaanite woman "Yes, Lord, 'I am a dog,' for the whelps also eat the crumbs that fall from their master's table."[2] At other times, turn to some spiritual book and read it attentively until your mind is awakened and restored within you. Sometimes you can arouse your heart by some act or movement of exterior devotion, such as prostrating yourself on the ground, crossing your hands before your breast, or embracing a crucifix. It is understood that you are in some retired place.

After this if you have not received any consolation do not be disturbed, no matter how great the dryness may be, but continue to keep a devout posture before God. How many courtiers go a hundred times a year into the prince's audience chamber without any hope of speaking to him but merely to be seen by him and do their duty. We too, my dear Philothea, ought to approach holy prayer purely and simply to do our duty and testify to our fidelity. If it pleases his Divine Majesty to speak to us and aid us by his holy inspirations and interior consolations, it is certainly a great honor and the sweetest of delights. But if it does not please him to grant this favor and he leaves without speaking to us, just as if he did not see us at all or we were not in his presence, we must not leave on that account. On the contrary, we must remain with a respectful and devotional bearing in the presence of his sovereign goodness. He will unfailingly be pleased with our patience and take note of our diligence and perseverance, so that when we again come before him he will favor and help us by his consolations and enable us to see how sweet is holy prayer. Yet if he does not do so, Philothea, let us be content that it is the very greatest honor for us to stand before him and in his sight.

10. THE MORNING EXERCISE

In addition to complete, formal, mental prayer and the various vocal prayers that we should say during the day, there are five other shorter kinds of prayer. They are divisions and branches, as it were, of the principal kind of prayer. Among them the first is morning prayer, which is made as a general preparation for all the day's actions. It may be made in the following manner.

1. Adore God profoundly and thank him for the grace of preserving you during the preceding night and implore his pardon if you committed any sin during the course of it.

2. Remember that the present day is given to you in order to gain the future day of eternity and make a firm purpose to employ the day well for this intention.

3. Anticipate what tasks, transactions, and occasions for serving God you may meet on this day and to what temptations of offending him you will be exposed, whether by anger, vanity, or some other irregularity. By a holy resolution prepare yourself to make the best use of the means that will be offered to you to serve God and advance in devotion. On the other hand, carefully prepare to avoid, resist, and overcome whatever may be encountered that is opposed to your salvation and God's glory. It is not sufficient simply to make this resolution; you must also prepare means of putting it into practice. For example, if I foresee that I will have to discuss some matter with a man who is emotional and prone to anger, I will not only resolve to keep from giving him offense but I will think of pleasant words to prevent his anger or get the assistance of

someone who can keep him in good humor. If I foresee an opportunity to visit a sick person I will arrange the time and the comforts and helps I can bring to him. So also for the rest of such things.

4. This done, humble yourself in the presence of God and acknowledge that by yourself you can do none of the things you have decided on, whether of avoiding evil or of doing good. As though holding your heart in your hands, offer it along with all your good purposes to his Divine Majesty, beseeching him to take it under his protection and strengthen it so that it may turn out successfully in his service. Do this by such unspoken words as the following or their like: "Lord, here is this wretched heart of mine, which through your goodness has conceived many good affections. Alas, it is too weak and miserable to do the good that it desires to do unless you impart your heavenly blessing. For this purpose I humbly beg your blessing, O merciful Father, through the merits of the passion of your Son, in whose honor I consecrate this day and all the remaining days of my life." Invoke our Lady, your guardian angel, and the saints that they may assist you to this effect.

All these spiritual acts must be made briefly and fervently and if possible before leaving your room, so that by means of this exercise whatever you do throughout the day may be watered by God's blessing. Philothea, I beg you never to omit this exercise.

11. THE EVENING EXERCISE AND EXAMINATION OF CONSCIENCE

Just before the day's dinner you prepare a spiritual repast by means of meditation, so before supper you must prepare a light devotional and spiritual supper or collation. Set aside a free period a little before the hour for supper, prostrate yourself before God and place your soul before Jesus Christ crucified. You may represent him to yourself by a simple consideration and interior glance, rekindle in your heart the fire of your morning meditation by a dozen lively aspirations, acts of humility, and loving transports directed towards this divine Savior of your soul, or by repeating the points in your morning meditation you liked best or arousing yourself to devotion by some new subject, as you may prefer.

As to the examination of conscience, which must always be made before going to bed, everyone knows how it is to be performed.

1. We give thanks to God for having kept us during the past day.

2. We examine how we conducted ourselves throughout the whole course of the day. To do so more easily, we may reflect on where, with whom, and in what work we have been engaged.

3. If we find that we have done any good, we must thank God for it. On the other hand, if we have done anything wrong in thought, word, or deed, we must ask pardon of his Divine Majesty with a resolution to confess it at the first opportunity and to make careful amendment for it.

4. After this we recommend to God's providence our body and soul, the Church, our relatives, and friends. We beg our Lady, our guardian angel, and the saints to watch over us and for us. Thus with God's blessing we go to take the rest that he has decreed as necessary for us.

This exercise, like that in the morning, must never be forgotten. By the morning exercise you open the windows of your soul to the Sun of Justice and by this evening exercise you close them against the shadows of hell.

12. SPIRITUAL RETREAT

At this point, Philothea, I strongly urge you to accept my counsel since in this article is found one of the most certain means to spiritual advancement.

During the course of the day recall as often as possible by one of the four ways I have indicated that you are in God's presence. Consider what God does and what you are doing. You will see his eyes turned toward you and constantly fixed on you with incomparable love. Then you will say to him: "O God, why do I not look always at you, just as you always look at me? Why do you think so often of me, O my Lord, and why do I think so seldom of you? Where are we, O my soul? God is our true place, and where are we?"

Birds have nests in trees and can retire to them when need arises and stags have bushes and thickets where they take cover, hide, and enjoy the cool shade during the summer. So also, Philothea, our hearts should each day pick and choose some place, either on Mount Calvary or within our Lord's wounds or in some other place near him, as a retreat where they can retire at various times to refresh and restore themselves during their exterior occupations. There, as in a stronghold, they can defend themselves against temptations. Blessed will be the soul that can truly say to our Lord: "You are my place of strength and my stronghold to give me safety, my roof against the rain, my shade against the heat."[1]

Always remember, then, Philothea, to retire at various times into the solitude of your own heart even while outwardly engaged in discussions or transactions with others. This mental solitude cannot be violated by the many people who surround you since they are not standing around your heart but only around your body. Your heart remains alone in the presence of God. Such was the exercise King David practiced amid his many occupations and he testifies to it countless times in the Psalms, as when he says: "O Lord, I am always with you."[2] "I see the Lord always before me."[3] "I have lifted up my eyes to you, O my God, who dwell in heaven."[4] "My eyes are ever toward God."[5] Indeed, our tasks are seldom so important as to keep us from withdrawing our hearts from them from time to time in order to retire into this divine solitude.

When the father and mother of St. Catherine of Siena deprived her of all opportunity for time and place to pray and meditate, our Lord inspired her to build a little oratory within her soul where she could retire mentally and enjoy this holy heartfelt solitude while going about her outward duties. Afterwards when the world attacked her it caused her no trouble, she said, because she had shut herself up in her interior closet and there was comforted by her heavenly Spouse. Because of this she afterwards counseled her spiritual children to make a cell within their own hearts and dwell in it.

Therefore withdraw your spirit from time to time into your heart and there, apart from the world of men, you can converse heart to heart with God on your state of soul. Say with David: "I have watched and am become like a pelican of the wilderness. I have become like the night-raven or the owl in ruins, and like the sparrow alone on the rooftop."[6] In addition to their literal sense, which testifies that this great king spent solitary hours in contemplation of spiritual things, by their mystical sense these words tell us about three excellent places of retreats or hermitages where we may imitate the solitude of our Savior. On Mount Calvary he was like the pelican in the wilderness which revives her dead chicks with her own blood. At his Nativity in a desolate stable he was the owl in a ruined building, mourning and weeping for our offenses and sins. At his Ascension he was like the sparrow flying up to heaven, which is, as it were the rooftop of the world. To these three places we can retreat even amid the turmoil of our outward affairs. When Blessed Elzear, Count of Arian in Provence, had been away for a long time from his devout and chaste wife Delphina, she sent a messenger to him to inquire about his health and he returned this answer: "I am very well, my dear wife, but if you desire to see me, you must seek me in the wound in the side of our beloved Jesus, for it is there that I dwell and there that you shall find me. If you seek me elsewhere, you will seek in vain."[7] He was indeed a Christian knight.

13. ASPIRATIONS, EJACULATORY PRAYERS, AND GOOD THOUGHTS

We retire into God before we aspire to him, and we aspire to him so that we may retire into him. Hence aspirations to be with God and spiritual retirement support one another and both proceed and are born from good thoughts.

Make spiritual aspirations to God by short, ardent movements of your heart, Philothea. Marvel at his beauty, implore his help, cast yourself in spirit at the foot of the cross, adore his goodness, converse often with him about your salvation, present your soul to him a thousand times during the day, fix your interior eyes upon his sweet countenance, stretch out your hand to him like a little child to his father so that he may lead you on, place him in your bosom like a fragrant bouquet, plant him in your heart like a flag, and make a thousand different motions of your heart to provide you with love of God and arouse in yourself a passionate and tender affection for this divine Spouse.

Ejaculatory prayer was strongly recommended by the great St. Augustine to the devout Lady Proba.[1] Philothea, if our mind thus habituates itself to intimacy, privacy, and familiarity with God, it will be completely perfumed by his perfections. There is no difficulty in this exercise, as it may be interspersed among all our tasks and duties without any inconvenience, since in this spiritual retirement or amid these interior aspirations we only relax quickly and briefly. This does not hinder but rather assists us greatly in what we do. The pilgrim who takes a little wine to restore his heart and refresh his mouth stops for a while but does not interrupt his journey by doing so. On the contrary, he gains new strength to finish it more quickly and easily since he rests only in order to proceed the better.

Many people have made collections of vocal ejaculations and they can be very useful. However, my advice is not to restrict yourself to a set form of words but to pronounce either within your heart or with your lips such words as love suggests to you at the time. It will supply you with as many as you wish. It is true that there are certain words that have a special power to satisfy the heart in this respect. Such are the aspirations strewn so thickly throughout the Psalms of David, various invocations of the name of Jesus, and the loving thoughts uttered in the Canticle of Canticles. Spiritual songs also answer the same purpose when sung with attention.

To conclude, the thoughts of those moved by natural human love are almost completely fastened on the beloved object, their hearts are filled with affection for it, and their mouths full of its praises. When it is absent they lose no opportunity of testifying to their passions by letters, and they do not pass by a tree without inscribing the name of their beloved in its bark. Thus too those who love God can never stop thinking about him, longing for him, aspiring to him, and speaking about him. If it were possible, they would engrave the holy, sacred name of Jesus on the breasts of all mankind. All things call them to this and there is no creature that does not proclaim the praises of their Beloved. As St. Augustine, following St. Anthony, says, all things in this world speak to them in a silent but intelligible language in behalf of their love.[2] All things arouse them to good thoughts, and they in turn give birth to many flights and aspirations to God. Here are some examples.

St. Gregory, bishop of Nazianzus, told his people[3] of how he walked on the seashore and observed how the waves advancing on the beach left behind them shells, little conches, bits of weed, small oysters, and the like which the sea had cast up and spat out as it were on the shore. Then it returned with other waves and took some of them back and swallowed them up again, but all the while the nearby rocks stood firm and immovable although the waters beat against them with great violence. He made the following fine reflection on all this. Like the shells, conches, and bits of weed, weak souls let themselves be carried away, sometimes by affliction, sometimes by consolation, at the mercy of the tides and waves of fortune, while courageous souls stand firm and unmoved before storms of every kind. From this thought he went on to those aspirations of David: "Save me, O Lord, for the waters have come even into my soul. O Lord, deliver me out of the depths of the waters. I have come to the depths of the sea, and the storm has overwhelmed me,"[4] for at the time he was afflicted by the unhappy usurpation of his bishopric attempted by Maximus.

St. Fulgentius, bishop of Ruspa, was present at a general assembly of the Roman nobility when Theodoric, king of the Goths, addressed them, and as he looked at the splendor of so many great lords, each standing according to his rank, he said: "O God, how glorious must the heavenly Jerusalem be, since here below we see earthly Rome in such pomp! If in this world such splendor is granted to the lovers of vanity, what must be the glory reserved in the next world for those who contemplate the truth!"[5]

It is said that St. Anselm, archbishop of Canterbury, by whose birth our mountains have been so highly honored, was admirable in this practice of forming good thoughts. Once when this holy prelate was making a journey, a hare pursued by dogs ran under his horse as to a place of refuge suggested by the imminent danger of death. The dogs barked around him but did not dare to violate the sanctuary to which their prey had run. This extraordinary sight made the whole company burst out laughing but the great Anselm wept and groaned and cried out, "Ah, you laugh but the poor beast does not laugh! The enemies of the soul, after hunting and driving her on through various twists and turns into every kind of sin, lie in wait at the narrow passage of death to seize and devour her. Terrified, she looks on every side for help and refuge and if she does not find any her enemies mock and laugh at her."[6] When the saint had thus spoken he rode on sighing to himself.

Constantine the Great wrote respectfully to St. Anthony and the religious with him were greatly surprised at this. "Why are you astonished that a king should write to a private citizen? You should marvel that the eternal God has written his law to mortal men, and more than that, has spoken to them by the mouth of his Son."[7] When St. Francis saw a sheep standing alone among a flock of goats, he said to a companion, "See how gentle that poor little sheep is among the goats! Our Blessed Lord walked in the same meek and humble way among the Pharisees."[8] At another time when he saw a little lamb being devoured by a hog, he burst into tears and said, "Poor little lamb, how clearly do you represent the death of my Savior!"[9]

While he was still Duke of Gandia, that great man of our own times, St. Francis Borgia, had a thousand devout thoughts while out hunting. Afterwards he said, "I marveled how the falcons come back to the hand, let themselves be hooded, and tied to the perch, while men are so opposed to God's voice."[10] The great St. Basil said that the rose among the thorns makes this objection to men: "O you mortal men, the most pleasant things in this world are mixed with sorrow. Nothing here is pure, grief follows joy, widowhood marriage, care fruitfulness, ignominy glory, expense honor, loathing delight, and sickness health." "The rose is a beautiful flower," says this holy man, "yet it makes me very sorrowful since it reminds me of my sin, for which the earth has been condemned to bring forth thorns."[11]

A certain devout person standing by a brook on a very clear night looked at the heavens and the stars reflected in the brook and said, "O my God, these very stars shall one day be beneath my feet when you have lodged me in your holy tabernacles. Just as the stars of heaven are reflected here on earth, so also men on earth are reflected in heaven in the living fountain of divine charity." When another man watched a river as it flowed swiftly on he said, "My soul will never find rest until it is swallowed up in the sea of divinity, its first source." When St. Frances knelt in prayer on the bank of a pleasant brook and contemplated it, she was rapt with ecstasy and repeated over and over these beautiful words, "The grace of God flows gently and sweetly like this little stream."[12] Another saint looked at trees in bloom, sighed, and said, "Ah, why am I the only one without blossom in the garden of the

Church!" Another looked at little chickens gathered under the hen and said, "Lord, keep us under the shadow of your wings."[13] Another looked at a sunflower and said, "When will it be, O my God, that my soul will follow the attractions of your goodness?" He also looked at pansies in a garden, which are without fragrance, and said, "Ah, such are my thoughts, beautiful to express, but without effect or result."

So you see, Philothea, how we may extract good thoughts and holy aspirations from everything found amid the changes of this mortal life. Unhappy are those who turn creatures away from their Creator in order to turn them into instruments of sin! Blessed are they who turn creatures to the glory of their Creator and use their own vanity to honor the truth. Indeed, as St. Gregory Nazianzen says, "It is my custom to refer all things to my spiritual profit."[14] Read the devout epitaph of St. Paula composed by St. Jerome and see how good it is to find it strewn with the aspirations and holy thoughts that he drew from occurrences of every kind.[15]

Since the great work of devotion consists in such use of spiritual recollection and ejaculatory prayers, it can supply the lack of all other prayers, but its loss can hardly be repaired by other means. Without this exercise we cannot properly lead the contemplative life, and we can but poorly lead the active life. Without it rest is mere idleness, and labor is drudgery. Hence I exhort you to take up this practice with all your heart and never give it up.

14. HOW TO ATTEND HOLY MASS

1. Thus far I have said nothing of the sun of all spiritual exercises—the most holy, sacred, and supremely sovereign sacrament and sacrifice of the Mass, center of the Christian religion, heart of devotion, and soul of piety, the ineffable mystery that comprises within itself the deepest depths of divine charity, the mystery in which God really gives himself and gloriously communicates his graces and favors to us.

2. Prayer made in union with this divine sacrifice has inestimable power, Philothea, so that by it the soul overflows with heavenly favors as if "leaning on her Beloved."[1] He fills our soul with such spiritual odors and delights that it resembles, as is said in the Canticle, "a pillar of smoke from aromatic wood, of myrrh and incense and all the powders of the perfumer."[2]

3. Make every effort therefore to assist every day at Holy Mass so that together with the priest you may offer up the sacrifice of your Redeemer to God his Father for yourself and for the whole Church. "Hosts of angels are always present to honor this adorable mystery,"[3] says St. John Chrysostom. If we are there with them and have the same intention, we cannot help receiving many favorable influences from this association. The choirs of the Church triumphant and those of the Church militant are united to our Lord in this divine action, so that with him, in him, and through him they may ravish the heart of God the Father and make his mercy all our own. What happiness it is for a soul devoutly to contribute its affections in order to obtain so precious and so desirable a treasure!

4. If some strict duty keeps you from being present in person at the celebration of this sovereign sacrifice, try at least to transport your heart to it and assist at Mass by your spiritual presence. Sometime during the morning go in spirit into the church, if you cannot do so otherwise, unite your intention with that of all Christians, and in the place you are make the same interior acts that you would make if you were really present in church at the offering of Holy Mass.

5. To hear Mass in a proper manner either actually or spiritually: (1) From the beginning until the priest goes up to the altar make your preparation with him. This consists in placing yourself in the presence of God, recognizing your unworthiness, and asking pardon for your sins. (2) From the time he goes up to the altar until the Gospel consider our Lord's coming and his life in this world by a simple, general consideration. (3) From the Gospel until after the Creed consider our

Savior's preaching and affirm that you are resolved to live and die faithful and obedient to his holy word and in union with the holy Catholic Church. (4) From the Gospel to the Our Father apply your heart to the mysteries of the passion and death of our Redeemer. They are actually and essentially represented in this Holy Sacrifice. Together with the priest and the rest of the people you will offer them to God the Father for his honor and for your own salvation. (5) From the Our Father to the communion strive to excite a thousand desires in your heart and ardently wish to be joined and united forever to our Savior in everlasting love. (6) From the communion to the end of Mass give thanks to Jesus Christ for his incarnation, life, passion, and death, and for the love he manifests in this Holy Sacrifice. Implore him always to be merciful to you, your parents, friends, and the whole Church. Humble yourself with all your heart and devoutly receive the blessing our Lord gives you through the ministry of his minister.

If you wish to meditate during Mass on the mysteries you have proposed from day to day, there is no need to change your plan and make all these particular acts. It will suffice that at the beginning you direct your intention to adore and offer this Holy Sacrifice by the exercise of meditation and prayer. In all meditations the aforesaid acts are found either explicitly or implicitly and virtually.

15. OTHER PUBLIC AND COMMUNAL EXERCISES

Besides hearing Mass on Sundays and holy days, Philothea, you should assist at the office of the hours[1] and vespers as far as convenience permits. As these days are dedicated to God, we must perform more acts in his honor and glory on them than on other days. By this means you will experience countless sweet feelings of devotion, as did St. Augustine, who testifies that at the beginning of his conversion when he heard the

Divine Office his heart melted with happiness and his eyes with tears of piety.[2] In fact, to say it once and for all, there is always more benefit and consolation to be derived from the public offices of the Church than from private particular acts. God has ordained that communion in prayer must always be preferred to every form of private prayer.

Be glad to join in the confraternities of the place where you reside and especially those whose exercises are most productive of good results and edification. In so doing you practice a type of obedience most acceptable to God. Although confraternities are not commanded, still they are recommended by the Church. To show its wish that many of the faithful be enrolled in them, the Church grants indulgences and other privileges to their members. Moreover, it is always a very charitable act to concur and cooperate with others in their good purposes. Although it may be that when alone we perform exercises as good as those with others in a confraternity and perhaps take more pleasure in performing them in private, yet God is more glorified by the union and contribution of our good works with those of our brethren and neighbors.

I say the same of all kinds of public prayers and devotions. As much as possible we ought to bring them our good example, for the edification of our neighbor and concern for God's glory and the common purpose.

16. OUR DUTY TO HONOR AND INVOKE THE SAINTS

Since God often sends us inspirations by means of his angels, we should frequently return our aspirations to him by the same messengers. The holy souls of the dead who dwell in paradise with the angels and, as our Savior says, are equal "and like the angels,"[1] also perform this office of inspiring us and interceding for us by their holy prayers. Philothea, let us join our hearts to these heavenly spirits and blessed souls. Just as young nightingales learn to sing in company with the old, so also by our holy associations with the saints let us learn the best way to pray and sing God's praise. "In the presence of the angels I will sing your praises"[2] says David.

Honor, reverence, and respect with a special love the sacred and glorious Virgin Mary. She is the Mother of our sovereign Father and consequently she is our own Mother in an especial way. Let us run to her and like little children cast ourselves into her arms with perfect confidence. At every moment and on every occasion let us call on this dear Mother. Let us invoke her maternal love and by trying to imitate her virtues let us have true filial affection for her.

Become familiar with the angels and see how they are often present though unseen in your life. Above all, have particular love and reverence both for the guardian angel of the diocese where you live and those of the persons with whom you live, and especially for your own guardian angel. Pray often to them, praise them constantly and use their aid and assistance in all your affairs, both spiritual and temporal, so that they may cooperate with your intentions.

When the great Peter Faber,[3] first priest, first preacher, and first lector in theology in the holy Company of the Name of Jesus, and first companion of the Blessed Ignatius,[4] its founder, was on his return journey one day from Germany where he had performed great services for the glory of our Lord and was traveling through this diocese, the place of his birth, he told one day how he had passed through many heretical places and had gained countless consolations from the guardian angels of the various parishes and on repeated occasions had received the most sensible and convincing proofs of their protection. Sometimes they preserved him from the snares of his enemies, at other times they rendered several souls more mild and tractable for receiving from him the doctrine of salvation. He related this so earnestly that a gentlewoman[5] then young who heard it from his own mouth repeated it with great feeling only four years ago, that is to say, about sixty years after he had told it. Last year I had the consolation of consecrating an altar on the spot where God was pleased that this holy man would be born, in a little village called Villaret in the midst of our most craggy mountains.

Choose certain particular saints whose lives you can best appreciate and imitate and in whose intercession you may have particular confidence. The saint whose name you bear was already assigned to you at baptism.

17. HOW WE MUST HEAR THE WORD OF GOD

Be devoted to the word of God whether you hear it in familiar conversation with spiritual friends or in sermons. Always listen to it with attention and reverence; make good use of it; do not let it fall to earth but take it into your heart like a precious balm. Do all this after the example of the most holy Virgin, for she carefully kept in her heart all the words spoken in praise of her Child.[1] Remember that our Lord gathers up the words we speak to him in prayer in measure with the way we gather up those he speaks to us by his preaching.

Always have at hand some approved book of devotion, such as those of St. Bonaventure,[2] Gerson,[3] Denis the Carthusian,[4] Louis of Blois,[5] Granada, Stella,[6] Arias, Pinelli,[7] Du Pont,[8] Avila, the *Spiritual Combat*,[9] St. Augustine's *Confessions*, St. Jerome's letters, and the like. Read a little of them every day with great devotion, just as if you were reading a letter that the saints had sent you from heaven to show you the way and give you the courage to go there.

You should also read stories and lives of the saints for there, as in a mirror, you can see a picture of the Christian life and adapt their deeds to your use in keeping with your vocation. Acts of the saints cannot be strictly imitated by people living in the world, yet they can be followed either closely or from a distance. The solitary life of St. Paul, the first hermit, is imitated by both spiritual and actual retirement, which we shall discuss later and have already discussed, the extreme poverty of St. Francis by such practices of poverty as we have already noted, and so on of the rest. It is true that some stories provide more light for the conduct of our lives than others do. Such, for instance, are the life of the Blessed Mother Teresa, the lives of the first Jesuits, those of St. Charles Borromeo, archbishop of Milan, St. Louis, and St. Bernard, the *Chronicles of St. Francis*, and others like them. There are others again that contain more material for us to marvel at than to imitate, such as the life of St. Mary of Egypt, St. Simeon Stylites, St. Catherine of Siena, St. Catherine of Genoa, St. Angela, and others like them.[10] Nevertheless, they give us great liking in general for the holy love of God.

18. HOW WE SHOULD RECEIVE INSPIRATIONS

By inspirations we mean all those interior attractions, motions, acts of self-reproach and remorse, lights and conceptions that God works in us and predisposes our hearts by his blessings,[1] fatherly care, and love in order to awaken, stimulate, urge, and attract us to holy virtues, heavenly love, and good resolutions, in short, to everything that sends us on our way to our everlasting welfare. This is what the Spouse calls knocking at the door and speaking to the heart of his bride, awaking her when she is asleep, calling and crying after her when absent, inviting her to partake of his honey, to gather apples and flowers in his garden, and to sing and sound her sweet voice in his ears.[2]

For the complete arrangement of a marriage there must be three acts that relate to the lady a man wishes to marry. First, the other party is proposed to her; secondly, she approves the proposal; thirdly, she accepts him. In like manner, when God wishes to do some great act of charity in us, by us, or with us, he first proposes it to us by inspiration, secondly, we approve it, and thirdly, we consent to it. Just as there are three steps by which we descend to sin, namely, temptation, delectations, and consent, so also there are three steps by which we ascend to virtue. They are inspiration, which is contrary to temptation, delight taken in the inspiration, which is contrary to that delight taken in temptation, and consent to the inspiration, which is contrary to the consent given to temptation.

Even if the inspiration lasted throughout our whole life, we would be completely unacceptable to God if we took no joy in it. On the contrary, his Divine Majesty would be offended with us, just as he was with the Israelites whose conversion, as he says, he had sought for forty years. During this time they would not listen to him and in his wrath he swore against them that they would never enter into his rest.[3] In like manner, the gentleman who served a young lady for a long time would be very much offended if after all this she would not hear of the marriage he desired.

To find joy in inspirations is a great advance to God's glory and by it we have already begun to please his Divine Majesty. Although this delectation is as yet not complete consent, yet it is a kind of predisposition to it. If it is a good sign and a very useful thing to have pleasure in hearing the word of God, which is like an outward inspiration and it is also something and pleasing to God to take pleasure in his inward inspirations. The sacred Spouse says about this kind of pleasure, "My soul melted when my beloved spoke."[4] Thus too a gentleman is already very pleased with the lady he serves and considers himself favored when he sees that she is pleased by his devotion to her.

But in the end it is consent that perfects the virtuous act. If we have received an inspiration and taken pleasure in it but still refuse to give our consent to God, we are extremely ungrateful and we give great offense to his Divine Majesty since we seem to despise his favors. Thus it was with the Spouse, for although the sweet voice of her Beloved had touched her heart with holy pleasure, she would not open the door to him but excused herself for a frivolous reason. The Spouse was justly displeased at this and went away and left her.[5] So too if a gentleman has long paid addresses to a lady and made his service agreeable to her but is finally rejected and spurned, he would have more reason for discontent than if his suit had never been accepted and favored.

Philothea, resolve to accept willingly all the inspirations it may please God to send you. When they come, receive them as ambassadors sent by the King of Heaven who desires to enter into a marriage contract with you. Listen calmly to his proposal, think of the love with which you are inspired, and cherish that holy inspiration. Give it your complete, loving, and permanent consent. In this way God, whom you cannot put under any obligations, will hold himself greatly obligated to your good will. But before you consent to inspirations with regard to important or extraordinary things, always consult your adviser so that he may examine the inspiration and see whether it is true or false. When the enemy sees a soul ready to consent to inspirations he often proposes false ones in order to deceive it. He can never accomplish this as long as that soul humbly obeys its director.

Once the consent has been given, you must diligently procure its effects and hasten to put the inspiration into practice. This is the height of true virtue. To have consent within your heart without putting it into effect is like planting a vine with no intention that it bear fruit.

What contributes marvelously to all this is practice of the morning exercise and the spiritual retirement already discussed. By such means we get ready to do what is good by a preparation that is not only general but particular as well.

19. HOLY CONFESSION

Our Savior gave the sacrament of penance and confession to his Church so that we may be cleansed from all our iniquities no matter how often and how greatly we have been defiled by them. Never let your soul remain long infected by sin, Philothea, since you have a remedy so near at hand and so easy to apply. A lioness that has been with a leopard hastens to wash herself and get rid of the stench the meeting has left with her lest her mate be offended and angered.[1] So too a soul that has consented to sin must have horror for itself and be washed clean as soon as possible out of the respect it must have for the eyes of God's Divine Majesty who sees it. Why should we die a spiritual death when we have this sovereign remedy at hand?

Make a humble, devout confession every week and always, if possible, before you go to communion even though you are not conscious of being guilty of mortal sin. In confession you not only receive absolution from the venial sins you confess but also great strength to avoid them in the future, light to see them clearly, and abundant grace to repair whatever damage you have incurred. You will also practice the virtues of humility, obedience, simplicity, and charity. In the single act of confession you will exercise more virtues than in any other act whatsoever.

However small the sins you confess may be, always have sincere sorrow for them together with a firm resolution to correct them in the future. Many who confess their venial sins out of custom and concern for order but without thought of amendment remain burdened with them for their whole life and thus lose many spiritual benefits and advantages. If you confess that you have told a lie, even though a harmless one, or have spoken some improper word or played cards too much, be sorry and make a firm resolution to amend. It is an abuse to confess any kind of sin, whether mortal or venial, without a will to be rid of it since confession was instituted for no other purpose.

Do not make mere pointless accusations as many do in a routine way, such as: I have not loved God as much as I should; I have not prayed with as much devotion as I should; I have not loved my neighbor as I should; I have not received the sacraments as reverently as I should, and the like. The reason is that when you say such things you say nothing definite to help your confessor know your state of conscience. Every saint in heaven and every man on earth might say the same thing if they went to confession. Examine the particular reason you have for making such accusations and having found it accuse yourself of not loving your neighbor as much as you should. Perhaps it was because you saw some poor person in great need and you could easily have helped him but did not care to do so. Well, accuse yourself of this precise thing and say, "I saw a poor man in want but out of negligence, hardness of heart, or contempt for him I did not help him as I could have done," according to whatever you find to be the occasion of this fault. Similarly, do not accuse yourself of not praying to God with as much devotion as you ought. If you have had voluntary distractions or neglected to choose a place, time, or posture needed for keeping attentive in prayer, then accuse yourself of this with complete simplicity as to what you find wrong without making such general charges. In confession they are neither hot nor cold.

Don't be satisfied with confessing your venial sins merely as to the fact but accuse yourself of the motive that led you to commit them. For example, don't be satisfied with saying that you told a lie without harming anyone by it. State whether it was done out of vainglory, to praise or excuse yourself, or told as a foolish joke or through obstinacy. If you have sinned by playing cards, state whether it was from a desire for gain or from pleasure in such company and so on. Tell if you have continued a long time in your sin, since length of time ordinarily greatly increases sin. There is great difference between some passing act of vanity that has slipped into the soul for a quarter-hour and one our heart has indulged in for one, two, or three days. Hence we must state the fact, the motive, and the duration of our sins. Although we are usually not bound to be so punctilious in declaring venial sins, nor are we absolutely obliged to confess them, still those who wish to cleanse their souls perfectly and attain to holy devotion must be careful to acquaint their spiritual physician with the evil they desire to be healed of, no matter how small it may be.

Do not fail to tell whatever is needed for a full understanding of the nature of your offense, such as the reason for getting angry or for cooperating with someone in his fault. For example, a man whom I dislike jokingly says some light word and I take it badly and get angry, while another whom I like says something sharper and I take it in good part. In this case I should not neglect to say that I have spoken harsh words against a certain person because I took offense at something he said, not because of the words themselves but because I disliked him. If there is still need to particularize the actual words in order to make yourself clear, I think that it is a good thing to state them. By accusing myself unaffectedly you not only disclose the sin but also the evil inclinations, customs, habits, and other roots of the sin. By this means your spiritual director gains full knowledge of the soul he is dealing with and of the proper remedies for it. You must always conceal a person who has had any part in your sin as far as this is possible.

Be on guard against a number of sins that frequently live and rule undetected in your conscience. In order to confess them and be able to cleanse yourself of them, read carefully Chapters 6, 26, 28, 29, 35, and 36 of Part Three, and Chapter 8 of Part Four.

Do not change your confessor needlessly, but having once chosen one, continue to render him an account of your state of conscience on the days appointed for this, simply and frankly naming the sins you have committed. From time to time, every month or every two months, tell the state of your inclinations even though you have not sinned because of them: for instance, if you have been tormented by sadness or melancholy or have been inclined to undue gaiety, a desire to acquire worldly goods, and similar inclinations.

20. FREQUENT COMMUNION

Mithridates, King of Pontus, is said to have invented the mithridate and by repeated use of it made his body so strong that later when he tried to poison himself to escape slavery under the Romans he could not carry out his plan.[1] Our Savior has instituted the most august sacrament of the Eucharist, which contains his flesh and blood in their reality, so that whoever eats of it shall live forever.[2] Therefore whoever turns to it frequently and devoutly so effectively builds up his soul's health that it is almost impossible for him to be poisoned by evil affection of any kind. We cannot be nourished by this flesh of life and live on the affections of death. Just as men dwelling in the earthly paradise might have avoided bodily death by power of that living fruit which God had planted in it, so also they can avoid spiritual death by virtue of this sacrament of life. If fruits that are tenderest and most subject to decay, such as cherries, apricots, and strawberries, can be easily preserved for a whole year with sugar or honey, it is no wonder if our hearts, no matter how frail and weak, are preserved from the corruption of sin when sweetened by the incorruptible flesh and blood of the Son of God. Philothea, those Christians who will be damned will stand without any defense when the just Judge shows them their crime in suffering spiritual death. It was easy for them to have kept themselves in life and health by eating his body, which he left them for that purpose. "Wretched men," he will say, "why did you die when you had the fruit and the meat of life at your command?"

"I neither recommend nor do I condemn daily reception of the Eucharist; but I persuade and exhort everyone to receive Communion every Sunday, provided his soul is without any affection for sin."[3] These are the exact words of St. Augustine. With him I neither condemn nor unreservedly approve daily Communion, but leave it to the discretion of the spiritual director of the one wishing instruction in this matter. As the dispositions required for daily Communion should be very precise, it is not well to recommend it generally. However, since such dispositions, although strict, can be found in many holy souls, it is not good to divert and dissuade people in general from it, but it should be regulated by consideration of the interior state of each individual. It would be imprudent to advise everyone indiscriminately to receive Communion frequently, but it would also be imprudent to blame anyone for doing so, especially if he follows the advice of a prudent director. St. Catherine of Siena gave a tactful answer when she was criticized for frequent Communion on the ground that St. Augustine neither praised nor condemned daily Communion. "Well," she said, "since St. Augustine does not condemn it, I beg you not to condemn it and I will be satisfied."[4]

As you see, Philothea, St. Augustine exhorts and advises us to communicate every Sunday. Do this as far as you can. Since I presume that you have no affection for either mortal or venial sin, you have the disposition St. Augustine requires and even a better one since you have not only an aversion to sin but do not even retain an affection for sin. If your spiritual director thinks it proper, you can profitably communicate even oftener than every Sunday.

Many legitimate impediments may arise, perhaps not on your own part but on the part of those with whom you live, and these may lead a prudent director to advise you not to go to Communion so often. For example, if you have certain obligations to others and those to whom you owe obedience or respect are so badly instructed or confused as to be disturbed or bothered at seeing you communicate so frequently, all things considered it would perhaps be good to adapt yourself a little to their weakness and receive Holy Communion only once every two weeks. It is understood that you are really unable to remove the difficulty. No set rule can be made for such cases and we must do as our spiritual director says. However, I may safely say that the longest time between Communions should not exceed a month for those who wish to serve God devoutly.

If you act prudently, neither mother nor wife nor husband nor father will stop you from receiving Communion often. On Communion days you will not fail in your proper duties. You will be even more cheerful and pleasant to others and not refuse them any due service. Hence there is no likelihood that they will try to keep you from a practice that doesn't inconvenience them in any way, unless their attitude is utterly perverse and unreasonable. In this case, as I have already said, your director will advise you to accommodate yourself to them.

I must say a word to married people. In the Old Law, God forbade creditors to exact payment of debts on festival days[5] but he never condemned debtors for paying and discharging debts to those demanding it. It is improper, although not a grave sin, to solicit payment of the marriage debt on Communion days, but it is not improper but meritorious to pay it. Hence no one ought to be kept from Communion for paying this debt, if otherwise their devotion incites them to seek Communion. It is certain that in the primitive Church Christians communicated every day, although married and blessed with children. Hence I have said that frequent Communion is by no means inconsistent with the state of parents, husbands, and wives, provided the person who communicates is prudent and discreet.

As for bodily disease, there is none that might be a lawful impediment to partake in holy devotion except one that would bring on frequent vomiting.

To receive Communion every week it is required that one be free from mortal sin and from any affection for venial sin and have a great desire to communicate. To communicate every day it is necessary in addition that we overcome the great part of our evil inclinations and that we follow the advice of our spiritual director.[6]

21. HOW WE OUGHT TO COMMUNICATE

Begin your preparation for Holy Communion on the evening before by many loving aspirations and transports and retire a little earlier so that you may rise earlier in the morning. If you awake during the night, immediately fill your heart and mouth with words redolent of love by which your soul will be perfumed to receive its Spouse. Since he is awake even while you sleep, he is prepared to bring you countless graces and favors if on your part you are ready to receive them. In the morning get up with great joy because of the happiness you hope for. Having made your confession, go with great confidence and with great humility to receive this heavenly food which nourishes you for everlasting life. After you have said those sacred words, "Lord, I am not worthy,"[1] do not move your head or lips to pray or sigh but open your mouth gently and moderately and lift up your head as much as is necessary for the priest to see what he is about, then, full of faith, hope, and charity, receive him in whom, by whom, and for whom you believe, hope, and love. Represent to yourself, Philothea, that just as after a bee has gathered from flowers the dews of heaven and the choicest juices of the earth and changed them into honey, it carries it to her hive, so also the priest, having taken from the altar the Savior of the world, who as true Son of God is like dew come down from heaven, and as true Son of the Virgin is like a flower sprung from the earth of our humanity, puts him as the sweetest food into your mouth and into your body. After you have received him, excite your heart to do homage to the King of salvation. Converse with him concerning your inmost concerns. Reflect that he is within you and has come there for your happiness. In fine, make him as welcome as you possibly can and conduct yourself in such manner that by your actions all may know that God is with you.

When you cannot enjoy the benefit of communicating in reality at Holy Mass, go to Communion at least in heart and spirit by uniting yourself in ardent desire to the life-giving Body of the Savior.

Your great intention in receiving Communion should be to advance, strengthen, and comfort yourself in the love of God. You must receive with love that which love alone has caused to be given to you. No, you cannot consider our Savior in an action more full of love or more tender than this. In it he abases himself, if we may so express it, and changes himself into food, so that he may penetrate our souls and unite himself most intimately to the heart and body of his faithful.

If worldly people ask you why you receive Communion so often, tell them that it is to learn to love God, be purified from your imperfections, delivered from misery, comforted in affliction, and supported in weakness. Tell them that two classes of people should communicate frequently: the perfect, because being well disposed they would be very much to blame if they did not approach the source and fountain of perfection, and the imperfect, so that they rightly strive for perfection; the strong lest they become weak, and the weak that they may become strong; the sick that they may be restored to health, and the healthy lest they fall sick. Tell them that for your part you are imperfect, weak, and sick and need to communicate frequently with him who is your perfection, strength, and physician. Tell them that those who do not have many worldly affairs to look after ought to communicate often because they have leisure to do so and those who have great undertakings because they have need to do so, since one who labors hard and is weighed down with troubles should eat solid food and do so frequently. Tell them that you receive the Blessed Sacrament often so as to learn how to receive it well, for we hardly do an action well which we do not practice often.

Go often to Communion, Philothea, as often as you can with the advice of your spiritual director. And, believe me, just as hares in our mountains become white in winter because they neither see nor eat anything but snow,[2] so by adoring and eating beauty, purity, and goodness itself in this divine sacrament you will become wholly beautiful, wholly good, and wholly pure.

THE THIRD PART OF THE INTRODUCTION

Instructions on the Practice of Virtue

1. THE CHOICE WE MUST MAKE IN THE EXERCISE OF VIRTUES

The king of the bees never goes out into the fields without being surrounded by his little subjects. In like manner, charity never enters a heart without lodging both itself and its train of all the other virtues which it exercises and disciplines as a captain does his soldiers. It does not put them to work all at once, nor at all times and in all places. The just man is "like a tree planted near running water, that yields its fruit in due season,"[1] for charity waters the soul and produces in it virtuous deeds, each in its proper time. No matter how pleasant it may be in itself, music is out of place at times of mourning, as the proverb says.[2] A great fault in many who undertake the exercise of some particular virtue is thinking they must practice it in every situation. Like certain ancient philosophers, they wish either always to weep or always to laugh. What is still worse, they condemn and censure others who do not practice the same virtues they do. The apostle says, "Rejoice with those who rejoice; weep with those who weep,"[3] and "charity is patient, is kind,"[4] generous, prudent, discreet, and considerate.

Some virtues have almost general use and must not only produce their own acts but also communicate their qualities to the acts of all other virtues. Occasions do not often present themselves for the exercise of fortitude, magnanimity, and great generosity, but meekness, temperance, integrity, and humility are virtues that must mark all our actions in life. We like sugar better than salt but salt is in more common and frequent use. We must always have on hand a good supply of these general virtues since we must use them almost constantly.

In practicing the virtues we should prefer the one most conformable to our duties rather than one more agreeable to our tastes. St. Paula was inclined to carry out severe bodily mortifications so as more easily to enjoy spiritual joys, but she had a greater duty to obey her superiors. For that reason St. Jerome said it was wrong for her to practice excessive fasts against her bishop's advice.[5] On the other hand, the apostles had been commissioned to preach the gospel and distribute the bread of heaven to souls and hence rightly concluded that it would be wrong to break off this holy activity in order to help the poor, even though that is a very great virtue.[6] Every state of life must practice some particular virtue. A bishop's virtues are of one kind, a prince's of another, a soldier's of a third kind, and those of a married woman are different from a widow's. All men should possess all the virtues, yet all are not bound to exercise them in equal measure. Each person must practice in a special manner the virtues needed by the kind of life he is called to.

Among virtues pertaining to our special duties we must prefer the more excellent to the more obvious. As a rule comets seem bigger than stars and hold a larger place in our eyes. Actually they cannot be compared to the stars in either size or quality and only seem great because they are closer to us and made of cruder matter than the stars. Certain virtues are greatly esteemed and always preferred by the general run of men because they are close at hand, easily seen, and as it were material. Thus many people prefer bodily to spiritual alms, hair shirts, fasting, going barefoot, using the discipline, and bodily mortifications to meekness, mildness, modesty, and other mortifications of the heart, although the latter are loftier virtues. Hence, Philothea, you should choose the best virtues, not the most popular, the noblest, not the most obvious, those that are actually the best, not the most spectacular.

It is helpful for everyone to practice some particular virtue, not to the extent of giving up all the rest but to keep his mind better ordered and occupied. A beautiful young girl, brighter than the sun, royally adorned and attired, and crowned with an olive wreath, appeared to St. John, bishop of Alexandria,[7] and said to him: "I am the eldest daughter of the king. If you can take me as your friend, I will lead you to his presence." He recognized that she was mercy toward the poor, which God had recommended to him, and afterwards he devoted himself so completely to this virtue that he is universally called St. John the Almoner. Wishing to render some special service to God but not having sufficient courage to enter the solitary life or place himself under obedience to another, Eulogius of Alexandria took into his own home an unfortunate man eaten up by leprosy. He did this to exercise charity and mortification in his behalf, and to do so better he vowed to honor, accept, and serve him as a servant does his lord and master. Both Eulogius and the leper were tempted to leave each other and they turned to the great St. Anthony who said, "Be very careful, my children, don't separate from one another. Both of you are near the end of life. If the angel does not find you together, you are in great danger of losing your crowns."[8]

St. Louis the king visited hospitals and with his own hands tended the sick as if serving for pay. St. Francis loved poverty above all things and called it Lady Poverty. St. Dominic loved preaching and from this fact his order takes its name. Following Abraham's example, St. Gregory the Great liked to entertain pilgrims and like Abraham he received the King of Glory in the form of a pilgrim. Tobias practiced charity by burying the dead. Great princess that she was, St. Elizabeth had a special love for self-abasement. St. Catherine of Genoa as a widow dedicated herself to work in a hospital. Cassian relates[9] that a devout lady who wished to practice patience went to St. Athanasius who at her request placed her with a poor widow who was complaining, short-tempered, troublesome, and hard to put up with. She constantly scolded the devout lady and gave her ample opportunity to practice the virtues of meekness and charity.

Thus among God's servants some dedicated themselves to serve the sick, others to help the poor, others to spread knowledge of Christian doctrine among children, others to reclaim souls lost and gone astray, others to beautify churches and decorate altars, others to restore peace and concord among men. In all this they imitate embroiderers who put silk, gold, and silver on different backgrounds in beautifully varied designs that resemble flowers of every kind. So too these pious souls choose some particular devotion to serve as a ground for the spiritual embroidery on which they practice all the other virtues, thereby keeping all their actions and affections more unified and better ordered by relating them to their principal exercise. They thus reveal their character:

> *In golden garments, rich and rare,*
> *Embroidered o'er with figures fair.*[10]

When attacked by some vice we must practice the contrary virtue as much as we can and refer all the others to it. By this means we will vanquish our enemy and at the same time advance in all the virtues. Thus if assaulted by pride or anger, I must devote and direct all my actions to humility and meekness and adapt all exercises of prayer, the sacraments, prudence, constancy, and sobriety to this end. To sharpen his tusks the wild boar rubs and polishes them with his other teeth and thus files and sharpens them all. So also a virtuous man who undertakes to perfect himself in the virtue most needed for his own protection must file and polish it by exercise of the other virtues. By refining one of them all are made more excellent and better polished. It was thus with Job. He particularly strove to be patient under the many temptations that disturbed him and he thus became completely holy and established in every kind of virtue. Thus it comes about, St. Gregory Nazianzen says,[11] that by perfect practice of a single virtue a person can reach the heights in all virtue. He cites the example of Rahab who carefully practiced the virtue of hospitality and thus attained a high degree of glory.[12] This is to be taken of a virtue that is practiced with great fervor and charity.

2. DISCUSSION OF THE CHOICE OF VIRTUES CONTINUED

St. Augustine well says[1] that beginners in devotion commit certain mistakes that according to the strict laws of perfection deserve blame but are also praiseworthy since they give good indication of future excellence in piety, to which they serve as a disposition. The low, servile fear that begets excessive scruples in the souls of new converts from a sinful life is a commendable virtue in this first period and a sign of future purity of conscience. The same fear would be blameworthy in those far advanced, men in whose hearts love ought to reign, and little by little love drives out such servile fear.

At the beginning of his career St. Bernard[2] was full of rigor and sharpness toward those put under his direction and would tell them they must leave the body behind and come to him in soul only. When he heard their confessions he reprimanded with extraordinary severity faults of every kind, no matter how slight, and urged on those poor apprentices to perfection in such a way that instead of pushing them on he pulled them back. They lost heart and breath at seeing themselves unrelentingly driven up so steep and high an ascent. Philothea, note that it was most ardent zeal for perfect purity that induced this great saint to adapt this method. His zeal was a great virtue but a virtue open to criticism. Hence God himself in a holy vision corrected him and infused into his soul a spirit so meek, gentle, amiable, and tender that he was completely changed by it. He not only charged himself with being too strict and severe but became so gracious and considerate to everyone that he became "all things to all men"[3] in order to save all of them.

St. Jerome tells how his dear daughter, St. Paula, was not only excessive but even so obstinate in practice of bodily mortifications that she would not give in to the contrary advice that Epiphanius, her bishop, gave in this matter. Moreover, she let herself be carried away by such grief at the death of her dear ones that she was herself in danger of dying. He concludes in this way: "Some will say that instead of writing in praise of this holy woman I write criticism and dispraise. I call as my witness Jesus, whom she served and whom I desire to serve, that I am not lying either on one side or on the other but put down sincerely what relates to her, as Christian to Christian. That is to say, I write her history, not her panegyric, and I say that her vices are virtues in others."[4] His meaning is that St. Paula's faults and defects would be considered virtues in a soul less perfect, just as there are actions looked on imperfections in the perfect that would be held great perfections in the imperfect. It is a good sign when the legs of a sick person swell at the end of an illness since it shows that nature has now gained strength and expels superfluous liquids. The same symptom would be bad in a well person, since it would show that nature lacked sufficient power to dissolve and dissipate such humors. Philothea, we must have a good opinion of those we see practicing virtues, even though imperfectly, since we know that the saints themselves have often practiced them in this manner. As for ourselves, we must be careful to practice them not only faithfully but prudently. For this purpose we must strictly follow the advice of the Wise Man not to rely on our own prudence but on the judgment of those whom God has given us for directors.[5]

There are various things that many people think are virtues but in reality are not such. I mean ecstasies or raptures, states of insensibility and impassibility, deific unions, levitations, transformations, and similar perfections discussed in certain books that promise to elevate the soul to purely intellectual contemplation, essential application of the spirit, and supereminent life. Note well, Philothea, that such perfections are not virtues. More correctly, they are rewards that God grants for virtues or slight indications of the happiness of the life to come. Sometimes they are granted to men to make them desire what is complete in heaven above. In spite of all that it is not expedient to aspire to such graces. They are in no way necessary to serve and love God well and this should be our only intention. Nor are they graces that can be gained by labor and skill. They are passions rather than actions and we can receive them but cannot produce them in ourselves. I add that all that we must try for is to make ourselves good men and women, devout men and women, pious men and pious women. We must try hard to achieve this end. If it pleases God to elevate us to those angelical perfections we shall then be good angels. In the meantime let us try sincerely, humbly, and devoutly to acquire those little virtues whose conquest our Savior has set forth as the end of our care and labor. Such are patience, meekness, self-mortification, humility, obedience, poverty, chastity, tenderness toward our neighbors, bearing with their imperfections, diligence, and holy fervor.

Let us gladly leave those supereminent favors to lofty souls; we do not deserve so high a rank in God's service, and we should be more than happy to serve him in his kitchen or pantry or to be his lackeys, porters, or chamberlains. Afterward if it seems good to him he may admit us into his cabinet or private council. Yes, Philothea, the King of Glory does not reward his servants according to the dignity of the offices they hold but according to the love and humility with which they fulfill their offices. Saul sought his father's asses and found the kingdom of Israel.[6] Rebecca watered Abraham's camels and became his son's wife.[7] Ruth gleaned after Boaz's reapers and lay down at his feet, and then she was raised to his side and made his wife.[8] Those high and elevated pretensions to extraordinary favors are very subject to illusions, deception, and deceit. Sometimes it happens that those who imagine themselves to be angels are not even good men and there is more sublimity in their words and expressions than in their way of thought and deeds. We must neither rashly despise nor censure anything. While blessing God for the supereminence of others, let us keep to our lower but safer way. It is less excellent but better suited to our lack and littleness. If we conduct ourselves with humility and good faith in this, God will raise us up to heights that are truly great.

3. PATIENCE

"For you have need for patience that, doing the will of God, you may receive the promise,"[1] says the apostle. True, for our Savior himself has declared, "By your patience you will win your souls."[2] It is man's great happiness to possess his own soul, Philothea, and the more perfect our patience the more completely do we possess our souls. We must often recall that our Lord has saved us by his suffering and endurance and that we must work out our salvation by sufferings and afflictions, enduring with all possible meekness the injuries, denials, and discomforts we meet.

Do not limit your patience to this or that kind of injury and affliction. Extend it universally to all those God will send you or let happen to you. Some men wish to suffer no tribulations except those connected with honor, for example, or to be wounded or made a prisoner in war, persecuted for religion, or impoverished by some lawsuit they win. Such people do not love tribulation but the honor that goes with it. The truly patient man and true servant of God bears up equally under tribulations accompanied by ignominy and those that bring honor. To be despised, criticized, or accused by evil men is a slight thing to a courageous man, but to be criticized, denounced, and treated badly by good men, by our own friends and relations is the test of virtue. I admire the meekness with which the great St. Charles Borromeo suffered for a long time the public criticisms an important preacher of a strictly reformed order uttered against him from the pulpit more than all the attacks he endured from others. Just as the sting of a bee is much more painful than that of a fly, so the wrongs we suffer from good men and the attacks they make are far harder to bear than those we suffer from others. Yet it often happens that two good men, both with good intentions, because of conflicting ideas stir up great persecutions and attacks on one another.

Be patient not only with regard to the big, chief part of the afflictions that may come to you but also as to things accompanying them and accidental circumstances. Many people would be ready to accept evils provided they were not inconvenienced by them. "I wouldn't be bothered by poverty," one man says, "if it didn't keep me from helping my friends, educating my children and living as respectably as I would like." "It wouldn't bother me," another says, "if people didn't think that it was my own fault." Another would be willing to suffer patiently false reports about him, provided no one believed his detractor. Others are willing to endure part of the evil, so they think, but not the whole of it. They say that they don't complain about being ill but about their lack of money to get cured or because they are so much bother to those about them. Now I say, Philothea, that we must have patience not merely at being ill but at having the illness that God wishes, where he wishes, among the people he wishes, and with whatever difficulties he wishes. The same must be said about other tribulations.

When any evil happens to you, apply whatever remedies you can and do this in a way agreeable to God, since to do otherwise is to tempt God. Having done this, wait with resignation for the results it may please God to send. If it is his will that the remedies overcome the evil, then humbly return him thanks. If it is his will that the evils overcome the remedies, then bless him with patience.

I am of St. Gregory's opinion[3] that when you are justly accused of some fault you have committed you must genuinely humble yourself and confess that you deserve the charge brought against you. If the accusation is false, excuse yourself meekly and deny your guilt, for you owe respect to truth and to the edification of your neighbor. If they continue to accuse you after you have made your true and legitimate explanation, don't be disturbed and don't try to make them accept your explanation. When you have discharged your duty to the truth, you must also do the same to humility. In this way you offend against neither the care you must have for your own good name nor the concern you must have for peace, meekness of heart, and humility.

Complain as little as possible about the wrongs you suffer. Undoubtedly a person who complains commits a sin by doing so, since self-love always feels that injuries are worse than they really are. Above all, do not complain to irascible or fault-finding persons. If there is just occasion for complaining to someone either to correct an offense or restore your peace of mind, do so to those who are even-tempered and really love God. Instead of calming your mind the others will stir up worse difficulties and in place of pulling out the thorn that is hurting you they will drive it deeper into your foot.

When sick, afflicted, or injured by others many men refrain from complaining or showing what they suffer. In their opinion, and it is true, to do so is clear proof of lack of strength and generosity. However, they greatly desire and contrive by various devices for others to have pity and great sympathy for them and regard them not only as badly treated but also as patient and courageous. This is patience, true enough, but false patience. In effect it is nothing but very subtle and refined ambition and vanity. "They have glory but not before God,"[4] the apostle says. The truly patient man neither complains of his hard lot nor desires to be pitied by others. He speaks of his sufferings in a natural, true, and sincere way, without murmuring, complaining, or exaggerating them. If he is pitied by others, he patiently accepts this pity, unless he is pitied for some ill that he does not suffer. In that case he modestly states that he does not suffer from it and thus maintains peace between truth and patience for he admits it but does not complain about it.

Amid the difficulties you meet in the exercise of devotion, remember the words of our Lord: "A woman about to give birth has great sorrow, but when she has brought forth her child, she no longer remembers the anguish for joy that a man is born into the world."[5] Within your soul you have Jesus Christ, the most precious child in the world, and until he is entirely brought forth and born you cannot help suffering from your labor. But be of good heart for these sorrows will pass and everlasting joy will remain with you for having brought forth such a man into the world. He will be wholly brought forth for you when you have wholly formed him in your heart and deeds by imitating his life.

When you are sick offer up all your grief, pain, and weakness as a service to our Lord and beseech him to join them to the torments he suffered for you. Obey your physician, take your medicine, food, and other remedies out of love of God, remembering the gall he drank out of love of you. Desire to get well so that you may serve him, but do not refuse to lie ill so that thus too you may obey him and prepare for death, if that is his will, so that you may praise him and be happy with him forever. Remember that while bees are making honey they live and feed on bitter food, and that we can never perform acts of greater sweetness and patience, or better, compose the honey of excellent virtues, than while we eat the bread of bitterness and live amid afflictions. Just as the best honey is gathered from the blossoms of thyme, a small, bitter herb, so also the virtue practiced in the bitterness of the most vile, low, and abject humiliations is the most excellent of all.

Look often with your inward eyes on Christ Jesus, crucified, naked, blasphemed, slandered, forsaken, and overwhelmed by every kind of weariness, sorrow, and labor. Remember that your sufferings are not comparable to his either in quality or quantity and that you can never suffer for his sake anything equal to what he has suffered for you. Think of the torments the martyrs endured and those so many people now endure that are incomparably more grievous than yours. Then say: "Alas! are not my hardships consolations and my thorns roses in comparison with those who without help, assistance, or relief live a continual death under the burden of afflictions infinitely greater than mine?"

4. OUTWARD HUMILITY

To a poor widow Eliseus said, "Borrow some empty vessels and pour oil into them."[1] To receive God's grace into our hearts they must be emptied of our own vainglory. The kestrel cries out and stares at birds of prey and thus frightens them away by some secret power and property it has[2] and because of this fact doves love the kestrel better than any other kind of bird and live near it in safety. In the same way humility drives away Satan and keeps the graces and gifts of the Holy Spirit safe within us. For this reason all the saints, and particularly the King of Saints and his Mother, have always honored and cherished this precious virtue more than any other among all the moral virtues.

We apply the term vainglory to whatever we assign to ourselves, whether something that is not actually in us or something in us but not of us, or something in us and of us but not such that we can glory in it. Noble ancestry, patronage of great men, and popular honor are things that are not in us but either in our ancestors or in the esteem of other men. Some men become proud and overbearing because they ride a fine horse, wear a feather in their hat, or are dressed in a splendid suit of clothes. Is anyone blind to the folly of all this? If there is any glory in such things it belongs to the horse, the bird, and the tailor. It is a mean heart that borrows honor from a horse, a bird, feather, or some passing fashion. Others value and pride themselves because of a fine moustache, well-trimmed beard, carefully curled hair, soft hands, ability to dance, play cards well, or sing. Such light-minded men seek to increase their reputation by frivolous and foolish things. Others would like to be honored and respected by men because of a little learning, as if everyone should go to school to them and take them as their teachers. They are called pedants for this reason. Other men have handsome bodies and therefore strut about and think that everybody dotes on them. All this is extremely vain, objectionable, and foolish and the glory based on such weak foundations is called vain, foolish, and frivolous.

We recognize genuine goodness as we do genuine balm. If balm sinks down and stays at the bottom when dropped into water, it is rated the best and most valuable. So also in order to know whether a man is truly wise, learned, generous, and noble, we must observe whether his abilities tend to humility, modesty, and obedience for in that case they will be truly good. If they float on the surface and seek to show themselves, they are so much less genuine in so far as they are more showy. Pearls conceived and nourished by wind or thunder claps are mere crusts, devoid of substance.[3] So also men's virtues and fine qualities conceived and nurtured by pride, show, and vanity have the mere appearance of good, without juice, marrow, and solidity.

Honors, dignities, and rank are like saffron, which thrives best and grows most plentifully when trodden under foot. It is no honor to be handsome if a man prizes himself for it; if beauty is to have good grace, it should be unstudied. Learning dishonors us when it inflates our minds and degenerates into mere pedantry. If we are demanding about rank, place, and title, then we not only expose our qualities to examination, judgment, and condemnation but make all of them base and contemptible. Just as honor is an excellent thing, when given to us freely, so also it becomes base when demanded, sought after, and asked for. A peacock spreads his tail in self-admiration and by the very act of raising up his beautiful feathers he ruffles all the others and displays his own ugliness. Flowers that are beautiful as they grow in the earth wither and fade when plucked. Like men who smell the mandrake from afar and while passing it sense its great fragrance, whereas those who smell it closely for a long time become ill and stupefied, so honors afford pleasure and satisfaction to those who view them from a distance and lightly without being deceived by them or becoming serious over them. Those who dote and feed on them deserve great blame and reproof.

For us the pursuit and love of virtue provide a start in virtue but the pursuit and love of honor make us contemptible and deserving of blame. Generous minds do not amuse themselves with the petty toys of rank, honor, and titles. They have other things to do. Such things belong only to idle minds. A man who can own pearls does not bother about shells, and those who aspire to virtue do not trouble themselves over honors. It is true that everyone can take and keep his proper rank without damage to humility if this is done unaffectedly and without quarreling. Travelers returning from Peru bring back gold and silver, but they also bring back apes and parrots because they cost little and don't burden the ships. So also men who aspire to virtue need not reject rank and honor due to them if this does not cost them too much care and attention or involve them in trouble, anxiety, disputes, and quarrels. I do not refer to men whose dignity concerns the public or to certain particular occasions attended with great consequences. In these matters everyone ought to keep what belongs to him with prudence and discretion accompanied by charity and courtesy.

5. DEEPER INTERIOR HUMILITY

You wish me to lead you still further into humility, Philothea, since to do what I have already said pertains to wisdom rather than humility, and I will now do so. Many men neither wish nor dare to think over and reflect on the particular graces God has shown them because they are afraid that this might arouse vainglory and self-complacence. They deceive themselves in this. Since the true means to attain to love of God is consideration of his benefits, as the great Angelic Doctor states,[1] the more we know about them the more we shall love him. As the particular benefits he has conferred on us affect us more powerfully than those we share with others, they must be considered more attentively.

Certainly nothing can so effectively humble us before God's mercy as the multitude of his benefits and nothing can so deeply humble us before his justice as our countless offenses against him. Let us consider what he has done for us and what we have done against him, and as we reflect on our sins one by one let us also consider his graces one by one. There is no need to fear that knowledge of his gifts will make us proud if only we remember this truth, that none of the good in us comes from ourselves. Do mules stop being dull, disgusting beasts simply because they are laden with a prince's precious, perfumed goods? What good do we possess that we have not received? And if we have received it, why do we glory in it?[2] On the contrary, a lively consideration of graces received makes us humble because knowledge of them begets gratitude for them. But if we are deceived by vanity on seeing the grace of God conferred on us, it will be an infallible remedy to consider our own ingratitude, imperfection, and misery. If we reflect on what we did when God was not with us, we will easily perceive that what we do when he is with us is not the result of our own efforts. We will of course enjoy it and rejoice in it because we possess it, but we will glorify God because he alone is its author. Thus the Blessed Virgin proclaims that God has done great things for her, but she does so only to humble herself and to glorify God. "My soul magnifies the Lord, because he has done great things for me,"[3] she says.

We often say that we are nothing, that we are misery itself and the refuse of the world, but we would be very sorry if anyone took us at our word or told others that we are really such as we say. On the contrary, we make a show of flying away and hiding ourselves so that people will run after us and seek us out. We pretend to want to be last in the company and to be seated at the foot of the table, but it is with a view to moving more easily to the upper end. True humility does not make a show of itself and hardly speaks in a humble way. It not only wants to conceal all other virtues but most of all it wants to conceal itself. If it were lawful to lie, dissemble, or scandalize our neighbor, humility would perform arrogant, haughty actions so that it might be concealed beneath them and live completely hidden and unknown.

My advice then, Philothea, is for us not to speak words expressing humility or else to speak them with a sincere interior feeling in keeping with what we utter outwardly. Let's not lower our eyes except when we humble our hearts. Let's not make a show of wanting to be the lowest unless we desire with all our hearts to be such. I maintain that this rule is so general that I don't admit any exception to it. I add only that sometimes good manners require us to offer precedence to those who will surely refuse it, and this is neither duplicity nor false humility. In such cases, the offer of precedence is only the beginning of honor and since we cannot give it to them entirely, it is not wrong to give them its beginning. I say the same about certain words of honor or respect which do not seem to be strictly true but are sufficiently so, provided the speaker's heart contains a sincere intention to honor and respect the man addressed. Although it is with some exaggeration that the words mean what we say, we do not act wrongly in using them when common usage requires it. However, I would truly like our words always to be suited as closely as possible to what we feel, so that in all things and through all things we may maintain heartfelt sincerity and candor. A truly humble man prefers that another tell him that he is a sorry fellow, that he is nothing at all and that he is worth nothing, than to say it himself. At least if he knows that someone says this about him, he does not contradict it but heartily agrees with it. Since he firmly believes it he is satisfied if others adopt his opinion.

Many people say that they leave mental prayer to the perfect and that they themselves are unworthy to use it. Others protest that they do not dare to receive holy Communion frequently because they do not feel themselves to be sufficiently pure. By reason of their great misery and weakness, others fear that they will bring disgrace on devotion if they take part in it. Others refuse to use their talents in the service of God and their neighbors because, they say, they know their weakness and fear they'll become proud if they are instruments of any good and that by giving light to others they would be consumed. All this is merely artifice and a form of humility that is not only false but even malicious. By it they silently and subtly try to find fault with the things of God, or at least to conceal love for their own opinions, moods, and sloth under the pretext of humility. "Ask for a sign from the Lord your God either unto the height of heaven above or unto the depths of the sea below," said the prophet to the unfortunate Achaz, and he answered, "I will not ask, and I will not tempt the Lord."[4] Oh, wicked man! He pretends to show great reverence for God and under the color of humility excuses himself from aspiring to the grace to which God's mercy calls him. Does he not see that when God desires to give us his graces, it is pride to refuse them, that God's gifts obligate us to accept them, and that it is humility to obey and comply as nearly as we can with his desires? It is God's will that we become perfect[5] by uniting ourselves to him and imitating him as closely as possible. The proud man who trusts in himself has good reason not to attempt anything. The humble man is all the more courageous because he recognizes his own impotence. The more wretched he esteems himself the more daring he becomes because he places his whole trust in God who rejoices to display his power in our weakness and raise up his mercy on our misery. We may therefore humbly and devoutly presume to undertake all that is judged proper for our advancement by those who direct our souls.

To think that we know what we do not know is complete folly. To desire to pass as knowing what we are well aware we don't know is inexcusable vanity. For my part, just as I would not parade knowledge even of what I actually know, so contrariwise I would not pretend to be ignorant of it. When charity requires it, we must candidly and gladly share with our neighbor not only what is necessary for his instruction but also what is useful for his consolation. Humility conceals and covers over virtues in order to preserve them, but it reveals them when charity so requires in order that we may enlarge, increase, and perfect them. In this respect humility imitates a certain tree found on the island of Tylos. At night it contracts and closes up its beautiful carnation blossoms and only opens them again in the morning sun. Hence the natives of the country say that they sleep at night.[6] In like manner humility covers over and hides all our purely human virtues and perfections and never displays them except for the sake of charity. Since charity is not a natural but a supernatural and not a moral but a theological virtue, it is the true sun of all the virtues and should have dominion over them. Hence we may conclude that acts of humility that are offensive to charity are certainly false.

I don't want to play either the fool or the wise man, for if humility forbids me to play the sage, candor and sincerity forbid me to act the fool. Just as vanity is opposed to humility, so artifice, affectation, and dissimulation are contrary to honesty and sincerity. If certain great servants of God have pretended to be fools in order to render themselves more abject in the eyes of the world, we must admire but not imitate them. They had their motives to act in this unusual fashion and those motives were so special and extraordinary that no one should draw conclusions from them for himself. When David danced and leaped before the Ark of the Covenant[7] with a vigor that ordinary decorum does not require, this was not because he wished to act foolishly. With all simplicity and without any affectation he made use of such outward movements to express the extraordinary and excessive joy he felt within his heart. It is true that when Michol, his wife, reproached him for it as a foolish act, he was not sorry to see himself criticized. Continuing in a natural and genuine manifestation of joy, he testified that he was glad to be criticized for the sake of God. In consequence, I tell you that if people think you are abject or foolish because of acts of true, genuine devotion, humility will cause you to rejoice at such fortunate criticism for its cause is not in you but in those who make it.

6. HUMILITY CAUSES US TO LOVE OUR OWN ABJECTION

I now move on to tell you, Philothea, that in all things and through all things you should love your own abjection. In Latin abjection signifies humility and humility means abjection. Thus when our Lady says in her sacred canticle that because our Lord "has regarded the humility of his handmaid all generations shall call her blessed,"[1] she means that our Lord has graciously looked down on her abjection, meanness, and lowliness in order to heap graces and favors upon her. However, there is a difference between the virtue of humility and abjection, for abjection is lowliness, meanness, and baseness in us although we are not aware of that fact, whereas humility is true knowledge and voluntary acknowledgement of our abjection. The chief point of such humility consists not only in willingly admitting our abject state but in loving it and delighting in it. This must not be because of lack of courage and generosity but in order to exalt God's Majesty all the more and to hold our neighbor in higher esteem than ourselves. I urge you to do this, and that you may understand me more clearly I point out that among the evils we suffer some are abject and others are honorable. Many men can easily adapt themselves to evils that bring honor with them but hardly anyone can do so to those which are abject. You see a devout old hermit covered with rags and shivering with cold. Everyone honors his tattered habit and sympathizes with his sufferings. If a poor tradesman, a poor gentleman, or a poor gentlewoman is in the same condition people laugh and scoff at them. Thus you see that their poverty is abject poverty. A monk meekly receives a sharp rebuke from his superior or a child from his father, and everyone calls it an instance of mortification, obedience, and wisdom. If a lord or lady suffers the same thing from someone, then even though it is accepted out of love for God it is called cowardice and lack of spirit. Hence you see here another abject evil. One man has a cancer in his arm and another on his face; the first has only the disease, while the other suffers contempt, disgrace, and abjection along with the disease. Hence I hold that we must not only love the disease, which is the duty of patience, but we must also embrace the abjection, and this is done by the virtue of humility.

Moreover, there are virtues that are abject and virtues that are honorable. Patience, meekness, simplicity, and even humility itself are virtues that worldly people consider mean and abject. On the other hand, they hold prudence, courage, and liberality in the highest esteem. There are also acts of one and the same virtue, some of which are despised and others held in honor. To give alms and to forgive injuries are both charitable acts, yet the first is held in honor by everyone while the second is despised by the eyes of the world. A young gentleman or a young lady who refuses to take part in the dissipated conduct of a debauched group or to talk, play, dance, drink, or dress like the rest will be scorned and criticized by the others and their modesty will be called fanaticism or prudery. To love this is to love our own abjection. Take abjection of another kind. We visit the sick, and if I am sent to the most miserable among them it will be abjection for me in the eyes of the world, and for that reason I will love it. If I am sent to persons of quality, it is spiritual abjection for there is not so much virtue or merit in it, and hence I will love this abjection. One man falls down in the public street and in addition to the fall incurs shame. We must love such abjection.

There are even faults that involve no other ill except abjection. Humility does not require that we should deliberately commit such faults but it does require that we should not disturb ourselves when we have committed them. Among them are certain kinds of folly, incivility, and inadvertency that we should avoid out of regard for good manners and discretion. But if they have been committed, we should endure the abjection we incur and willingly accept it so as to practice humility. I add further that if in passion or anger I have spoken any unbecoming words by which God or my neighbor may have been offended, I will sincerely repent and be sorry for the offense and make the best reparation I can. At the same time I will accept the abjection and contempt it has brought upon me. If the one could be separated from the other, I would gladly cast away the sin and humbly keep the abjection.

Although we love the abjection that follows an evil, we must not forget to correct by just and lawful means the evil that caused it, especially when it is serious. If I should have some disagreeable infection in my face, I will try to have it cured, although not with an intention to forget the abjection I received from it. If I have done something that has offended nobody, I will not apologize for it since although it were an offense yet it was not lasting. That being the case, I could not excuse it except with a view of ridding myself of the abjection and humility does not permit this. However, if through inadvertence or folly I have offended or scandalized anyone, I will correct the offense by some true explanation, for evil is lasting and charity obliges me to remove it. Moreover, it sometimes happens that charity requires us to remove the abjection for the good of a neighbor before whom our good name must be preserved. In such cases, although we remove the abjection from our neighbor's sight in order to prevent scandal, yet we must carefully enclose it in our heart for our own edification.

If you wish to know which are the best kinds of abjection, Philothea, I tell you plainly that the ones most profitable to our souls and most acceptable to God are those which come to us accidentally or because of our state in life. The reason is that we have not chosen them ourselves but have accepted them as sent by God and his choice is always better than our own. If we were to choose any form of humiliation, we should prefer the greatest, and those most contrary to our inclinations are such, provided that they are in keeping with our vocations. To say it once and for all, our own choice and selection spoil or lessen almost all our virtues. Who will say with the great king, "I have chosen to be abject in the house of God, rather than to dwell in the tabernacles of sinners?"[2] No one can say this, Philothea, except him who to exalt us lived and died in such manner as to become "the reproach of men and the outcast of the people."[3]

Many of the things I have told you may seem hard when you reflect on them, but believe me, they will be sweeter than sugar or honey when you put them to practice.

7. HOW WE ARE TO PRESERVE OUR GOOD NAME WHILE PRACTICING HUMILITY

Praise, honor, and glory are not given to men as rewards for a mere virtue but for some outstanding virtue. By praise we try to persuade others to esteem the excellence of a certain man. By honor we testify that we ourselves esteem him. Glory, in my opinion, is only a kind of luster pertaining to a man's reputation and springing from the concurrence of many acts of praise and honor. Hence honor and praise are like precious stones and out of a collection of them glory proceeds like an enamel. Humility does not permit us to have any opinion of our own excellence or right to be preferred before others, and therefore it cannot allow us to seek after praise, honor, and glory, which are things due only to excellence. Yet humility agrees with the counsel of the Wise Man who warns us to "take care of our good name,"[1] because to esteem our good name is not to esteem an excellence but only ordinary honesty and integrity of life. Humility does not forbid us to acknowledge this within ourselves or to desire a reputation for it. It is true that humility would despise a good name if charity had no need for it, but because good name is one of the bases of human society and without it we are not only useless but harmful to the public by reason of the scandal it would provoke, charity requires and humility agrees that we should desire to have a good name and carefully preserve it.

Moreover, just as leaves growing on a tree are not themselves of much value but serve important purposes, not only to beautify the tree but also to preserve its tender young fruit, so with a good reputation. Of itself it is not very desirable but it is very useful not only for the adornment of our life but also for preservation of virtue, especially of virtues which are as yet only weak and tender. The duty of preserving our reputation and of being actually such as we are thought to be urges a generous spirit to go forward with a strong and agreeable impulse. Let us preserve our virtues, my dear Philothea, because they are acceptable to God, the great and sovereign object of all our actions. But just as those who want to preserve fruit are not satisfied merely with covering them over with sugar, but put them into vessels that can keep them, so too although love of God is the principal preservative of our virtues, we can also employ our good name as very proper and useful for that purpose.

We must not be too ardent, precise, and demanding in regard to preserving our good name. Men who are overly tender and sensitive on this point are like persons who take medicine for slight indispositions. Although they think they are preserving their health, they actually destroy it. In like manner those who try too carefully to maintain their reputation lose it entirely. By such sensitivity they become captious, quarrelsome, and unbearable and thus provoke the malice of detractors. Generally speaking, to ignore and despise an injury or calumny is a far more effectual remedy than resentment, fighting, and revenge. Contempt for injuries causes them to vanish, whereas if we become angry, we seem to admit them. Crocodiles harm only those who are afraid of them and detraction hurts only those who are vexed by it. Excessive fear of losing our good name reveals great distrust in its foundation, which is really a good life. Towns that have wooden bridges over great rivers are afraid that they will be swept away by every little rise of water, but those with stone bridges fear only extraordinary floods. In like manner those with souls solidly grounded on Christian virtue usually despise the floods let loose by harmful tongues, while those who know that they are weak are upset by every report. In a word, Philothea, a man who is too anxious to keep his reputation loses it. The person who tries to win reputation with those whose vices have made them truly infamous and dishonorable deserves to lose honor.

Reputation is like a sign pointing to where virtue dwells and therefore this virtue must be preferred in all things and through all things. Hence if anyone calls you a hypocrite because you are devout or a coward because you have pardoned some injury, laugh at him. Although such judgments are passed on us by foolish and stupid people, we must not forsake the path of virtue even if we suffer loss of reputation. We must prefer the fruit before the leaves, that is, interior spiritual graces above all external goods. It is legitimate to be jealous of our reputation but not to be idolatrous of it. Also, just as we must not offend the eyes of good men, so also we must not try to please the eyes of the wicked. A beard is an ornament on a man's face and hair is such on a woman's head. If a man's beard is plucked from his face or a woman's hair from her head it will hardly grow on again, but if it is only cut off or even shaved close, it will soon come back and grow stronger and thicker than ever. So also if our reputation is cut off or even shaved away clean by the tongues of detractors—David says that they are like a sharp razor[2]—we must not disturb ourselves. It will grow out again, not only as beautiful as before but even much stronger. If our vices, base deeds, and evil life ruin our reputation, it will hardly return again since it has been pulled up by the roots. The root of a good name is virtue and probity. As long as they remain in us it can always regain the honor due to it.

If some vain way of life, idle habit, foolish love, or custom of keeping improper company should injure our reputation, we must give them up. Our good name is of more value than any such empty pleasures. But if because of exercise of piety, advancement in devotion, or progress toward heaven men grumble, murmur, and speak ill of us, let us leave them to bay at the moon. If at times they can cast aspersions on our good name and thus cut and shave off the hair and beard of our reputation, it will quickly grow out again. The razor of detraction will be as useful toward our honor as the pruning knife is to the vine, which makes it abound and multiply in fruit.

Let us always keep our eyes fixed on Jesus Christ crucified and go forward in his service with confidence and sincerity but with prudence and discretion. He will protect our reputation. If he permits it to be taken away from us, it will either be to give us a better one or to make us profit by holy humility, of which a single ounce is preferable to a thousand pounds of honor. If we are condemned unjustly, let us calmly oppose truth to calumny. If the calumny continues, let us continue to humble ourselves. By surrendering our reputation together with our soul into God's hands, we safeguard it in the best way possible. Let us serve God "by evil report and good report,"[3] after the example of St. Paul, so that we may say with David, "Because for your sake, O Lord, I have borne reproach, shame has covered my face."[4] Nevertheless, I except from this certain crimes so horrid and infamous that no man should put with being falsely charged with them if he can justly acquit himself of it. I also except certain persons on whose reputation the edification of many others depends. According to the opinion of theologians, in such cases we must quietly seek reparation of the wrong received.

8. MEEKNESS TOWARD OUR NEIGHBOR AND REMEDIES FOR ANGER

The holy chrism, which by apostolic tradition we use in the Church of God for confirmation and consecration, is made up of olive oil mixed with balm. Among other things it represents to us two favorite and beloved virtues that shone forth in the sacred person of our Lord. He has strongly recommended them to us as though to indicate by them that our hearts must be in a special way consecrated to serve him and dedicated to imitate him. "Learn of me," he says, "for I am meek and humble of heart."[1] Humility perfects us with respect to God, and meekness with respect to our neighbor. As I have already remarked,[2] balm, which sinks deeper than any other liquid, symbolizes humility, while olive oil, which always rises to the top, symbolizes meekness and mildness, which rise above all things and stand out among the virtues as the flower of charity. According to St. Bernard,[3] it is perfect when it is not only patient but also meek and mild.

Take care, Philothea, that this mystical chrism compounded of meekness and humility is found within your heart. It is one of the great tricks of the enemy to lead many people to be deceived by expressions and outward appearances of these two virtues. Without making a thorough examination of their interior affections, they think that they are humble and meek but actually they are not. This may be discovered because in spite of all their ceremonious mildness and humility they show unparalleled arrogance at the least cross word or the least little injury they receive. It is reported that those who have taken a preservative called St. Paul's grace[4] do not swell up if bitten and stung by a viper, provided the preservative is of the best quality. In like manner, when humility and meekness are good and true they preserve us from the inflammation and swelling that injuries usually cause in our hearts. If we are proud, puffed up, and enraged when we are stung and bitten by detractors and enemies, it is a sure sign that in us neither humility nor meekness is genuine and sincere but only apparent and artificial.

When Joseph, that holy and illustrious patriarch, sent back his brothers from Egypt to his father's house, he gave them this single piece of advice: "Do not be angry on the way."[5] I say the same to you, Philothea. This wretched life is only a journey to the happy life to come. We must not be angry with one another on the way, but rather we must march on as a band of brothers and companions united in meekness, peace, and love. I state absolutely and make no exception, do not be angry at all if that is possible. Do not accept any pretext whatever for opening your heart's door to anger. St. James tells us positively and without reservation, "The anger of man does not work the justice of God."[6]

Constantly and courageously but meekly and peacefully we must resist evil and restrain the vices of those under our charge. Nothing so quickly calms down an angry elephant as the sight of a little lamb, and nothing so easily breaks the force of a cannon ball as wool. We do not set much value on correction that comes from passion, even though accompanied by reason, as to that which proceeds from reason alone. By nature the reasonable soul is subject to reason and therefore it is never subject to passion except through tyranny. Therefore, when reason is accompanied by passion it becomes odious, for its just government is debased by association with tyranny. When princes visit their people with a peaceable retinue they honor them and cause them great joy, but when they come at the head of armies, even though for the common good, their visits are always disagreeable and harmful. Even though they enforce strict military discipline among their troops, they can never do it so effectively that there will not be disorders in which good men are oppressed. In like manner, as long as reason rules and peaceably chastises, corrects, and warns, even though severely and exactly, everyone loves and approves it. When reason brings along anger, passion, and rage, which St. Augustine calls soldiers of reason,[7] it is feared rather than loved. Even reason's own heart is depressed and mistreated. "It is better," says St. Augustine writing to Profuturus, "to deny entrance to just and reasonable anger than to admit it, no matter how small it is. Once let in, it is driven out again only with difficulty. It comes in as a little twig and in less than no time it grows big and becomes a beam."[8] If anger can only gain the night on us and if the sun sets on it, which the apostle forbids,[9] it turns into hatred, from which we have hardly any way of ridding ourselves. It is nourished by a thousand false pretexts; there never was an angry man who thought his anger unjust.

It is better to attempt to find a way to live without anger than to pretend to make a moderate, discreet use of it. When we find ourselves surprised into anger through our own imperfections and frailty, it is better to drive it away quickly than to start a discussion with it. If we give it ever so little time, it will become mistress of the place, like the serpent that easily draws in his whole body where it can once get in its head. "But how shall I banish it?" you may ask me. My dear Philothea, at the first attack you must immediately muster your forces, not violently and tumultuously but mildly and yet seriously. Among the crowds in certain senate chambers and parliaments we see ushers crying, "Quiet, there!" thus making more noise than those they want to silence. So too it often happens that by trying violently to restrain our anger, we stir up more trouble within our heart than wrath excited before and being this agitated our heart can no longer be its own master.

After this meek effort, put to practice the advice St. Augustine gave in his old age to the young Bishop Auxilius. "Do what a man should do. If what the man of God speaks of in the Psalms happens to you, 'My eye is troubled with wrath,' turn to God and cry out, 'Have mercy on me, O Lord,'[10] so that he may stretch forth his right hand to restrain your anger."[11] I mean that when we find that we have been aroused to anger we must call for God's help like the apostles when they were tossed about by the wind and storm on the waters.[12] He will command your passions to cease and there will be a great calm. I constantly advise you that prayers directed against present and pressing anger must always be said calmly and peaceably and not violently. This rule must be observed in all steps taken against this evil. Moreover, as soon as you see that you are guilty of a wrathful deed, correct the fault right away by an act of meekness toward the person you were angry with. It is a sovereign remedy against lying to contradict the untruth upon the spot as soon as we see we have told one. So also we must repair our anger instantly by a contrary act of meekness. Fresh wounds are quickest healed, as the saying goes.

Again, when your mind is tranquil and without any cause for anger, build up a stock of meekness and mildness. Speak all your words and do all your actions, whether little or great, in the mildest way you can. Call to mind that just as the Spouse in the Canticle of Canticles not only has honey on her lips and at the end of her tongue, that is, in her breast, and not honey but milk as well,[13] so too we must have not only sweet words for our neighbor but also our entire breast, that is to say, the whole interior of our soul. We must not merely have the aromatic and fragrant sweetness of honey, namely, the sweetness of polite conversation with strangers, but also the sweetness of milk among our own family and neighbors. Those who appear in public as angels but are devils in their own homes greatly fail in this regard.

9. MEEKNESS TOWARD OURSELVES

One of the best exercises in meekness we can perform is when the subject is in ourselves. We must not fret over our own imperfections. Although reason requires that we must be displeased and sorry whenever we commit a fault, we must refrain from bitter, gloomy, spiteful, and emotional displeasure. Many people are greatly at fault in this way. When overcome by anger they become angry at being angry, disturbed at being disturbed, and vexed at being vexed. By such means they keep their hearts drenched and steeped in passion. It may seem that the second fit of anger does away with the first, but actually it serves to open the way for fresh anger on the first occasion that arises. Moreover, these fits of anger, vexation, and bitterness against ourselves tend to pride and they spring from no other source than self-love, which is disturbed and upset at seeing that it is imperfect.

We must be sorry for our faults, but in a calm, settled, firm way. When a judge is guided in his decisions by reason and proceeds calmly, he punishes criminals much more justly than when he acts in violence and passion. If he passes judgment hastily and passionately, he does not punish the crimes because of what they really are but because of what they seem to him. So also we correct ourselves much better by calm, steady repentance than by that which is harsh, turbulent, and passionate. Violent repentance does not proceed according to the character of our faults but according to our inclinations. For example, a man much concerned with chastity will be very bitterly disturbed at the least fault he commits against that virtue, while he will only laugh at an act of gross detraction he has committed. On the other hand, a man who hates detraction torments himself because of some slight whisper against another while he takes no account of a gross sin against chastity. So also for other sins. All this springs from this source, that such men form their consciences not by reason but by passion.

Believe me, Philothea, a father's gentle, loving rebuke has far greater power to correct a child than rage and passion. So too when we have committed some fault if we rebuke our heart by a calm, mild remonstrance, with more compassion for it than passion against it and encourage it to make amendment, then repentance conceived in this way will sink far deeper and penetrate more effectually than fretful, angry, stormy repentance.

For my own part, if I had made a firm resolution not to yield to the sin of vanity, for example, and yet had seriously fallen into it, I would not reprove my heart after this manner: "Aren't you wretched and abominable, you who have made so many resolutions and yet let yourself be carried away by vanity? You should die for shame. Never again lift up your eyes to heaven, blind, insolent traitor that you are, a rebel against your God!" I would correct it in a reasonable, compassionate way: "Alas, my poor heart, here we are, fallen into the pit we were so firmly resolved to avoid! Well, we must get up again and leave it forever. We must call on God's mercy and hope that it will help us to be steadier in the days to come. Let us start out again on the way of humility. Let us be of good heart and from this day be more on guard. God will help us; we will do better." On the basis of such correction I would build a firm, solid resolution never again to fall into that fault, using the proper means of avoiding it under the advice of my director.

However, if anyone finds that his heart is not sufficiently moved by this mild manner of correction, he may use a sharp, severe reproach and rebuke so as to excite it to deeper sorrow. This must be on condition that after he has curbed and chided his heart in this rough way he closes all his grief and anger with sweet, consoling confidence in God in imitation of that illustrious penitent who saw his afflicted soul and raised it up in this way: "Why are you sad, O my soul, and why do you disquiet me? Hope in God, for I will give praise to him, the salvation of my countenance and my God."[1]

Lift up your heart again whenever it falls, but do so meekly by humbling yourself before God through knowledge of your own misery and do not be surprised if you fall. It is no wonder that infirmity should be infirm, weakness weak, or misery wretched. Nevertheless, detest with all your powers the offense God has received from you and with great courage and confidence in his mercy return to the path of virtue you had forsaken.

10. WE MUST WATCH OUR AFFAIRS CAREFULLY BUT WITHOUT EAGERNESS OR SOLICITUDE

The care and diligence with which we should attend to our concerns are very different from solicitude, worry, and anxiety. The angels have care for our salvation and are diligent to procure it, yet they are not solicitous, worried, and anxious. Care and diligence may be accompanied by tranquillity and peace of mind but not by solicitude and worry, much less anxiety. Be careful and attentive, Philothea, to all the matters God has committed to your care. Since God has confided them to you, he wishes you have great care for them. If possible, do not be solicitous and worried, that is, don't exert yourself over them with uneasiness, anxiety, and forwardness. Don't be worried about them, for worry disturbs reason and good judgment and prevents us from doing well the very things we are worried about.

When our Lord corrected St. Martha, he said, "Martha, Martha, you are solicitous and troubled about many things."[1] Note that she would not have been troubled if she had been merely diligent, but she was overconcerned and disturbed and therefore hurried about and troubled herself.

It was for this reason that our Lord rebuked her. Rivers that flow gently through the plains carry along large boats and rich merchandise. Rains that fall gently on open fields make them fruitful in grass and grain. Torrents and rivers that spread over the land in great floods ruin the bordering country and are useless for commerce, just as in like manner heavy, tempestuous rains ruin the fields and meadows. A job done too eagerly and hurriedly is never well done. We must do things in a leisurely fashion, according to the proverb. "He who is hasty is in danger of stumbling and hurting his foot,"[2] says Solomon. We perform actions quickly enough when we do them well. Drones make more noise and work more eagerly than bees, but they make only wax and not honey. So also men who hurry about with tormenting anxiety and eager solicitude never accomplish much, nor do they do it well. Flies do not bother us because of their strength but because of their numbers, and so also affairs of importance do not give us as much trouble as do many trifling things. Undertake all your affairs with a calm mind and try to despatch them in order one after the other. If you make an effort to do them all at once or without order, your spirits will be so overcharged and depressed that they will likely sink under the burden without effecting anything.

In all your affairs rely wholly on God's providence through which alone you must look for success. Nevertheless, strive quietly on your part to cooperate with its designs. You may be sure that if you have firm trust in God, the success that comes to you will always be that which is most useful for you whether it appears good or bad in your private judgment. Imitate little children who with one hand hold fast to their father while with the other they gather strawberries or blackberries from the hedges. So too if you gather and handle the goods of this world with one hand, you must always hold fast with the other to your heavenly Father's hand and turn toward him from time to time to see if your actions or occupations are pleasing to him. Above all things, take heed that you never leave his hand and his protection, thinking that thus you can gather more or gain some advantage. If he should forsake you, you will not be able to go a step further without falling to the ground. What I mean, Philothea, is that in ordinary affairs and occupations that do not require strict, earnest attention, you should look at God rather than at them. When they are of such importance as to require your whole attention to do them well, then too you should look from time to time at God, like mariners who to arrive at the port they are bound for look at the sky above them rather than down on the sea on which they sail. Thus God will work with you, in you, and for you, and after your labor consolation will follow.

11. OBEDIENCE

Charity alone can establish us in perfection, but obedience, chastity, and poverty are the three principal means to attain to it. Obedience consecrates our heart, chastity our body, and poverty the means we take to God's love and service. These are the three main branches of the spiritual cross and all three are based on a fourth, namely, humility. I shall not discuss these three virtues as things solemnly vowed to God, since this concerns only those in the religious life, nor as things simply vowed. Although a vow adds great graces and merits to all the virtues, yet to make us perfect it is not necessary that they be vowed, provided only that they are observed. If vowed, especially if solemnly vowed, they place a man in the state of perfection,[1] so that to be perfect it suffices that they be observed, there is still a difference between the state of perfection and perfection itself. All bishops and religious are in the state of perfection, yet not all of them have arrived at perfection itself, as is only too plainly to be seen. Let us try, then, Philothea, to practice these virtues well, each of us according to his vocation. Although they do not place us in the state of perfection, yet they will bring us perfection itself. In fact, all of us are obliged to practice these three virtues, although not all in the same way.

There are two kinds of obedience, one necessary and the other voluntary. By reason of that which is of necessity, you must humbly obey your ecclesiastical superiors, such as the pope, your bishop, your parish priest, and those who have been commissioned by them. You must obey your civil superiors, such as your prince and the magistrates he has appointed for your well-being; and you must obey your domestic superiors, your father and mother, your master and mistress. Such obedience is called necessary because none of us can exempt himself from the duty of obeying superiors to whom God has given authority to command and govern us, each in the department assigned to him. Hence you must of necessity obey their commands. To be perfect, you must follow their counsels as well, even their desires and inclinations, as far as charity and prudence will permit. Obey them when they order something you like, for instance, to eat or take recreation. Although it seems no great virtue to obey in such cases, it would be very wrong to disobey. Obey them in indifferent things, such as to wear this or that kind of clothing, to take one path or another, to sing or keep silent, and it will be a very praiseworthy form of obedience. Obey in matters that are disagreeable, severe, and difficult, and that will be perfect obedience. In short, obey meekly and without arguing, quickly and without delay, cheerfully and without complaining. Above all, obey lovingly out of love of him who for love of us "made himself obedient unto death, even death on a cross,"[2] and as St. Bernard says, chose to lose life rather than obedience.[3]

In order to learn to obey your superiors with ease, adapt yourself easily to the will of your equals by giving in to their opinions in what is not sinful and by not being contentious or obstinate. Accommodate yourself cheerfully to your inferiors' wishes as far as reason permits and do not exercise imperious authority over them so long as they are good. It is an illusion for us to think that if only we were members of some religious community we would obey readily although we are slow and stubborn in obeying those God has placed over us.

We term obedience voluntary when we obligate ourselves by our own choice and when this choice is not imposed on us by someone else. Ordinarily a man does not choose his own prince, bishop, father, or mother and often women do not choose their husbands. However, each one chooses his own confessor and director. It may be that in making this choice we also make a vow to obey him—it is reported that in addition to the obedience solemnly vowed to the superior of her order Mother Teresa bound herself by a simple vow to obey Father Gratian—or without making a vow we dedicate ourselves to obey someone. Such obedience is called voluntary since it results from our own free will and choice.

We must obey all our superiors, at least in what concerns the authority each of them has over us. Thus in public policy and political matters we must obey the prince, in ecclesiastical affairs our prelates, in domestic matters father, master, or husband, and in what regards the particular conduct of our soul, our particular director and confessor.

Request your spiritual director to command you to do all the devout actions you must perform since they will thus be better and have a twofold grace and value. The one comes from the deeds themselves because they are works of piety; the other from obedience that accepts such commands and in virtue of which the acts are done. Blessed are the obedient for God will never let them go astray.

12. THE NECESSITY OF CHASTITY

Chastity is the lily of virtues and makes men almost equal to the angels. Nothing is beautiful except by purity, and in men purity is chastity. Chastity is referred as honesty[1] and to profess it is termed honor. It is called integrity, and its opposite corruption. In short, it has its own peculiar glory of being the fair, unspotted virtue of both soul and body.

It is never licit to derive shameful pleasure from our bodies in any way whatsoever except in lawful marriage, whose sanctity by just compensation can repair damage received in such pleasure. Moreover, in marriage too there must be a virtuous intention so that even if there is unseemliness in the pleasure taken there is nothing but virtue in the will that takes it. A chaste heart is like the mother-of-pearl, which cannot admit any drop of water except that which comes down from heaven,[2] for it can take no pleasure except that of marriage which is ordained by heaven. Outside of marriage it is not permissible even to entertain voluptuous, wilful, and deliberate thoughts about it.

For the first degree of this virtue, Philothea, be on guard against giving in to any kind of condemned and forbidden pleasure, such as all those taken outside of marriage or even those within marriage when taken contrary to its laws. For the second degree, refrain as much as possible from all useless, unnecessary pleasures even though lawful and permitted. For the third, do not set your affections on pleasures and delights that are ordained and commanded. While it is necessary to take such delights as are necessary—I mean those which concern the end and institution of holy marriage—one must never set his heart and mind on them.

For the rest, everyone greatly needs this virtue. Widows must have courageous chastity which not only despises present and future objects of pleasure but also resists impure images that pleasures lawfully had in marriage may produce in their minds, which are thus more susceptible to impure allurements. For this reason St. Augustine admired the purity of his friend Alypius who had completely forgotten and despised the fleshly pleasures he had once experienced in his youth.[3] In fact when fruits are whole and sound they can be preserved, some kinds in straw, others in sand, and still others in their own leaves. Once damaged, they are almost impossible to keep except when preserved in honey and sugar. In like manner, when chastity has not been harmed or violated it can be kept safe in various ways. Once broken, nothing can preserve it except extraordinary devotion, which is the true honey and sugar of the spirit, as I have often suggested.

For virgins complete, unalloyed, and tender chastity is a necessity so that they can banish from their minds all curious thoughts and look down with absolute contempt on unclean pleasures of every kind. In all truth, such things are not worthy of men's desires because they are more fitting for swine and asses. These pure souls must be on guard and never doubt that chastity is incomparably finer than anything incompatible with it. As the great St. Jerome says,[4] the enemy violently tempts virgins to desire to try such pleasures and pictures them as infinitely more pleasurable and delightful than they actually are. Such temptations disturb them very much since, as this holy father says, they think that what is unknown to them is very sweet. A little butterfly sees the flame and hovers curiously about it, trying to find out if it is as fine as it looks, and carried away by this fancy, it doesn't stop until it is destroyed at the very first test. In like manner, young people often become so enthralled by false and foolish ideas as to the pleasure found in those voluptuous flames that after many alluring thoughts they at last plunge into ruin and perish. More foolish than the butterflies, which have some cause to think that the fire is pleasant since it is so beautiful, they know what they are looking for is completely immoral and still do not stop putting too much value on that foolish animal pleasure.

As for the married, it is true that chastity is very necessary for them too, although many cannot conceive how this is. In their case chastity does not consist in complete abstinence from carnal pleasures but in self-restraint in them. The commandment, "Be angry but do not sin,"[5] in my opinion is harder to keep than simply, "Do not get angry." It is easier to abstain from anger than to regulate it, and so too it is easier to remain completely free from carnal pleasures than to maintain moderation in them. It is true that the holy liberty of marriage has a special power to extinguish the fires of concupiscence, but the frailty of those who enjoy this liberty easily passes from permission to license and from use to abuse. Just as we find that many rich men steal, not from need but from avarice, so also we see that many married people go to excesses by mere intemperance and lewdness, notwithstanding the lawful object to which they must and can confine themselves. Their concupiscence is like wildfire, which runs about and burns on every side without staying in any one place. It is always dangerous to take strong medicine for if we take more than we should or if it is not well prepared, it may lead to serious injury. Marriage was blessed and ordained partly as a remedy for concupiscence. Undoubtedly it is a very good remedy, still it is a violent and consequently a very dangerous remedy if not used with discretion.

I add that changes in human affairs and long illnesses often separate husbands from wives and hence married people have need of two kinds of chastity, one for absolute abstinence, when separated at such times as I have mentioned, and one for moderation, when with one another in the ordinary course of events. Among the damned St. Catherine of Siena saw many souls grievously tormented for having violated the sanctity of marriage. This resulted, she said, not from the enormity of the sin, for murders and blasphemies are even more enormous, but "because those who commit it do not make it a matter of conscience"[6] and hence continue in it for a long time.

You see then that chastity is necessary for all classes of people. "Strive for peace with all men, and for that holiness without which no man will see God,"[7] says the apostle. By holiness we here understand chastity, as St. Jerome[8] and St. John Chrysostom[9] observe. No, Philothea, "no one shall see God without chastity,"[10] no one shall dwell in his holy tabernacle who is not "clean of heart."[11] As our Savior himself says, "Dogs and the unchaste shall be banished from there,"[12] and "Blessed are the pure of heart for they shall see God."[13]

13. ADVICE ON HOW TO PRESERVE CHASTITY

Be very quick to turn away from whatever leads or allures to lewd conduct, for this evil works without our knowing it and from small beginnings moves on to great difficulties. Such things are always easier to avoid than to cure.

Human bodies are like glass vessels that cannot be carried about while touching one another without risk of breakage. They are also like fruits which though sound and well prepared are damaged by rubbing against one another. No matter how fresh the water within a vessel may be, once it has been touched by any beast of earth, it cannot keep its freshness for long. Never permit anyone to touch you improperly, Philothea, either playfully or fondly. Although chastity may perhaps be preserved in such actions if they are thoughtless rather than malicious, yet the freshness and flower of chastity always receive some harm and loss. To let oneself be touched immodestly is the utter ruin of chastity.

Chastity depends on the heart as its source, but looks to the body as its subject. For this reason it may be lost both by the body's external senses and by thoughts and desires within the heart. It is an act of impurity to look at, hear, speak, smell, or touch anything immodest if our heart is entertained thereby and takes pleasure in it. St. Paul states positively, "Do not let fornication even be named among you."[1] Bees not only dislike carrion but avoid and hate the stench that comes from it. The sacred Spouse in the Canticle of Canticles has "hands dripping myrrh," a liquid that preserves from corruption. Her lips are bound with a scarlet ribbon, the mark of modesty in speech. Her eyes are those of a dove because of their clearness. Her ears have gold earrings in token of purity. Her nose is compared to the cedars of Lebanon which are incorruptible wood.[2] Such must be the devout soul—chaste, clean, and pure in hands, lips, ears, eyes, and all its body.

For this purpose I recall to your mind an expression that an ancient father, John Cassian, relates as coming from the mouth of the great St. Basil. Speaking of himself, he said one day, "I have not known women, yet I am not a virgin."[3] Certainly chastity may be lost in as many ways as there are immodest and wanton acts. According as they are great or little, some weaken it, others wound it, and still others cause it to die completely. There are certain indiscreet, foolish, sensual familiarities and passions, which, to speak properly, do not violate chastity but weaken it, leave it languid, and tarnish its beautiful whiteness.

There are other familiarities and passions that are not only indiscreet but vicious, not merely foolish but immoral, and not only sensual but carnal. Chastity is at least grievously wounded and damaged by them. I say at least because from them it dies and perishes utterly when such foolish acts and wanton deeds cause in the flesh the final effect of impure pleasure. Chastity then perishes in a more unworthy, wicked, and unfortunate way than when lost by fornication or even adultery and incest. These latter kinds of filthiness are simply sins, but the others, as Tertullian says in his work *On Chastity*,[4] are monsters of iniquity and sin. Cassian does not believe, nor do I, that St. Basil spoke of any such perversity when he accused himself of not being a virgin. I believe that he referred only to evil and voluptuous thoughts which, although they had not caused bodily defilement, had contaminated his heart. Generous minds are exceedingly solicitous for purity of heart.

Do not associate with immodest persons, especially if they are also loose in speech, as is generally the case. Just as when goats touch sweet almond trees with their tongues they make them turn bitter,[5] so too such corrupt souls and infected hearts can scarcely speak to anyone of their own or the other sex, without causing them to fall in some degree from modesty. Like basilisks they have poison in their eyes and on their breath.[6] On the contrary, associate with chaste, virtuous people and often think and read about sacred things, for "the word of God is chaste"[7] and makes those who delight in it chaste, which led David to compare it to the topaz,[8] a precious stone that has the power to allay the heat of concupiscence.[9]

Always keep yourself close to Jesus Christ crucified, both spiritually by meditation and really by Holy Communion. Just as those who lie on the herb called *agnus castus* become chaste and modest,[10] so too if you rest your heart on our Lord, who is the true chaste and immaculate Lamb, you will see that your soul and your heart will soon be cleansed of all stain and lewdness.

14. THE POVERTY OF SPIRIT TO BE OBSERVED
IN THE MIDST OF RICHES

"Blessed are the poor in spirit, for theirs is the kingdom of heaven."[1] Accursed, then, are the rich in spirit, for the misery of hell is their portion. A man is rich in spirit if his mind is filled with riches or set on riches. The kingfisher shapes its nests like an apple, leaving only a little opening at the top, builds it on the seashore, and makes it so solid and tight that although waves sweep over it the water cannot get inside. Keeping always on top of the waves, they remain surrounded by the sea and are on the sea, and yet are masters of it.[2] Your heart, dear Philothea, must in like manner be open to heaven alone and impervious to riches and all other transitory things. Whatever part of them you may possess, you must keep your heart free from the slightest affection for them. Always keep it above them and while it may be surrounded by riches it remains apart from riches and master over them. Do not allow this heavenly spirit to become captive to earthly goods. Let it always remain superior to them and over them, not in them.

There is a difference between having poison and being poisoned. Pharmacists keep almost every kind of poison in stock for use on various occasions, yet they are not themselves poisoned because they merely have it in their shops and not in their bodies. So also you can possess riches without being poisoned by them if you merely keep them in your home and purse and not in your heart. To be rich in effect and poor in affection is a great happiness for a Christian. By this means he has the advantages of riches for this world and the merit of poverty for the world to come.

Unfortunately, Philothea, no one is ready ever to admit that he is avaricious. Everyone denies having so base and mean a heart. One man excuses himself on the score that he has to take care of his children, that this fact puts him under obligations to them, and that prudence requires that he be a man of property. He never has too much; he always finds need for more. The most avaricious men not only deny that they are avaricious but even think in their conscience that they are not such. Avarice is a raging fever that makes itself all the harder to detect the more violent and burning it is. Moses saw the sacred fire that burned but did not consume the bush.[3] On the contrary, avarice is a profane, unholy fire that both consumes and devours but does not burn an avaricious man. In the most violent heat of his avarice he boasts about the most agreeable coolness in the world and esteems an insatiable drought to be a natural and pleasing thirst.

You are truly avaricious if you longingly, ardently, anxiously desire to possess goods that you do not have, even though you say that you would not want to acquire them by unjust means. A man shows that he has a fever if he longingly, ardently, and anxiously desires to drink, even though he wants to drink nothing but water.

Philothea, I do not know whether the desire to have justly what someone else possesses justly is itself just. It seems that by such desire we want to serve our own advantage to the disadvantage of others. Doesn't a man who possesses something justly have greater right to keep it justly than we do to desire it justly? Why then do we extend our desires so far as to deprive him of his possessions? At most, even if this desire is just, it certainly is not charitable. We would not like to have another man desire, even justly desire, what we want to keep justly. Such was the sin of Achab, who desired to possess justly Naboth's vineyard, while Naboth much more justly desired to keep it.[4] Achab longingly, ardently, anxiously desired this and therefore offended God. It is soon enough, dear Philothea, to desire your neighbor's property when he wants to get rid of it, for then his desire will make yours not only just but charitable as well. I willingly grant that you may take care to increase your wealth and resources, provided this is done not only justly but properly and charitably.

If you are strongly attached to the goods you possess, are too solicitous about them, set your heart on them, always have them in your thoughts, and fear losing them with a strong, anxious fear, then, believe me, you are still subject to such fever. When feverish men are given water they drink it with a certain eagerness, concentration, and satisfaction that the healthy are not accustomed to have. It is impossible to take great pleasure in a thing without having extraordinary affection for it. If you find your heart very desolated and afflicted at the loss of property, believe me, Philothea, you love it too much. The strongest proof of love for a lost object is suffering over its loss.

Don't have a full and explicit desire for wealth you do not possess. Don't set your heart deeply in what you have. Don't grieve over losses you incur. Then you will have some grounds to believe that although rich in effect you are not so in affection but poor in spirit and consequently blessed because the kingdom of heaven belongs to you.[5]

15. HOW TO PRACTICE GENUINE POVERTY ALTHOUGH REALLY RICH

Parrhasius the artist painted the people of Athens in a very ingenious way and represented their various changing dispositions—irascible, unjust, unstable, polite, gentle, merciful, haughty, proud, humble, resolute, and timid—all these together.[1] Dear Philothea, I would like to instill into your heart both wealth and poverty together, that is, great care and also great contempt for temporal things.

Have greater care than worldly men do to make your property profitable and fruitful. Princes' gardeners are more careful and faithful in cultivating and beautifying the gardens in their charge than if they were their own property. Why is this? Undoubtedly it is because they see the gardens as the property of princes and kings to whom they want to make themselves acceptable by their services. Philothea, our possessions are not our own. God has given them to us to cultivate and he wants us to make them fruitful and profitable. Hence we perform an acceptable service by taking good care of them. It must be a greater and finer care than that which worldly men have for their property. They labor only out of self-love and we must labor out of love of God. Just as self-love is violent, turbulent, and impetuous, so the care that comes from it is full of trouble, uneasiness, and disquiet. As love of God is sweet, peaceable, and calm, so also the care that proceeds from such love, even if it is for worldly good, is amiable, sweet, and agreeable. Therefore let us exercise this gracious care of preserving and even of increasing our temporal goods whenever just occasions present themselves and so far as our condition in life requires, for God desires us to do so out of love for him. But be on guard so that self-love does not deceive you. Sometimes it counterfeits love of God so closely that one might say it is the same thing. In order that it may not trick you and that care of temporal possessions may not degenerate into avarice, in addition to what I said in the preceding chapter we must practice real poverty in the midst of all the goods and riches God has given us.

Frequently give up some of your property by giving it with a generous heart to the poor. To give away what we have is to impoverish ourselves in proportion as we give, and the more we give the poorer we become. It is true that God will repay us not only in the next world but even in this. Nothing makes us so prosperous in this world as to give alms, but until such time as God shall restore it to us we remain the poorer in the amount we have given. Oh, how holy and how rich is the poverty brought on by giving alms!

Love the poor and love poverty, for it is by such love that you become truly poor. As the Scripture says, we become like the things we love.[2] Love makes lovers equal.[3] "Who is weak and I am not weak?"[4] says St. Paul and he might have also said, "Who is poor and I am not poor with him?" for love made him like those he loved. If you love the poor you will share their poverty and be poor like them. If you love the poor be often with them. Be glad to see them in your own home and to visit with them in theirs. Be glad to talk to them and be pleased to have them near you in church, on the street, and elsewhere. Be poor when in conversing with them and speak to them as their companions do, but be rich in assisting them by sharing some of your more abundant goods with them.

Do you wish to gain another benefit, Philothea? Don't be satisfied merely with being poor like the poor but be poorer than the poor themselves. How may this be brought about? The servant is less than the master;[5] therefore make yourself a servant of the poor. Go and wait on them when they are sick in bed, wait on them, I say, with your own hands. Prepare their food for them yourself and at your own expense. Be their seamstress and laundress. Philothea, such service is more glorious than that of a king.

I can never sufficiently admire how zealously this counsel was observed by St. Louis, one of the greatest kings the sun has ever shone upon. He was a great king, I say, with every kind of greatness. He often served at table the poor whom he supported and had three of them dine with him almost every day. Many times he ate what was left over of their food with incomparable love. When he visited the hospitals of the sick, as he often did, he usually served those who had the most loathsome diseases, such as lepers, the ulcerous, and others like them. He performed all his services with uncovered head and kneeling on the ground, thus honoring in their persons the Savior of the world and cherishing them with as tender a love as a fond mother cherishes her child. St. Elizabeth, daughter of the king of Hungary, often visited the poor. For recreation among her ladies she sometimes clothed herself like a poor woman, saying to them, "If I were poor I would dress in this manner." O God, dear Philothea, how poor were this prince and this princess in the midst of all their riches and how rich was their poverty!

"Blessed are they who are poor in this manner, for to them belongs the kingdom of heaven." "I was hungry and you gave me to eat; I was cold and you clothed me; come, possess the kingdom prepared for you from the foundation of the world."[6] He who is King of the poor and of kings will say this at his great judgment.

There is no one who at some time or other has not felt the lack and want of some convenience. It sometimes happens that we are visited by a guest whom we would and should entertain very well but at the time lack means to do so. At other times our best clothes are in one place and we need them in another where we must appear publicly. Again, sometimes the wines in our cellar ferment and turn sour so that only bad or green wines are left. At another time we are out in the country and have to stay in some hovel where everything is lacking and we have neither bed, room, table, nor service. In fine, it is often very easy to lack something, no matter how rich we are. This is to be poor in effect with regard to the things we lack. Rejoice on such occasions, Philothea, accept them with a good heart and put up with them cheerfully.

If you meet with losses that impoverish you either very much or a little, as in the case of tempests, fires, floods, droughts, thefts, or lawsuits, that is the proper time to practice poverty by accepting your losses meekly and patiently and by courageously submitting to such impoverishment. Esau presented himself to his father with his hands covered with hair, and Jacob did the same,[7] but because the hair on Jacob's hands did not belong to his skin but only to his gloves it might be taken away without injuring the skin. On the contrary, the hair on Esau's hands adhered to his skin, which was naturally very hairy, so if anyone had tried to pluck it off it would have hurt him and he would have cried out, been angry, and defended himself. Thus when our worldly goods cleave to our hearts, what complaints, what trouble, and what impatience do we fall into if a storm, a thief, or a cheat takes any part of them away from us. When our goods do not cleave to our hearts and we think of them only because of such care as God wants us to have for them, we don't lose reason or peace of mind if they are taken from us. Hence the difference as to clothing between men and beasts. The garments of beasts, namely, their skins, adhere to their flesh, while those of men are merely put on them and can be taken off at will.

16. HOW TO PRACTICE RICHNESS OF SPIRIT
IN REAL POVERTY

If you are really poor, dearest Philothea, then out of love of God you must be poor in spirit as well. Make a virtue of necessity and put the precious jewel of poverty at its high value. Its brilliance is not seen by the world but it is surpassingly rich and beautiful. Be patient, you are in good company. Our Lord himself, our Lady, the apostles, and countless saints, both men and women, have been poor. Even though they might have been rich they scorned to be so. How many men high in the world, against great opposition and with unequalled zeal, have sought holy poverty in cloisters and hospitals! They have gone to great trouble to find her, as witness St. Alexius, St. Paula, St. Paulinus, St. Angela, and so many others. Philothea, see how holy poverty is even more gracious to you and presents herself to you at your own door. You have met her without seeking her and without trouble. Embrace her, then, as the dear friend of Jesus Christ, for he was born, lived, and died in poverty. Poverty was his nurse throughout his entire life.

Your poverty enjoys two great privileges, Philothea, and by their means you may win great merit. The first privilege is that it has come not by your choice but solely by God's will. He has made you poor without any concurrence of your own will. Whatever we receive wholly from God's will is always most agreeable to him, provided that we accept it with a sincere heart and out of love for his holy will. Where there is the least of our will, there is the most of God's. Simple, pure acceptance of God's will makes our suffering pure in the highest degree. The second privilege of such poverty is this: it is poverty that is truly poor. Poverty that is praised, caressed, esteemed, supported, and helped along is closely allied to wealth. At least it is not complete poverty. But poverty despised, rejected, reproached, and abandoned is truly poor. Such is ordinary poverty among lay people, for since they are not poor by their own choice but by necessity, their poverty is not rated highly, and because it is not rated highly their poverty is poorer than that of the religious, although otherwise religious poverty is much higher and more praiseworthy because of the vow and intention for which it is chosen.

Don't complain about your poverty, my dear Philothea. We complain only of things we don't like, and if poverty displeases you, you are not poor in spirit but rich in desire. Don't be downcast at not being as well cared for as might seem necessary, for in this consists the excellence of poverty. To want to be poor and yet not suffer any hardships is asking too much: it is to desire both the honor of poverty and the advantages of wealth.

Don't be ashamed of being poor or of asking alms in the name of charity. Humbly accept whatever is given to you and put up meekly with refusals. Recall often the journey our Lady undertook into Egypt in order to bring her beloved Son there and remember all the contempt, poverty, and misery she had to endure. If you live in this way you will be very rich in your poverty.

17. ON FRIENDSHIP, AND FIRST, ON EVIL AND
FRIVOLOUS FRIENDSHIPS

Among the passions of the soul love holds first place. It reigns as king of all movements of the hearts. It turns all other things toward itself and causes us to be like what we love.[1] Hence, Philothea, you must be on guard against having any evil love, for thus you would soon become completely evil yourself. Friendship is the most dangerous of all types of love, since other kinds may be had without intercommunication, but friendship is completely based on it and we can hardly have such communication with a person without sharing in its qualities.

All love is not friendship, first, because we can love without being loved. In such cases there is love but not friendship since friendship is mutual love, and if it is not mutual it is not friendship. Secondly, it is not sufficient for it to be merely mutual. Persons who love each other must be aware of their reciprocal affection and if they are unaware of their love it is not friendship. Thirdly, there must also be some kind of communication between them, and this is the basis of friendship.

According to different kinds of communication friendships also differ, and communications differ according to the variety of goods exchanged. If the goods are false and empty, the friendship is false and empty. If they are true goods, the friendship is true, and the better the goods are, the better is the friendship. Just as the best honey is gathered from blossoms of the most exquisite flowers, so too the love based on the most exquisite communication is the best. At Heraclea in Pontus there is a kind of honey that is poisonous and deprives those eating it of reason because it is gathered from aconite, which abounds in that country.[2] In similar fashion friendship based on the communication of false and vicious goods is itself completely false and vicious.

Exchange of carnal pleasures involves mutual inclination and animal allurement. It has no more right to the title of friendship among men than that of asses and horses for like effects. If there were no other exchange in marriage, there would be no true friendship there at all. However, in marriage there is communication of life, work, goods, affection, and indissoluble fidelity and therefore married friendship is true, holy friendship.

Friendship based on exchange of sensual pleasures is utterly gross and unworthy of the name of friendship, and so too is that based on vain and frivolous qualities since these also depend on the senses. I call those pleasures sensual which are immediately and principally attached to the external senses, such as pleasure in looking at beautiful things or hearing a sweet voice, pleasures of touch, and the like. To certain useless talents and qualities, which weak minds call accomplishments and perfections, I apply the term frivolous qualities. Listen to how most girls, women, and young men talk. They do not hesitate to say that so and so is a very accomplished gentleman and has many fine qualities.

He is a good dancer, plays all sorts of games well, dresses fashionably, sings delightfully, chats pleasantly, and makes a fine appearance. Mountebanks think that the biggest clowns are the most accomplished men in their group. All such things concern the senses and therefore friendships proceeding from them are termed sensual, vain, and frivolous and deserve to be called folly rather than friendship. Ordinarily such are the friendships of young people when based on a fine moustache or head of hair, smiling glances, fine clothes, superior attitudes, and idle talk. They are friendships proper to the age of lovers whose virtue is still only in blossom and whose judgment is only in bud. Such friendships are only passing things and melt away like snow in the sun.

18. FOND LOVES

When playful friendships like these are between persons of different sexes with no intention of marriage they are called fond loves. They are only abortive births, or rather phantoms of friendship, and deserve the name neither of friendship nor of love by reason of their complete vanity and deep imperfection. By them the hearts of men and women are caught, bound, and entangled together in empty, foolish affections, based on frivolous exchanges and low pleasures of which I will now speak. Ordinarily such foolish loves collapse and are engulfed in carnality and the most lewd and sordid conduct, although that was not the original intention of those who have them. Otherwise, their relations would not have begun as mere foolish flirtations but as manifest impurity. Sometimes many years may pass before anything directly contrary to bodily chastity occurs between those affected by such folly. They are satisfied with indulging in the pleasure of wishes, desires, sighs, love taps, and similar folly and vanity, all done under various excuses.

Some have the sole purpose of satisfying their hearts with loving and being loved, and in this way give in to their amorous inclinations.

In their choice of what they love they are concerned only with their own tastes and instincts. As soon as they meet someone who appeals to them, then without examining the person's character or conduct they begin this fond communication and get entangled in sordid nets and later have great difficulty in freeing themselves from them. Out of vanity others get involved in love affairs and esteem it no small glory to capture and bind hearts by love. Aiming at glory in the choice they make, they set their nets and lay their snares in well-known, exalted, exclusive, and illustrious places. Others are led away by their amorous inclinations and by vanity together. Although their hearts are disposed to love, they will not engage in it without gaining some glory.

Such friendships are always evil, foolish, and vain. They are evil because they lead to and finally end in carnal sin and rob God and a husband or wife of the love and consequently the heart that belong to them. They are foolish because they have neither foundation nor reason. They are vain because they yield neither profit, honor, nor contentment. On the contrary, they cause loss of time, compromise honor, and bring no pleasure but that of eagerly seeking and hoping without knowing what they want or seek. These weak, wretched minds always think that they have something to expect from the pledges of mutual love but they cannot tell what it is. Their desire for it can never end but goes on continually, oppressing their hearts with perpetual distrust, jealousy, and unquiet.

Writing to certain vain women, St. Gregory Nazianzen had some wonderful things to say on this subject. Here is a small part of it; it is addressed principally to women but it applies to men as well. "Your natural beauty is sufficient for your husband, but if it is set out for many men like a net spread out for a flock of birds, what will be the result? The man who is pleased by your beauty will be pleasing to you. You will return him glance for glance and look for look. Presently smiles and little amorous words will follow. At first dropped by stealth, they soon become more familiar and pass into open friendships. Take heed, my running tongue, of telling what will happen later! I will state this truth: nothing of all those things young men and women say and do together in this foolish intimacy is free from grievous stings. All the links of wanton love depend on one another and succeed one another, just as one piece of iron drawn by a magnet drags many others along with it."[1]

How wisely has this great bishop spoken! What do you think of doing? To give love or not to give it? No one voluntarily gives love without in turn receiving it of necessity, for in this game one who catches is likewise caught. As soon as the herb called aproxis sees fire it both receives and conceives fire.[2] Our hearts are the same. As soon as they see a soul on fire with love for them they are quickly inflamed with love for it. Someone will tell me, "I am willing to accept some of this love but not too much of it." Unfortunately, you deceive yourself, the fire of love is more active and penetrating than it appears to be. You think that you will take in only a spark but you will be amazed to see that in a moment it has seized your whole heart and reduced your resolutions to ashes and your reputation to smoke. The Wise Man cries out, "Who pities a snake charmer stung by a serpent?"[3] I cry out after him, "O foolish and senseless people, you think that you will charm love so as to manipulate it at will. You want to play with it, but it will cruelly sting and bite you. Do you know what men will say? Everyone will mock and laugh at you for trying to charm love and with a false sense of safety placing in your own bosom a dangerous serpent that ruins and destroys your soul and your honor."

O God, what blindness it is to gamble away the chief power of your soul for such trivial stakes! Yes, Philothea, God does not regard man except for his soul, nor his soul except for his will, nor his will except for his love. Alas, we do not have nearly so much love as we need. I mean, we would need an infinite amount to love God sufficiently, yet unfortunate creatures that we are, we lavish and spend it on foolish, useless, and frivolous things, as if we had some to spare. Ah, this great God has reserved for himself the whole love of our souls in acknowledgement of our creation, preservation, and redemption and he will demand a most strict account of all the mad deductions we make from it. If he makes so rigorous an examination of our idle words, what will he do with our idle, insolent, mad, and pernicious loves!

The walnut tree is very harmful to vines and fields in which it is planted, because it is so large that it draws the moisture from the earth, which is then unable to nourish other plants. Its leaves are so thick that they make a large, close shade. Lastly, it lures passersby to it and they spoil and trample on everything near it in order to knock down its nuts. Fond loves do the same sort of damage to the soul. They possess it in such a way and so powerfully draw its movements to themselves that it can no longer produce any good work. Their leaves, namely, their idle talk, amusements, and dalliance, are so numerous that all leisure time is wasted. Finally they bring on so many temptations, distractions, suspicions, and other effects that the whole heart is trampled down and ruined by them. In short, these fond loves not only banish heavenly love but also the fear of God from the soul, weaken the mind, and lower a man's reputation. In a word, they are a pastime at court but the plague itself within one's heart.[4]

19. TRUE FRIENDSHIP

Love everyone with a deep love based on charity, Philothea, but form friendships only with those who can share virtuous things with you. The higher the virtues you share and exchange with others, the more perfect your friendship will be. If this participation is in matters of knowledge, the resulting friendship is certainly very praiseworthy. It is still more so if you have virtues in common, namely, prudence, temperance, fortitude, and justice.[1] If your mutual and reciprocal exchanges concern charity, devotion, and Christian perfection, O God, how precious this friendship will be! It will be excellent because it comes from God, excellent because it leads to God, excellent because its bond will endure eternally in God.

How good it is to love here on earth as they love in heaven and to learn to cherish one another in this world as we shall do eternally in the next!

Here I do not refer to the simple love of charity we must have for all men but of that spiritual friendship by which two, three, or more souls share with one another their devotion and spiritual affections and establish a single spirit among themselves. Such fortunate souls may justly sing, "Behold how good and pleasant it is for brothers to dwell together in unity."[2] Yes, for the delicious balm of devotion is distilled from one heart into another by such unbroken participation that it may be said that God on this friendship has poured down "his blessing and life forevermore."[3] I hold that all other friendships are mere shadows in comparison with this and that their bonds are but chains of glass or jet when compared to this bond of holy devotion for it is made entirely of gold. Do not form any kind of friendship except this. I refer to friendships you must make for yourselves, for you must not give up or neglect friendships that nature or earlier duties oblige you to cultivate with parents, kindred, benefactors, neighbors, and others. I refer here only to those you yourself choose.

Many people may say, "We should not have any particular friendship or affection since it fills our hearts, distracts our minds, and causes envy." They are mistaken in their advice. They have read in the writings of many holy and devout authors that particular friendships and unusual affections cause the very greatest harm to persons in the religious life and they therefore imagine that it is the same for the rest of the world. There is a difference. In a well-ordered monastery the common purpose of all the members tends to true devotion. Hence it is not necessary to form particular associations, lest by seeking among individuals what is common to the whole community they should fall from particularities to partialities. For those who live in the world and desire to embrace true virtue it is necessary to unite together in holy, sacred friendship. By this means they encourage, assist, and lead one another to perform good deeds. Men walking on level ground do not have to lend one another a hand, while those who are on a rugged, slippery road hold on to one another in order to walk more safely. So also members of religious orders have no need for particular friendships, whereas people in the world need them to keep safe and assist one another in the many dangerous places they must pass through. Those in the world do not all have the same end, nor do they all have the same mind. Hence we must go separate ways and contract friendships according to our different purposes. Such particularity causes partiality, but it is a holy partiality and it creates no division except that which holds between good and evil, between sheep and goats, between bees and hornets. It is a distinction that must be made.

No one will deny that our Lord loved St. John, Lazarus, Martha, and Mary Magdalen with a very sweet and special friendship, for the Scriptures tell us so.⁴ We know that St. Peter tenderly cherished St. Mark and St. Petronilla, just as St. Paul did Timothy and St. Tecla. In many places St. Gregory Nazianzen boasts of his incomparable friendship with the great St. Basil and describes it in this way: "It seemed that in us there was only a single soul dwelling in two bodies. Although we do not believe those who say that all things are in all things, yet of us you can believe that we were both together in each of us and that each was in the other. We had each of us only one purpose, to cultivate virtue and to adapt all the purposes of our life to our future hopes, in this way leaving mortal earth before we died in it."⁵ St. Augustine testifies⁶ that St. Ambrose loved St. Monica solely for the rare virtue he saw in her and that she in turn loved him as an angel of God. I am wrong in detaining you so long on so obvious a subject. St. Jerome, St. Augustine, St. Bernard, and all the greatest servants of God have had very particular friendships without doing any harm to their perfection. When condemning the disorders of the pagans St. Paul accuses them of being people "without affection,"⁷ that is, they had no true friendships. Together with all good philosophers, St. Thomas states that friendship is a virtue. He speaks of "particular friendship" since, as he says, "perfect friendship cannot be extended to a great many persons."[8] Hence perfection consists not in having no friendships, but in having only those which are good, holy, and sacred.

20. THE DIFFERENCE BETWEEN TRUE AND VAIN FRIENDSHIPS

This is an important warning, Philothea. In Heraclea there is poisonous honey so like wholesome honey that there is great danger of taking it for the other, and even of mixing them together, for the good qualities of the one cannot cancel out the other's poison.[1] We must be on guard against deception in friendships, especially when they are contracted between persons of different sexes, no matter what the pretext may be. Satan often tricks those who are in love. They begin with virtuous love but if they are not very prudent, fond love will first be injected, next sensual love, and then carnal love. If one is not very much alert there is danger even in spiritual love, although there it is harder to be tricked because its purity and candor make the defilements that Satan tries to mingle with it more easily recognized. For this reason when he attempts to do so, he does it more subtly and tries to introduce impurity by almost insensible degrees.

You can distinguish worldly from holy and virtuous friendship in the same way as Heraclean honey is distinguished from the other. Heraclean honey is sweeter in taste than ordinary honey because of the aconite, which increases its sweetness. Worldly friendship generally produces a great profusion of honeyed words, little coaxing, passionate phrases, and praise of beauty, grace, and other bodily qualities. Sacred friendship uses plain, sincere language and praises nothing but virtue and God's grace, the only foundation on which such friendship rests. When swallowed, Heraclean honey makes a man's head dizzy. Similarly, false friendship brings on dizziness of mind, which in turn causes people to falter in chastity and devotion and carries them on to knowing, affected, improper looks, sensual caresses, deep sighs, little complaints about not being loved, slight but studied and enticing postures, acts of gallantry, requests for kisses, and other familiarities and indecent favors—all sure and unquestionable signs of the approaching ruin of chastity. Holy friendship has eyes that are clear and modest, caresses that are pure and sincere, sighs meant solely for heaven, familiarities that are wholly spiritual, complaints only that God is not loved—all infallible marks of purity. Heraclean honey affects the sight; worldly friendship impairs judgment to such an extent that those infected think they do well when they act wrongly and believe that their excuses, pretexts, and words are true acts of reason. They fear the light and love darkness, whereas holy friendship has clear-seeing eyes and never hides away but willingly appears before good men. In conclusion, Heraclean honey leaves a very bitter taste in the mouth. So too false friendships change and end in lewd, carnal words and demands and when refused in harmful acts, slander, trickery, sadness, confusion, and jealousy which often terminate in brutal degradation and madness. Chaste friendship is at all times and in all ways honest, courteous, and amiable. It never changes except into a purer and more perfect union of minds, a living image of the blessed friendship that exists in heaven.

St. Gregory Nazianzen says[2] that when the peacock utters his cry, struts about, and spreads his feathers, he greatly incites passion in the peahens that hear him. When we see a man strut about, deck himself out, and come to wheedle and whisper and bargain in a woman's ears with no intention of lawful marriage, beyond doubt it is to arouse her to impurity. Every virtuous woman will close her ears against this peacock's cries, the voice of the enchanter who seeks thus subtly to charm her.[3] O God, if she listens to him, what an evil omen it is of the future loss of her heart!

Young people who use postures, glances, and caresses or speak words in which they would not like to be caught by their parents, mothers, husbands, wives, or confessors, by that very fact testify that they are acting against honor and conscience. Our Lady was disturbed when she saw an angel in human form both because she was alone and because he gave her extraordinary, although heavenly, praise. O Savior of the world, if purity itself was fearful of an angel in human form, must not impurity fear a man, even though he should come in an angel's shape, especially when he lauds her with sensual human praise?

21. ADVICE AND REMEDIES AGAINST EVIL FRIENDSHIPS

What kind of remedies are we to take against this brood and swarm of fond loves, wanton acts, and impure deeds? As soon as you are aware of their first approach, turn right away. In absolute detestation of such vain things, run to your Savior's cross, take up his crown of thorns, and press it around your heart, so that the little foxes[1] cannot get near it. Guard well against making any compromise with such an enemy. Don't say, "I'll listen to him, but I won't do anything he tells me. I'll give him my ear, but I'll refuse to give him my heart." Philothea, for God's sake, be strict with yourself on such occasions. Heart and ear speak to one another. Just as it is impossible to stop a torrent coming down from a mountain peak, so also it is hard to stop love that has entered the ear from sweeping down into the heart. According to Alcmaeon, goats breathe through their ears, although Aristotle denies this,[2] and as for myself I do not know what is the case. But I well know that our heart breathes through the ear. Just as it breathes forth its thought by the tongue so it breathes in the thoughts of others through the ear. Let us keep close watch on our ears against breathing in the foul air of filthy words, for otherwise our heart will soon become infected. Do not listen to proposals of any kind under any pretext whatsoever. Only in that way is there no danger of being rude and uncivil.

Remember that you have vowed your heart to God and that since your love has been sacrificed to him it would be a sacrilege to take its least part away from him. Sacrifice it again to him by repeated resolutions and protestations, and keep yourself closed within them like a deer within its covert. Call on God, and he will help you and take you under his protection so that you will live for him alone.

If you are already caught in the nets of such fond loves, O God, how difficult it will be to extricate yourself from them! Place yourself before his Divine Majesty, acknowledge in his presence how great are your misery, weakness, and folly, and then by a supreme effort of your heart detest any such loves already entered into, repudiate the vain professions you have made, renounce all promises made to you, and by an absolutely firm act of the will determine within your heart and resolve nevermore to take part in such games and deeds of love.

If you can avoid the object of such love, I greatly recommend that you do so. Just as men bitten by serpents cannot be easily cured in the presence of others wounded by the same animal,[3] so also a person stung by love can hardly be cured of such passion as long as he is near the one wounded in like manner. Change of scene contributes greatly to allaying the heat and pain both of grief and love. The youth of whom St. Ambrose speaks in the second book of his work on penance[4] went on a long journey and returned home completely free from the fond love he had formerly entertained and changed so much that when his foolish mistress met him and said, "Don't you know me? I'm just the same as before," he answered, "Yes, but I'm no longer the same man." Absence had worked this fortunate change in him. St. Augustine testifies that to lessen the grief he suffered over a friend's death, he left Tagaste, where the friend had died, and went to Carthage.[5]

What is a man who cannot go away to do? He must absolutely cut off all particular familiarity, private conversations, amorous looks and smiles, and in general all kinds of associations and allurements that may nourish this shameful, smouldering fire. At most, if he must speak to the other party, let it be only to declare by a bold, brief, and serious protest that he has sworn an eternal divorce. I call aloud on everyone who has fallen into such wretched snares: Cut them! Break them! Rip them apart! Do not delay by unravelling these criminal friendships. You must tear and rend them apart. Do not untie their knots but break them or cut them, so that the cords and strings are made useless. Do not enter into any compromise with a love so opposed to love of God.

After I have broken the chains of such an infamous bondage, some remains of it will still be left. The marks and prints of the irons will still be stamped on my feet, that is, on my affections. They will not remain there, Philothea, if you have conceived as great a detestation of the evil as it deserves. If you do that, you will no longer be excited by any emotion but that of extreme horror for so base a love and all that goes with it. You will entertain no affection for the forsaken object but that of pure charity out of love for God. If by reason of imperfect repentance there should remain in you any evil inclination, arrange a mental solitude for your soul in accordance with what I have already taught you.[6] Return there as often as you can and by many repeated ejaculations, renounce all such inclinations and reject them with all your strength. Read devout books with more than ordinary applications; go to confession and Communion more frequently; speak humbly and sincerely to your director if you can, or at least to some faithful, prudent person concerning whatever suggestions and temptations of this kind may come to you. Do not doubt that God will deliver you from all passion, provided you continue faithfully in these exercises.

But you may say, "Won't it be ungrateful on my part to break off a friendship so ruthlessly?" Oh, how blessed is ingratitude that makes us pleasing to God! No, Philothea, before God, it will not be ingratitude but a great blessing that you will confer on your lover. When you break your own bonds asunder, you will also break his, since they are common to both of you. Although he may not now recognize his happiness, he will soon admit it and with you he will sing in thanksgiving, "O Lord, you have broken my bonds. I will sacrifice a sacrifice of praise to you, and call upon your holy name."[7]

22. FURTHER ADVICE ON THE SUBJECT OF FRIENDSHIPS

Friendship requires close communication between friends, since otherwise it can neither come into existence nor remain in existence. Because of this fact it often happens that with the exchange of friendship many other exchanges imperceptibly pass and slip from one heart to another by mutual infusion and reciprocal sharing in affection, inclinations, and impressions. This especially occurs when we have a high esteem for the one we love, since we then open our heart to his friendship in such wise that along with it inclinations and impressions, whether good or bad, quickly and completely enter into us. Certainly Heraclean bees seek nothing but honey, but with the honey they unknowingly suck in the poisonous qualities of the aconite from which they draw it. Hence, Philothea, at such times we must carefully practice what the Savior of our souls was accustomed to say, as the ancients have informed us, "Be good bankers,"[1] or money changers. That is, don't take in bad money along with the good or base gold along with the fine. "Separate the precious from the vile."[2] Yes, for there is hardly anyone who is entirely free from imperfections. Why should we indiscriminately absorb a friend's tares and imperfections together with his friendship? Certainly we must love him in spite of his faults, for friendship requires us to share the good, not evil. Hence just as those who dig gravel out of the river Tagus also pick out the gold they find and take it away while leaving the sand on the banks, so also those who share in a good friendship ought to remove the sand of its imperfections and not let it get into their souls. In fact St. Gregory Nazianzen testifies[3] that many who liked and admired St. Basil were unwittingly led to imitate him even in his outward faults, such as his habit of speaking slowly with an abstracted and pensive mind, his style of beard, and way of walking. We see husbands, wives, children, and friends who have great regard for their friends, parents, husbands, and wives but acquire in the course of association with them, either by giving in to them or by imitating them, a thousand little unfortunate ways. This should not be. Everyone has enough bad inclinations of his own without burdening himself with another's. Far from requiring this, friendship obliges us rather to aid and assist one another to free ourselves from every kind of fault. We must of course meekly put up with a friend's faults, but we must not lead him into faults, much less acquire his faults ourselves.

I speak only of imperfections. As to sins, we must neither occasion them nor tolerate them in our friends. It is either a weak or a sinful friendship that watches our friend perish without helping him, that sees him die of an abscess and does not dare to save his life by opening it with the lance of correction. Genuine, living friendship cannot continue in the midst of sin. Just as the salamander puts out a fire it lies on,[4] so sin destroys the friendship in which it lodges. If it is only a passing sin, friendship will soon put it to flight by correction. If it stops and remains there friendship immediately perishes, for it lives only on true virtue. How much less, then, should we commit sin for the sake of friendship! A friend who would lead us into sin has become our enemy. If he wishes to ruin and destroy his friend, he deserves to lose his friendship. One of the surest marks of false friendship is to see it given to a vicious person, no matter what his sins may be. If the person we love is vicious, then our friendship is undoubtedly also vicious. Since it does not look to true virtue, it is necessarily based on some frivolous virtue or sensual quality.

An arrangement made among merchants for material gain is only a mere show of true friendship, since it is not made for love of their fellow men but for love of gain.

Finally, two divine texts are two mighty columns for the firm support of a Christian life. The first is by the Wise Man: "He who fears God shall likewise have a good friendship."[5] The other is that of St. James the apostle, "The friendship of this world is the enemy of God."[6]

23. THE EXERCISE OF EXTERIOR MORTIFICATION

Men engaged in horticulture tell us that if a word is written on a sound almond seed and it is put back in its shell, bound up carefully, and planted, whatever fruit the tree bears will have that same written word stamped on it.[1] For myself, Philothea, I cannot approve the methods of those who try to reform a man by beginning with outward things, such as his bearing, dress, or hair. On the contrary, it seems to me that we ought to begin inside him. "Be converted to me with your whole heart,"[2] God said. "My son, give me your heart."[3] Since the heart is the source of our actions, as the heart is so are they. When the divine Spouse invites the soul, he says, "Put me as a seal on your heart, as a seal on your arm."[4] Yes, for whoever has Jesus Christ in his heart will soon have him in all his outward ways.

For this reason, dear Philothea, I have wished above all else to engrave and inscribe on your heart this holy and sacred motto, "Live, Jesus!" I am certain that your life, which comes from the heart just as the almond tree comes from its seed, will thereafter produce all its actions—which are its fruits—inscribed and engraved with this sacred word of salvation. As our beloved Jesus lives in your heart, so too he will live in all your conduct and he will be revealed by your eyes, mouth, hands, yes even the hair on your head. With St. Paul you can say these holy words, "It is no longer I that live, but Christ lives in me."[5] In short, whoever wins a man's heart has won the whole man. Yet even the heart, where we wish to begin, must be instructed as to how it should model its outward conduct and bearing so that by them men can see not only holy devotion but also great wisdom and prudence. For this purpose I will give you in summary fashion the following words of advice.

If you can stand fasting, you will do well to fast on certain days in addition to those prescribed by the Church. Besides the usual effects of fasting, namely, elevating our spirits, keeping the body in subjection, practicing virtue, and gaining a greater reward in heaven, it is valuable for restraining gluttony and keeping our sensual appetites and body subject to the law of the spirit. Although we may not fast very much, yet the enemy has greater fear of us when he sees that we can fast. Wednesdays, Fridays, and Saturdays are the days on which the early Christians chiefly observed abstinence, and you should therefore choose some of them to fast as far as your devotion and your director's judgment advise you.

I gladly agree with what St. Jerome said to the devout Leda. "Long, immoderate fasts displease me very much, especially by those who are still quite young. I have learned by experience that when an ass's foal grows tired, it tries to wander away,"[6] meaning that young people who are weakened by excessive fasting easily turn to soft living. Stags run poorly at two times—when too fat and heavy and when too lean. We are very much exposed to temptation both when our bodies are too pampered and when too run down, for the one makes the body demanding in its softened state and the other desperate with affliction. Just as we cannot support the body when it is too fat, so also it cannot support us when it is too thin. Lack of moderation in fasting, use of the discipline, hair shirts, and other forms of austerity makes many men's best years useless for the service of charity. This was the case even with St. Bernard and he regretted that he had been too austere with himself. The more some men mistreat the body in the beginning, the more they are led to pamper it in the end. Wouldn't they have done better to have a program that is balanced and in keeping with the duties and tasks their state in life obliges them to?

Both fasting and labor mortify and subdue the flesh. If your work is necessary for you to contribute to God's glory, I much prefer that you endure the pains of work rather than of fasting. Such is the mind of the Church, for it exempts those who are working in the service of God and our neighbor even from prescribed fasts. One man finds it difficult to fast, another to take care of the sick, visit prisoners, hear confessions, preach, comfort the afflicted, pray, and perform similar tasks. These last sufferings are of greater value than the first. Besides subduing the body, they produce much more desirable fruits. Generally speaking, therefore, it is better to maintain our bodily strength even more than necessary rather than to weaken it too much. We may always discipline the body when we wish, but we cannot always restore its strength when we like.

We should listen with great reverence to the words said to his disciples by our Savior and Redeemer: "Eat what is set before you."[7] It is, I believe, a greater virtue to eat without preference what is put before you and in the order it is put before you, whether you like it or dislike it, than always to choose the worst. Although this latter way of life seems more austere, the former demands more resignation for by it we renounce not only our taste but our choice as well. Moreover, it is no little mortification to adapt our taste to all kinds of food and keep it under control at all times. Again, mortification of this kind doesn't show in public, bothers no one, and is well adapted to social life. To set one kind of food aside in order to eat another kind, examine and criticize everything, find nothing properly prepared or good enough, and make a to do over every mouthful, all this reveals a soft character attached to dishes and dainties. I respect St. Bernard for drinking oil instead of water or wine more than if he had deliberately drunk wormwood. It is a proof that he did not think of what he drank. In such indifference as to what we must eat and drink is found the perfect practice of that sacred text, "Eat what is set before you." However, I except such foods as may injure one's health or badly affect one's spirits, as do certain hot, highly seasoned, smoked, windy foods, and certain occasions when nature needs restoration and help in order to carry out some work for God's glory. Steady, moderate sobriety is preferable to periods of violent abstinence, interspersed with periods of great self-indulgence.

Moderate use of the discipline has wonderful power to awaken the spirit of devotion. The hair shirt mortifies the flesh greatly, but in general its use is not proper either for married people or those with delicate constitutions or those who have to endure great suffering. However, on some special penitential days it may be used with the advice of a prudent confessor.

We must use the night for sleep, each one according to his disposition so as to get what is needed to spend the day usefully. Many Scriptural passages, the example of the saints, and natural reason all strongly recommend to us the morning as the best and most profitable part of the day. Our Lord himself is named "the rising sun,"[8] and our Lady is called "the dawning of the day."[9] Hence I think that it is prudent for us to go to rest early in the evening so we can awaken and get up early in the morning. Certainly it is the brightest, most pleasant and least troubled part of the day. The very birds invite us to awake and praise God so that early rising is helpful to both health and holiness.

Balaam was mounted on a she ass and going to visit King Balak, but because he did not have a right intention an angel waited for him on the road sword in hand to kill him. When the ass saw the angel, she stood still at three different times as if disturbed at something. Balaam beat her cruelly with his staff in order to make her move forward and on the third occasion she lay down beneath Balaam, miraculously spoke to him, and said, "What have I done to you? Why are you beating me for the third time?" Soon after Balaam's eyes were opened and he saw the angel, who said to him, "Why have you beaten your ass? If she had not turned away from me I would have slain you." Then Balaam said to the angel, "Lord, I have sinned, not knowing that you stood against me in the way."[10] You see, Philothea, although Balaam is the cause of the evil yet he strikes and beats a poor beast that could not prevent it.

It is often the same with us. A woman sees her husband or child lying ill and suddenly takes up fasting, a hair shirt, and discipline as David did on a similar occasion.[11] Unfortunately, my friend, you too beat the poor beast, you punish the body, but it cannot remedy the evil, nor is it the reason God's sword is drawn against you. Correct your heart, which idolizes your husband, tolerates many faults in the child, and prepares it for pride, vanity, and ambition. Again, a man sees that he often falls deep into the sin of impurity. Inward remorse assails his conscience like a sharp sword to pierce him with a holy fear and when his heart has got control of itself, he says, "Ah, wicked flesh, ah, treacherous body, you have betrayed me!" Immediately by immoderate fasting, excessive use of the discipline, and unbearable hair shirts, he inflicts great blows on his body. O poor soul, if your flesh could speak like Balaam's ass, it would say to you, "Wretched man, why do you strike me? It is against you, my soul, that God arms his vengeance. It is you who are the criminal. Why do you use my eyes, my hands, and my lips in wantonness? Why do you trouble me with impure imaginations? Cherish good thoughts and I shall have no evil movements. Shun immodest company and I will not be aroused to lust. It is you, alas! who hurl me into the flames and then do not want me to burn. You cast smoke into my eyes, but you do not want them to be inflamed." Beyond doubt in such cases God says to you: "Beat, break, rend, and crush your heart to pieces, for it is chiefly against it that my anger is aroused."[12] To cure the itch there is need not so much to wash and bathe as to cleanse the blood and purge the liver. So also, to be cured of our vices it is good indeed to mortify the flesh but it is still more necessary to cleanse our affections and purge our hearts.

But above all else and in every place, we must never undertake bodily austerities without the advice of our spiritual director.

24. SOCIETY AND SOLITUDE

Seeking familiar conversations with others and avoiding them are two extremes and both are blameworthy in devout people living in the world, whom we are now discussing. To avoid such conversations shows disdain and contempt of our neighbor; to seek them is a mark of sloth and idleness. We must love our neighbor as ourselves,[1] and to show that we love him we must not shun his company, and to show that we love ourselves we must dwell within ourselves. "Think first of yourself, and then of others,"[2] St. Bernard says. If you are not obliged to go out into society or entertain company at home, remain within yourself and entertain yourself within your own heart. If people visit you or if you are called out into society for some just reason, go as one sent by God and visit your neighbor with a benevolent heart and a good intention.

Associations are termed evil when made with an evil intention or when the company is vicious, imprudent, and dissolute. For these reasons we must avoid them in the way bees shun wasps and hornets. When anyone is bitten by a mad dog, his perspiration, breath, and even spittle become infectious, especially for children and those who have a delicate constitution. So also vicious, dissolute persons cannot be visited without the utmost risk and danger, especially by those whose devotion is as still tender and delicate.

There are some needless visits made merely for purposes of recreation and diversion from our serious occupations. We must not be too addicted to such visits, although they may be permitted during the leisure time assigned to recreation.

Other social gatherings have good manners as their object, as in the exchange of visits and certain gatherings made to pay respect to our neighbor. With respect to these, we must not be too meticulous in practice of them nor must we be impolite in condemning them. We must modestly do our duty in their regard so that we may equally avoid ill-breeding and frivolity.

It remains for us to speak of useful associations like those of devout and virtuous persons. To meet frequently with such persons will be of the very greatest benefit to you, Philothea. Just as vines planted among olive trees produce oily grapes with the taste of olives, so also a soul often in the company of virtuous people cannot help sharing in their good qualities. Drones cannot make honey without the help of bees, and in like manner it is a great help to us in the practice of virtue to associate with devout souls.

In all our associations with others sincerity, simplicity, meekness, and modesty are always to be preferred. Some people never make a gesture or movement without so much affectation that everybody is annoyed by it. Just as a man unable to walk without counting his steps or speak without singing would be annoying to others, so those who affect an artificial manner and do nothing in a natural way are very disagreeable in society. There is always a sort of presumption in such people. Ordinarily moderate cheerfulness should predominate in our associations with others. St. Romuald and St. Anthony have been highly praised because in spite of all their austerity they always had their countenance and speech adorned with joy, gaiety, and courtesy. "Rejoice with them that rejoice,"[3] and with the apostle I tell you, "Again I say, rejoice always, but in the Lord. Let your modesty be known to all men."[4] To rejoice in the Lord, the reason for your joy must be not only lawful but also suitable. I say this because there are some things that are lawful but not fitting. That your moderation may be known to all, keep free from insolence, which certainly is always reprehensible. To cause one of the party to fall down, soil another's face, tease a third, or harm a feeble-minded person in some way, all these are foolish, insolent jokes and amusements.

Besides that mental solitude to which you may retreat even in the midst of the highest society, as I have already observed, you must also love real, physical solitude. You should not go out into the desert like St. Mary of Egypt, St. Paul, St. Anthony, Arsenius, and the other ancient solitaries did. You should remain for some time alone with yourself in your room or garden or some other place. There you will have leisure to withdraw your spirit into your heart and refresh your soul with pious meditations, holy thoughts, or a little spiritual reading after the example of the great bishop of Nazianzus. Speaking of himself he says: "I walked alone by myself about sunset and passed the time on the seashore, for it is my custom to use such recreation to refresh myself and shake off a little of my ordinary troubles."[5] Later he relates the pious reflections that he made, which I have already mentioned. There is also the example of St. Ambrose. St. Augustine says that often when he

went to St. Ambrose's home—he never denied entrance to anyone—
he found him reading. After remaining there for awhile St. Augustine
left without speaking a word for fear of interrupting him, since he
thought that he should not deprive this great shepherd of the little time
left to relax his mind after the rush of all his various duties.[6] Also, when
the apostles one day told our Lord about how they preached and how
much they had done, he said to them, "Come apart into a desert place
and rest a while."[7]

25. PROPRIETY IN DRESS

St. Paul desires that devout women—and the same may be said of
men—should be attired "in decent apparel, adorning themselves with
modesty and sobriety."[1] Decency in apparel and other ornaments depends on their matter, form, and cleanliness. As to cleanliness, it should
almost always be present in all our clothing, on which we should not
permit any kind of stain or soil to remain. To a certain extent outward
neatness represents inward cleanliness. God himself requires bodily
cleanliness in those who come near the altar and have the principal
charge of devotions.[2]

As to the material and style of our clothing, decency should be considered in reference to the various circumstances of time, age, rank,
company, and occasion. Ordinarily, people are better dressed on holi-
days and this is in proportion to the solemnity of the feast that is celebrated. In penitential seasons, like Lent, ornaments are laid aside. At
marriages people put on wedding garments and at funerals they wear
mourning. When in the company of princes they set themselves out in
state attire, which they take off when alone with others in their homes.
A married woman may and should adorn herself when she is with her
husband if he so wishes. However if she should do this when they are
separated by some distance the neighbors will ask whose eyes she wants

to favor in this way. More freedom in the way of ornament is allowed to young women, since they can lawfully desire to appear pleasing to others although there must be no intention except that of holy marriage. Nor are widows who propose to marry again to be criticized for adorning themselves, provided they do not display a frivolous spirit. Having already been mothers of families and having passed through the grief of widowhood, they should be looked on as having a more mature and settled mind. As for those who are widows indeed, not only in body but in heart as well, no ornament becomes them but humility, modesty, and devotion. If they are inclined to seek a man's love, they are not widows indeed. If they have no such desire, why do they carry about them the instruments of love? Old people are always ridiculous when they try to make themselves pretty. Such folly can be put up with only in youth.

Be neat, Philothea, don't allow anything negligent and careless to be about you. It is a sort of contempt of those you associate with to frequent their company in unbecoming attire. At the same time avoid all affectation and vanity, all extremes and frivolity. As far as possible keep always to the side of simplicity and modesty, for this is undoubtedly beauty's greatest ornament and the best excuse for its lack. St. Peter warns young women in particular not to wear their hair frizzed and curled in ringlets and braids.[3] Men so weak as to amuse themselves with such trifles are rightly laughed at for their effeminacy. Even women who are very vain in this regard are thought to be weak in chastity. At least, if they are chaste, it is not to be discovered among so many toys and fripperies. They say they mean no evil by such things and I reply here, as I do elsewhere,[4] that the devil thinks very differently. For my part, I would have devout people, whether men or women, always the best dressed in a group but the least pompous and affected. As the proverb says, I would have them adorned with grace, decency, and dignity. St. Louis says in a few words that "each one should dress according to his condition, so that the wise and the good may have no reason to complain that you do too much or young people say that you do too little."[5] In case young people are not content with what is proper, we must conform to the judgment of the prudent.

26. CONCERNING SPEECH, AND FIRST, HOW WE MUST SPEAK OF GOD

Physicians learn about a man's health or sickness by looking at his tongue and our words are a true indication of the state of our souls. "By your words you will be justified and by your words you will be condemned,"[1] says the Savior. We quickly move our hand to the pain we feel and our tongue to what we like. If you are truly in love with God, Philothea, you will often speak of God in familiar conversation with your servants, friends, and neighbors. "The mouth of the just man shall meditate on wisdom and his tongue shall speak of judgment."[2] Just as bees extract with their tiny mouths nothing but honey, so your tongue should always be sweetened with its God and find no greater pleasure than to taste the praise and benediction of his holy name flowing between your lips. It is said of St. Francis that he used to apply his tongue to his lips after pronouncing the Lord's holy name, he would moisten and lick his lips as if to draw from them the greatest sweetness in the world.[3]

Always speak of God as of God, that is, reverently and devoutly, not with outward show or affectation but in a spirit of meekness, charity, and humility. As is said of the Spouse in the Canticle of Canticles,[4] distill as much as you can of the delicious honey of devotion and divine things drop by drop, now into one person's ears and now into another's. Pray to God in the secret places of your soul that it may please him to send this holy dew deep into the heart of those who hear you. Above all, this angelic office must be done meekly and gently, not by way of correction but of inspiration. It is wonderful how powerfully a gentle, loving explanation of some good practice attracts men's hearts.

Never speak of God or devotion in a routine or thoughtless manner, but always with attention and reverence. I say this so that you may avoid the strange vanity found in many who make a profession of devotion and on every occasion speak of words of piety and godliness in a mechanical way without thinking of what they say. After they have spoken in this way, they think they are such as their words attest but they are not.

27. MODESTY IN SPEECH AND THE RESPECT DUE TO OTHERS

"If a man does not offend in word, he is a perfect man,"[1] says St. James. Be careful never to let an indecent word leave your lips, for even if you do not speak with an evil intention those who hear it may take it in a different way. An evil word falling into a weak heart grows and spreads like a drop of oil on a piece of linen cloth. Sometimes it seizes the heart in such a way as to fill it with a thousand unclean thoughts and temptations. Just as bodily poison enters through the mouth, so what poisons the heart gets in through the ear and the tongue that utters it is a murderer. Perhaps the poison the mouth casts forth does not always produce its effect because it finds its hearers' hearts guarded by some protective remedy. Still it was not for want of malice that it did not bring about their death. No man can tell me that he speaks without thinking. Our Lord, the searcher of hearts, has said, "Out of fullness of the heart the mouth speaks."[2] If we intend no evil on such occasions, the enemy still thinks very much about it and constantly and secretly uses immodest words to pierce into somebody's heart. It is said that those who eat the herb called angelica always have a sweet and pleasant breath. In like manner those who have modesty and chastity, the angelic virtue, within their hearts, always speak chaste and modest words. As for indecent and obscene things, the apostle will not let them be so much as named among us,[3] and he assures us that "nothing so much corrupts good manners as evil communications."[4]

When immodest words are subtly and hypocritically concealed

they become much more poisonous. The more pointed a dart is, the more easily it enters the body, and in like manner the sharper an obscene word is, the deeper it penetrates into the heart. Those who pride themselves on being sophisticated do not know the purpose of conversation when they speak such words. They should be like a swarm of bees gathered together to collect honey from some sweet virtuous object of interest and not like a lot of wasps gathered together to feed on corruption. If some insolent person speaks to you in a lascivious way, prove to him that your ears are offended either by immediately turning away or by some other sign that prudence will suggest to you.

To scoff at others is one of the worst states a mind can be in. God detests this vice and in past times inflicted strange punishments on it. Nothing is so opposed to charity, and much more to devotion, than to despise and condemn one's neighbor. Derision and mockery are always accompanied by scoffing, and it is therefore a very great sin. Theologians consider it one of the worst offenses against one's neighbor that a man can be guilty of.[5] Other offenses may be committed with some esteem for the person offended, but by this he is treated with scorn and contempt.

As for certain good-humored, joking words, spoken by way of modest and innocent merriment, they belong to the virtue called eutrapelia by the Greeks, which we can call pleasant conversation. By their means we take friendly, virtuous enjoyment in the amusing situations human imperfections provide us. However, we must be careful not to pass from honest mirth to scoffing. Scoffing arouses laughter by way of scorn and contempt of our neighbor. Mirth and banter cause laughter by unaffected freedom, confidence, and familiarity cleverly expressed. When a religious wanted to speak to St. Louis after dinner about certain lofty subjects the king told those present: "This is not the time to quote texts, but to regale ourselves with jokes and puns. Everybody can say whatever innocent things come into his head."[6] He said this to set at ease the noblemen present to receive marks of kindness from his Majesty. Let us remember, Philothea, to pass our recreation time in such a way that we may gain a holy eternity by devotion.

28. RASH JUDGMENT

"Judge not, and you shall not be judged," says the Savior of our souls. "Condemn not, and you shall not be condemned."[1] "No," says the Apostle, "Judge not before the time: until the Lord comes, who will both bring to light the hidden things of darkness and will make manifest the counsel of hearts."[2] How offensive to God are rash judgments! The judgments of the children of men are rash because they are not the judges of one another, and when they pass judgment on others they usurp the office of our Lord. They are rash because the principal malice of sin depends on the intention and counsel of the heart, and to us they are "the hidden things of darkness." They are rash because every man has enough on which he ought to judge himself without taking it upon him to judge his neighbor. To avoid future judgment it is equally necessary both to refrain from judging others and to judge ourselves. Just as our Lord forbids the one, so also the apostle enjoins the other for he says: "If we would judge ourselves, we should not be judged."[3] But, O God, how differently do we act! By judging our neighbor on every occasion we never stop doing what is forbidden and we never do what is imposed on us, namely, judge ourselves.

Remedies against rash judgments must be based on their different causes. Some dispositions are naturally sour, so sour, bitter, and harsh as to make equally bitter and harsh everything they receive. They convert "judgment into wormwood,"[4] as the prophet says, by never judging their neighbors except with the strictest rigor and severity. Such people have great need to place themselves under the care of a good spiritual physician. Since their bitterness of heart is natural to them it is difficult to overcome. Although it is in itself not a sin but only an imperfection, it is dangerous because it introduces and causes rash judgment and detraction to dominate in their souls. Some men judge harshly not through rashness but because of pride. They think that in the same proportion as they lower other men's honor they raise their own. Arrogant, presumptuous minds who admire and rate themselves very high in their own esteem look down on others as base and low. "I am not like the rest of men,"[5] said the foolish Pharisee.

Some men do not have such obvious pride, but when they see the defects of others they feel a certain little satisfaction so as to preen themselves more and bring others to admire the contrary good qualities they think they possess. Such self-satisfaction is so secret and imperceptible that a man must have sharp eyes to discover it, and even those affected by it do not recognize it when it is shown to them. To flatter and excuse themselves and soften their own remorse of conscience, others are quite willing to judge their fellow men to be guilty of the very vices they are addicted to or of vices equally great. They think that many offenders will make their own sin less guilty. Many men make a habit of rash judgment merely because they like to play the philosopher and probe into men's moods and morals as a way of showing their own keen intelligence. Unfortunately, if they sometimes happen to be right in their judgments, their rashness and desire to go further increase so much that they have difficulty turning away from them. Others judge out of passion. They always think well of things they love and ill of those they dislike. There is a single exception to this, wonderful but real, where excess of love arouses them to pass harsh judgments on what they love. This is a monstrous effect that always comes from a love that is impure, imperfect, disturbed, and diseased. It is jealousy. As everyone knows, because of a mere look or the least smile in the world, it condemns a person loved as guilty of infidelity and adultery. To conclude, fear, ambition, and similar mental weaknesses often contribute to the birth of suspicion and rash judgment.

What is the cure for this? Men who drink the juice of an Egyptian herb called ophiusa imagine that they see serpents and other frightful objects on every side.[6] Men who have drunk in pride, envy, ambition, and hatred think that everything they see is evil and reprehensible. To be cured the first class must drink palm wine, and to the second I say: Drink as deeply as you can of the sacred wine of charity. It will set you free from the perverse moods that cause you to make such tortured judgments. Charity is fearful of meeting evil, so she never looks for it. Whenever she encounters it, she turns away her face and does not look at it. At the first threat of evil, she closes her eyes, and later believes with a holy simplicity that it was not really evil but a shadow or mere appearance of evil. If sometimes she cannot help admitting that it is a real evil, she quickly turns away and tries to forget even its form. Charity is the supreme remedy for every evil, and especially for this kind. "All things look yellow to the jaundic'd eye,"[7] and it is said that to cure their disease the jaundiced must wear leaves of celandine under the soles of their feet.[8] The sin of rash judgment is truly spiritual jaundice and causes all things to appear evil to the eyes of those infected with it. Whoever wants to be cured must apply remedies not to his eyes or intellect but to his affections, which are feet in relation to his soul. If your reflections are kind, your judgments will also be kind. If your affections are charitable, your judgments will be the same.

Here I offer you three wonderful examples of this. Isaac had stated that Rebecca was his sister, and when Abimelech saw him playing with her, that is, tenderly caressing her, he immediately concluded that she was his wife.[9] A malicious eye would have concluded that she was a harlot or, if actually his sister, that Isaac had committed incest. Abimelech chose the most charitable opinion he could about such an action. We must always do the same, Philothea, and as far as possible pass favorable judgments on our neighbors. If an action has many different aspects, we must always think of which is the best. Our Lady was with child and St. Joseph clearly saw this fact. On the other hand, he saw that she was all holy, all pure, all angelic, and he could never believe that she had conceived in an unlawful manner. Hence he resolved to leave her and leave judgment on her case to God. Although there was strong argument leading him to form an ill opinion of the Virgin, he would never pass judgment on her. Why? Because, says the Spirit of God, "he was a just man."[10] When a just man can no longer explain either the fact or the intention of someone whom he otherwise knows to be virtuous, he still will not pass judgment on him but puts it out of his mind and leaves the judgment to God. Thus the crucified Savior could not entirely excuse the sin of those who crucified him, but he extenuated its malice by pleading their ignorance.[11] When we cannot excuse a sin, let us at least make it worthy of compassion by attributing the most favorable cause we can to it, such as ignorance or weakness.

Can we never pass judgment on our neighbor? No, never. In courts of justice, Philothea, it is God who judges the criminals. It is true that he uses the voices of magistrates so as to make himself intelligible to our ears. They are his officers and interpreters and they must make no pronouncement except such as they have learned from him, since they are his spokesmen. If they act otherwise and follow their own passions, then it is truly they who judge and who consequently will be judged. In their character as men it is forbidden for men to judge other men.

To see or know something is not to pass judgment on it. Judgment, at least according to the words of Scripture, presupposes some difficulty, great or small, real or only apparent, that must be settled. Hence Scripture says that "they who do not believe are already judged,"[12] because there is no doubt as to their damnation. Is it not a sin then to doubt our neighbor? No, for we are forbidden not to doubt but to judge. However, it is permissible to doubt or suspect in the strict sense and as far as proof and arguments compel us to do so. Otherwise our doubts and suspicions are rash. Suppose some one had cast a malicious eye on Jacob as he kissed Rachel[13] at the well or on Rebecca as she accepted bracelets and earrings from Eliezer, a man unknown in her country.[14] Such a one would undoubtedly have had a bad opinion of those two patterns of chastity but without reason or foundation. When an action is in itself indifferent, it is rash suspicion to draw evil conclusions from it unless many circumstances give weight to the argument. Again, it is rash judgment to draw a conclusion from an action in order to condemn the person. I will explain this later on.

To conclude, those who look carefully into their consciences are not very likely to pass rash judgments. Just as bees in misty or cloudy weather stay in their hives to prepare honey, so also the thoughts of good men do not go out in search of things concealed among the cloudy actions of our neighbors. To avoid meeting them they retire into their own hearts and make good resolutions for their own amendment. It is the part of an unprofitable soul to amuse itself with examining the lives of other people.

I except those who are placed in charge of others, whether within a family or in the state. For them a great part of their duties consists in inspecting a watching over the conduct of others. Let them discharge their duty with love. This done, they must then look to themselves in regard to their own conduct.

29. SLANDER

Rash judgment begets uneasiness, contempt of neighbor, pride, self-satisfaction, and many other extremely bad effects. Slander, the true plague of society, holds first place among them. I wish that I had a burning coal taken from the holy altar to purify men's lips so that their iniquities might be removed and their sins washed away, as did the seraphim who purified Isaiah's mouth.[1] The man who could free the world of slander would free it of a large share of its sins and iniquity.

Whoever robs his neighbor of his good name in addition to committing sin has the obligation of making reparation, although this must be done in different ways according to the different types of slander. No man can enter heaven in possession of another man's property, and of all external goods a good name is the best. Slander is a form of murder. We have three kinds of life: spiritual, which consists in God's grace, corporeal, which depends on the body and soul, and social, which consists in our good name. Sin deprives us of the first kind of life, death takes away the second, and slander the third. By a single stroke of his tongue the slanderer usually commits three murders. He kills his own soul and the soul of anyone who hears him by an act of spiritual homicide and takes away the social life of the man he slanders. As St. Bernard says,[2] the one who slanders and the one who listens to a slanderer have the devil in their company—one man has Satan on his tongue and the other in his ear. Speaking of slanderers David says, "They have made their tongues sharp as those of serpents."[3] The serpent's tongue is forked and two-pointed, as Aristotle says,[4] and such too is the slanderer's tongue. At one stroke he stings and poisons the listener's ear and the reputation of the man he is speaking against.

I earnestly exhort you, dearest Philothea, never to slander anyone either directly or indirectly. Beware of falsely imputing crimes and sins to your neighbor, revealing his secret sins, exaggerating those that are manifest, putting an evil interpretation on his good works, denying the good that you know belongs to someone, maliciously concealing it or lessening it by words. You would offend God in all these ways but most of all by false accusations and denying the truth to your neighbor's harm. It is a double sin to lie and harm your neighbor at the same time.

Men who preface slander with protestations of honorable intentions or make little compliments and private jokes are the most subtle and venomous slanderers of all. "I must say that I like him," they protest. "In every other way he is a very fine man. However, the truth must be told. He was wrong to do so treacherous an act." "She was a very good girl, but she was caught off her guard," and similar little tricks. You see what they are up to. The archer draws back the arrow as near himself as he can so that he can shoot his dart with greater force. Such men seemingly draw the slander towards themselves, but it is merely to shoot it out more forcibly so that it can pierce deeper into their hearers' hearts.

Slander spoken in a joking way is even crueler than all the rest. Taken alone, hemlock is not a quick but a rather slow poison and can easily be cured, but when taken with wine there is no antidote for it.[5] So also slander that might by itself pass lightly in one ear and out the other, as we say, sticks in the hearers' minds when expressed in some subtle, funny story. "The venom of asps is under their lips,"[6] as David says. The bite of an asp is hardly felt and at first the poison produces merely a pleasant itching sensation but by this means the heart and bowels are expanded and absorb a poison for which there is later no remedy.

Do not say that so and so is a drunkard even though you have seen him intoxicated, or that so and so is an adulterer even if you saw him in his sin, or that he is incestuous because he has been guilty of a certain depraved deed. A single act is not enough to justify the name of vice. The sun stood still once for the sake of Joshua's victory[7] and at another time it was darkened for our Savior's victory,[8] yet no one will say that the sun is stationary or dark. Noah got drunk once[9] and Lot twice and Lot also committed the great sin of incest,[10] yet neither one was a drunkard and Lot was not an incestuous man. Because St. Peter once shed blood[11] does not mean that he was bloodthirsty, nor was he blasphemous because he once blasphemed.[12] To deserve the name of a vice or a virtue, there must be some advance in an act and it must be habitual. Hence it is untrue to say that so and so is bad-tempered or a thief simply because we once saw him in a fit of anger or guilty of theft.

Even if a man may have been addicted to a vice for a long time, we are in danger of falsehood if we call him a vicious man. Simon the leper called Mary Magdalen a sinner,[13] because she had been one not long before, but he spoke untruly since she was no longer a sinner but a most sincere penitent. Hence our Savior took her under his protection. The foolish Pharisee took the publican for a great sinner, perhaps even an unjust man, an adulterer, and an extortioner.[14] He was much deceived for at that very hour the publican was justified. Since God's goodness is so immense that a single moment suffices for us to ask for and receive his grace, what certainty can we have that a man who yesterday was a sinner is such today? A day that is past must not judge the present day and the present day must not judge the day that is past. It is only the Last Day that judges all days. Hence we can never say that a man is wicked without exposing ourselves to the danger of telling a lie. If we must say something it is only that he did such and such a bad deed, that he lived a bad life at such a time, or that he does ill at present. We must never draw conclusions from yesterday to today, nor from today to yesterday, and still less to tomorrow.

While we must be extremely cautious of slandering our neighbor, we must avoid another extreme into which some men fall. To avoid slander, they praise and speak well of vice. If a person is actually a slanderer, don't say in excuse of him that he speaks frankly and freely. If a person is obviously vain, don't say that he is genteel and well-mannered. Never call dangerous familiarity mere natural, simple association. Don't adorn disobedience with the name of zeal, insolence with the name of frankness, or lewd familiarity with the name of friendship. No, dear Philothea, to avoid the vice of slander we must not favor, flatter, or cherish vice. We must freely and frankly speak evil of evil and condemn things that need condemnation. By doing so we glorify God, provided we observe the following conditions.

To speak rightly against another's vices it must be for the profit of either the person spoken about or the persons spoken to. Someone talks in the presence of young girls of the imprudent and manifestly dangerous familiarities of such and such persons or about dissolute conduct of such and such a man or woman either with words or gestures that are clearly lascivious. If I do not boldly condemn such evil or even wish to excuse it, the tender minds that hear all this will take occasion to yield to similar things. For their good I must boldly rebuke such liberties on the spot, unless I can postpone this duty to a later date when it can be done better and with less disadvantage to the persons spoken of. Besides, when I am one of the principal members of a group it is my duty to speak about the matter, for if I do not speak out I will seem to approve of

the vice. But if I am one of the least important present, I must not presume to pass censure. Above all, I must be very cautious in my remarks
and not say a single word too much. For example, if I criticize the familiarity of a certain young man and young girl because it is very indiscreet
and dangerous, it is most important, Philothea, that I hold the balance so
even as not to make the matter a single bit heavier. If there is only slight
evidence of imprudence, I will say nothing about it. If it is merely a case
of imprudence, I will not give it a worse name. If there is neither imprudence nor any real appearance of evil but only the probability that some
malicious mind may take the situation as an excuse to speak slander, I
will say nothing at all or only mention this latter fact. Whenever I speak
of my neighbor, the tongue in my mouth is like a scalpel in the hand of a
surgeon who wishes to cut between the nerves and the tendons. The
stroke I give must be neither more nor less than the truth. To conclude,
we must be especially careful when condemning a vice to spare as far as
possible the person in whom it is found.

It is true that we can speak openly of infamous, public, notorious
sinners, provided it is in a spirit of charity and compassion and not
arrogantly and presumptuously. Nor should we take any pleasure from
the evils of others, for this last is always the act of a mean, debased
heart.[15] However, I exclude the declared enemies of God and his
Church. It is our duty to denounce as strongly as we can heretical and
schismatic sects and their leaders. It is an act of charity to cry out
against the wolf when he is among the sheep,[16] wherever he is.

Everyone takes the liberty to judge and criticize princes and to
speak ill of whole nations according to the different attitudes they have
towards them.[17] Avoid this fault, Philothea, for besides the offense
against God, it can get you into a thousand quarrels.

When you hear anyone spoken ill of, make the accusation doubtful
if you can do so justly. If you cannot, excuse the intention of the
accused party. If that cannot be done, express sympathy for him,
change the subject of conversation, remembering yourself and causing

the rest to recall that those who do not fall into sin owe it all to God's grace. Recall the slanderer to himself in a mild way and tell of some good deed of the offended party if you know of any.

30. ADDITIONAL ADVICE WITH REGARD TO CONVERSATION

Your language should be restrained, frank, sincere, candid, unaffected, and honest. Be on guard against equivocation, ambiguity, or dissimulation. While it is not always advisable to say all that is true, it is never permissible to speak against the truth. Therefore, you must become accustomed never to tell a deliberate lie whether to excuse yourself or for some other purposes, remembering always that God is the "God of truth."[1] If you happen to tell a lie inadvertently, correct it immediately by an explanation or making amends. An honest explanation always has more grace and force to excuse us than a lie has.

Although we may sometimes discreetly and prudently hide and disguise the truth by an equivocal statement, this must never be done except when the matter is important and God's glory and service clearly require it. In any other case such tricks are dangerous. As the sacred word tells us,[2] the Holy Spirit does not dwell in a deceitful and tricky soul. No artifice is so good and desirable as plain dealing. Worldly prudence and carnal artifice belong to the children of this world, but the children of God walk a straight path and their heart is without guile. "He that walks sincerely walks confidently,"[3] says the Wise Man. Lying, double-dealing, and dissimulation are always signs of a weak, mean mind.

In the fourth book of his *Confessions*[4] St. Augustine says that his soul and that of his friend were but a single soul and after his friend's death he had a horror of this life because he did not want to live by halves. Yet for that same reason he was unwilling to die lest his friend should die wholly. Afterwards these words seemed so artificial and affected that he retracted them and called them absurd in his *Retractions*.[5] Dear Philothea, see how tender this holy, beautiful soul is with respect to the least artifice in words. Fidelity, simplicity, and sincerity of speech are certainly a great ornament of a Christian life. David says: "I will take heed to my ways so that I do not sin with my tongue. Set a watch, O Lord, beside my mouth and a door about my lips."[6]

It was St. Louis' advice that to avoid quarrels and disputes we should not contradict anyone unless it were either sinful or very harmful to agree with him.[7] If we must contradict someone or oppose another's opinion to his, we must do so very mildly and carefully so as not to arouse his anger. Nothing is ever gained by harshness. To speak little—a practice highly recommended by ancient sages—does not consist in uttering only a few words but in uttering none that are useless. With regard to speech, we must not look to the quantity but rather to the quality of our words. It seems to me that we ought to avoid extremes. To be too reserved and to refuse to take part in conversation looks like lack of confidence in the others or some sort of disdain. To be always babbling or joking without giving others time or chance to speak when they wish is a mark of shallowness and levity.

St. Louis did not like to engage in private or confidential conversation when in a group of people, particularly when at table, lest it give others occasion to suspect that some evil was spoken about them. He said: "A man sitting at table and in good company who has something humorous and amusing to say should speak so that the whole company can hear him. If it is an important matter, he should keep it for a more suitable occasion."[8]

31. PASTIMES AND RECREATIONS, AND FIRST, THOSE THAT ARE LAWFUL AND PRAISEWORTHY

It is sometimes necessary for us to relax both mind and body by some kind of recreation. As Cassian relates, when a hunter one day found St.

John the Evangelist holding a partridge in his hand and stroking it by way of amusement, he asked how a man like him could spend time on so common and trivial a thing. St. John replied to him, "Why don't you always carry your bow taut?" "If it were always bent I'm afraid it would lose its spring and be useless when I needed it," the hunter answered. To this the apostle replied, "Don't be surprised then if I sometimes relax my close application and attention of mind a bit and enjoy a little recreation so that I may afterwards apply myself fervently to contemplation."[1] It is undoubtedly a defect to be so strict, ill-bred, uncouth, and austere as neither to take any recreation ourselves nor to allow it to others.

To get out into the open air, be entertained by happy, friendly conversation, play the lute or some other musical instrument, sing to a musical accompaniment, and go hunting are all such innocent forms of recreation that to use them properly all that is needed is the common prudence that gives due order, time, place, and measure to all things.

Games in which gain serves as recompense for skill and bodily or mental activity, such as tennis, pall-mall, charging the ring, chess, and backgammon, are by nature good and licit forms of recreation. We need only to provide against going to extremes as to the time spent on them or the amount played for. If we spend too much time on them, they are no longer amusements but tasks in which neither mind nor body is refreshed but rather stupefied and worn out. To play tennis for a long time does not refresh the body but tires it out. If the stakes played for are too high, the players' emotions get out of control. Moreover, it is unjust to gamble so much money on skill and labor so unimportant and useless as that exercised in games of chance.

Above all, Philothea, you must take particular care not to become absorbed in such amusements. No matter how innocent some kind of recreation may be, it is wrong to set heart and affections on it. I don't say that you must take no pleasure out of games of chance since then it would not be a means of recreation. I do say that you must not fasten your affections on them, spend too much time on them, or be too eager for them.

32. PROHIBITED GAMES

Games of dice, cards, and the like in which winning depends principally on chance are not only dangerous as recreations, just as dancing is, but are of their own simple nature bad and reprehensible. This is why they have been forbidden both by civil and ecclesiastical law. "But," you will ask, "what great harm can there be in them?" Gain is not acquired at these games by reason but by chance, which often falls to one whose ability or industry deserves nothing. This in itself is an offense against reason. "But that was what we agreed on," you will tell me. This is all right as far as proving that the winner does no wrong to the others, but it does not follow that either the agreement or the game is reasonable. Gain ought to be a reward for labor but here it is made the reward of chance. Chance deserves no reward whatever since it in no way depends on us.

Moreover, although such games are called recreation and are designed for it, they are by no means such. Actually they are strenuous occupations. Is it not an occupation to keep one's mind caught and bound by unremitting concentration and disturbed by constant worry, apprehension, and care? Can there be any sadder, gloomier, or more depressing concentration than that of gamblers? You must neither speak, laugh, nor cough while they are playing for fear of offending them.

In fact, there is no pleasure in gambling except to win, and pleasure that comes solely from our companions' loss and pain is certainly evil. For these three reasons gambling is forbidden. When the great King St. Louis heard that his brother the Count of Anjou and M. Gautier de Nemours were gambling, he became very angry with them, got out of bed where he lay ill, staggered to their room, took the tables, dice, and some of the money, and threw them all out of the window and into the

sea.[1] A holy and chaste maiden, Sarah, says in reference to her own innocence, "You know, O Lord, that I have never joined with them that play."[2]

33. PARTIES AND LAWFUL BUT DANGEROUS PASTIMES

Balls and dances are forms of recreation that are in themselves morally
indifferent but because of the way in which they are conducted lean very
much towards evil and are consequently full of risk and danger. Generally held at night in partial or complete darkness, it is easy for many dark
and vicious things to take place in them since the situation is of itself so
favorable to evil. Since dancers stay up late at night, they lose the following morning and hence an opportunity for serving God. In a word, it is
always foolish to exchange day for night, light for darkness, and good
works for wanton deeds. Everyone tries to see who will bring the most
vanity to the ball, and vanity is so favorable to evil affections that dangerous and reprehensible acts of love easily occur at dances.

For my part, Philothea, I have the same opinion of dances that a
physician has of pumpkins and mushrooms. In his opinion the best of
them are good for nothing, and I claim that even the best dances are not
much good. Nevertheless, if you must eat pumpkins, be sure that they
are well prepared. If you must go to a ball on some occasion that you
cannot very well avoid, see to it that you yourself dance properly. You
will ask me how this is to be done, and I answer, with modesty, dignity,
and a good intention. Eat mushrooms only sparingly and seldom, the
physicians say, for no matter how well they are prepared, a large quantity
makes them poisonous. Dance only a little and very seldom, Philothea,
since by doing otherwise you put yourself in danger of loving it.

According to Pliny,[1] because mushrooms are spongy and porous
they readily attract all the poisons that are around them. Thus if near
serpents, they absorb their venom. Balls, dancing, and other such noc-
turnal gatherings usually attract the vices and sins rife in such places,

namely, quarrels, envy, scoffing, and wanton love. Such affairs open up the bodily pores of those taking part in them and they also open up the pores of the hearts. They are thus exposed to the danger that a serpent will seize a favorable opportunity to breathe into their ears loose words, foolish deeds, or wanton acts, or that a basilisk will cast an impure look or wanton glance of love into their hearts which, being thus opened, are easily caught and poisoned. Philothea, idle recreations are usually dangerous. They extinguish the spirit of devotion, weaken its powers, cool the fervor of charity, and arouse countless evil affections in the soul. This is why they must be used only with the greatest caution.

Physicians say that after eating mushrooms we must drink good wine, and I say that after dancing we must turn to consideration of good and holy things to prevent the baneful effects that the empty pleasure taken in dancing might stamp on our minds. What are such considerations?

(1) While you were at the ball many souls were burning in the flames of hell for sins committed at dances or occasioned by their dancing. (2) At that very time many devout, religious persons were in God's presence, singing his praises and contemplating his beauty. How much more usefully was their time spent than yours! (3) While you were dancing, many souls departed out of this world in great anguish, and thousands of men and women were suffering dreadful pain in their beds, in hospitals, or out on the streets from gout, kidney stones, and burning fever. Alas, they had no rest. Will you have no pity on them? Do you not know that some day you shall groan like them while others will dance as you did? (4) Our Lord, our Lady, the angels, and the saints saw you at the ball. Ah, how greatly they pitied you when they saw your heart filled with pleasure by so vain an amusement and taken up with such childish trifles! Alas! while you were there time was passing away and death was drawing nearer. See how he mocks at you and invites you to join his dance! In that dance of death the sighs of your friends will be

the violin and you will take the single step from this life to the next. This latter dance is the true pastime of mortal men since by it we pass in an instant from time to an eternity of either reward or punishment.

I have set down these little considerations for you but if you fear God he will bring to your mind many more to the same effect.

34. WHEN IT IS PERMISSIBLE TO PLAY OR DANCE

For cards or dancing to be licit we must use them as recreation and at the same time not have any affection for them. We may engage in them for a short time but we must not continue until tired out or stupefied. We must engage in them only on rare occasions for if we indulge in them constantly we turn recreation into work. When can we play cards or dance? Proper occasions for dancing and legitimate games of chance are not frequent, while those of forbidden games are rarer still. Such games are far more open to criticism and far more dangerous. In short, dance and play cards according to the conditions I have noted, namely, when prudence and discretion direct you to be agreeable and join in the pastimes of the group you are with. To be agreeable is a part of charity and makes indifferent things good and dangerous things permissible. It even removes harm from things in some way evil. For this reason games of chance, which otherwise would be evil, are not so if we sometimes join in them because of legitimate friendliness.

It has been consoling to me to read in St. Charles Borromeo's life of how he adapted himself to Swiss customs in certain things about which he was otherwise very strict and how the Blessed Ignatius Loyola accepted invitations to play cards. When taking part in social affairs St. Elizabeth of Hungary sometimes played cards and danced without harm to her devotion. It was so deeply rooted in her soul that it increased in the midst of the pomps and vanities her position exposed her to, just as the rocks bordering the lake of Rietta grow larger because they are pounded by the waves.[1] Great fires are increased by the wind, but little ones are put out if we carry them without something to protect them.

35. WE MUST BE FAITHFUL TO BOTH GREAT AND LITTLE TASKS

The sacred Spouse in the Canticle of Canticles says that his bride has ravished his heart with one of her eyes and one of her hairs.[1] Of all the outer parts of the human body none is nobler in structure or activity than the eye and none of less value than the hair. Hence the sacred Spouse implies that he is pleased to accept the great deeds of devout persons, that their least and lowest deeds are also acceptable to him, and that to serve him as he wishes we must have great care to serve him well both in great, lofty matters and in small, unimportant things. With love we can capture his heart by the one just as well as by the other.

Philothea, you must be ready to suffer many great afflictions for our Lord, even martyrdom itself. Resolve to give him whatever you hold dearest if it pleases him to take it—father, mother, brother, husband, wife, child, your very eyes and life. Prepare your heart for all such sacrifices. However, as long as divine Providence does not send you such great, piercing afflictions and does not demand your eyes of you, give him your hair at least. I mean, bear patiently the slight injuries, the little inconveniences, the inconsequential losses that daily come to you. By means of such trifles as these, borne with love and affection, you will completely win his heart and make it all your own. These little daily acts of charity, this headache, toothache, or cold, this bad humor in a husband or wife, this broken glass, this contempt or that scorn, this loss of a pair of gloves, ring, or handkerchief, the little inconveniences incurred by going to bed early and getting up early to pray or receive Holy Communion, that little feeling of shame one has in performing certain acts of devotion in public—in short, all such little trials when accepted and embraced with love are highly pleasing to God's mercy. For a single cup of water[2] God has promised to his faithful a sea of perfect bliss. Since such opportunities present themselves from moment to moment it will be a great means of storing up vast spiritual riches if you only use them well.

When I saw in St. Catherine of Siena's life[3] so many raptures and elevations of spirit, words of wisdom and even sermons uttered by her, I did not doubt that by the eye of contemplation she had ravished the heart of her heavenly Spouse. But I was equally comforted when I saw her in her father's kitchen, humbly turning the spit, kindling fires, dressing meat, kneading bread, and doing the meanest household chores cheerfully and filled with love and affection for God. I do not have less esteem for the humble little meditations she made during these mean, lowly tasks than for the ecstasies and raptures she so often had. Perhaps they were granted to her only in recompense for her humility and self-abasement. Her manner of meditating was as follows. While preparing her father's food she imagined that like another Martha she was preparing it for our Savior and that her mother had the place of our Lady and her brothers that of the apostles. In this way she aroused herself to serve in spirit the whole court of heaven while joyously carrying out these humble tasks because she knew that such was God's will. I have cited this example, Philothea, so that you may know how important it is to direct all our actions, no matter how lowly they may be, to the service of his divine Majesty.

Therefore, I earnestly counsel you to imitate the valiant woman whom the great Solomon praises so highly. As he says, she puts her hand to strong, generous, and exalted things and yet does not disdain to spin and turn the spindle. "She has put her hand to strong things, and her fingers have taken hold of the spindle."[4] Put your hand to strong things, by training yourself in prayer and meditation, receiving the sacraments, bringing souls to love God, infusing good inspirations into their hearts, and, in fine, by performing big, important works according to your vocation. But never forget your distaff or spindle. In other words, practice those little, humble virtues which grow like flowers at the foot of the cross: helping the poor, visiting the sick, and taking care of your family, with all the tasks that go with such things and with all that useful diligence which will not let you stand idle. Among all these tasks mingle reflections like those I have related about St. Catherine.

Great opportunities to serve God rarely present themselves but little ones are frequent. Whoever will be "faithful over a few things" will be placed "over many"[5] says the Savior. "Do all things in the name of God,"[6] and you will do all things well. Provided you know how to fulfill your duties properly, then "whether you eat or drink,"[7] whether you sleep or take recreation or turn the spit, you will profit greatly in God's sight by doing all these things because God wishes you to do them.

36. WE MUST PRESERVE A JUST AND REASONABLE MIND

We are men solely because we possess reason, yet it is a rare thing to find men who are truly reasonable. Usually self-love leads us away from reason and directs us imperceptibly into countless small yet dangerous acts of injustice and iniquity, which, like the little foxes spoken of in the Canticle of Canticles,[1] destroy the vines. Because they are little we are not on guard against them, and because there are many of them they are sure to cause us great injury. I think you will agree that the things about which I am going to speak are both unjust and unreasonable.

We condemn every little thing in our neighbor and excuse ourselves of important things. We want to sell very dearly and to buy at bargain prices. We desire that justice be done in another's house but that mercy and generosity be granted to our own. We like to have things we say taken in good part but we are tender and touchy about what others say. We want our neighbor to give up his property and take our money for it.

Isn't it juster that we let him keep his property and he let us keep our money? We take it ill if he will not accommodate us, but doesn't he have greater reason for taking offense because we want to inconvenience him? If we like a certain practice we despise everyone else and oppose everything that is not to our taste. If one of our inferiors is poor-looking or if we have taken a dislike to him, we find fault with everything he does. We never stop plaguing him and are always ready to run him down. On the contrary, if we like someone because of his good looks, he can do nothing we won't excuse. There are some virtuous children whom their parents can scarcely look at because of some physical defect, while others are mean and still favorites because of some bodily grace.

In general we prefer the rich to the poor, even though they are neither of better condition nor as virtuous. We even prefer those who are better dressed. We rigorously demand our own rights, but want others to be considerate in insisting on theirs. We maintain our rank with exactness, but we want others to be humble and accommodating as to theirs. We complain easily about our neighbors, but none of them must complain about us. What we do for others always seems very great, but what is done for us seems nothing at all. In short, like the Paphlagonian partridges we have two hearts.[2] We have a mild, gracious, and courteous attitude toward ourselves and another that is hard, severe, and rigorous toward our neighbor. We have two weights: one to weigh goods to our own greatest possible advantage and another to weigh our neighbor's to his greatest possible disadvantage. As the Scripture says, they have spoken "with deceitful lips and with a double heart,"[3] that is, they have two hearts. To have two weights, one heavier with which to receive and the other lighter with which to dispense, "is an abominable thing before the Lord."[4]

Be just and equitable in all your actions, Philothea. Always put yourself in your neighbor's place and him in yours, and then you will judge rightly. Imagine yourself the seller when you buy and the buyer when you sell and you will sell and buy justly. All these injustices are slight and do not oblige us to restitution since we abide solely by rigorous terms that are in our favor. Yet we are obliged to make amendment since they are great faults against reason and charity. In the end they are simply acts of self-deceit, for a man loses nothing by living generously, nobly, courteously, and with a royal, just, and reasonable heart. Philothea, resolve to examine your heart often to see if it is such toward your neighbor as you would like his to be toward you were you in his place. This is the touchstone of true reason. When Trajan was criticized by his intimates for making, as they thought, the imperial majesty too accessible, he said, "Shouldn't I be such an emperor toward private citizens as I would desire an emperor to be toward me if I myself were a private citizen?"[5]

37. ON DESIRES

We all know that we must be on guard against desires for wrong things, since desire for evil makes us evil. I say more than this: Do not desire things that endanger your soul, such as parties, card games, or similar amusements. Desire neither honors and offices and neither visions nor ecstasies. There is a great danger, self-deceit, and vanity in such things. Do not desire faraway things, that is, things that cannot happen for a long time, as many people do, and by so doing wear out and waste their hearts to no purpose and expose themselves to the danger of becoming very discontented. If a young man greatly desires to be established in some position before the proper time, what help, I ask you, does this desire bring him? If a married woman wants to be a nun, to what purpose is it? If I want to buy my neighbor's property before he is ready to sell it, don't I waste my time by such desires? If I am sick in bed and yet want to preach, say Holy Mass, visit other sick people, and do the work of well men, are not all these empty desires since it is now beyond my ability to put them into effect? In the meantime these useless desires usurp the place of virtues I ought to have—patience, resignation, mortification, obedience, and meekness under suffering. They are what God wishes me to practice at this time. Our desires are often like those of expectant women who long for fresh cherries in autumn and for fresh grapes in spring.

I can in no way approve the idea that a person obligated to a certain duty or vocation should distract himself by longing for any other kind of life but one in keeping with his duties or by engaging in exercises incompatible with his present state. To do so dissipates his heart and renders it unfit for its needed work. If I want to live the secluded life of the Carthusian, I am wasting my time and such a desire displaces those I should have in order to do good work in my actual state in life. No, in my opinion no one should wish for better talents or better judgment, since such desires are frivolous and take the place of the wish everyone ought to have, namely, to cultivate his character such as it actually is. No one should desire means of serving God that he now lacks but rather should diligently use those he actually has. All this is to be understood only of desires that distract our minds. As to simple wishes, if they are not too frequent they do no harm whatever.

Do not desire crosses except in proportion to the way in which you have patiently carried those already sent to you. It is an abuse to desire martyrdom and lack courage to put up with an injury. The enemy often supplies us with great desires for absent things that we will never encounter in order to divert our minds from present things, from which, small as they may be, we might obtain great profit. In imagination we often do battle with monsters in Africa. In the meanwhile for want of vigilance we let ourselves be slain by little serpents that lie in our path. Do not desire temptations—to do so would be rashness—but prepare yourself to await them with courage and defend yourself against them when they come.

A variety of foods, especially if a large amount is eaten, overburdens the stomach and ruins it if it is weak. Don't overburden your soul with many desires, neither with worldly desires, which may completely corrupt you, nor with spiritual desires for they may cause you difficulty.

When our soul has been purged and feels free from evil passions, it experiences a great craving for spiritual things. Like a famished person, it longs for many different kinds of pious practices, mortification, penance, humility, charity, and prayer. To have so keen an appetite is a good sign, Philothea, but you must consider whether you can properly digest all you want to eat. From among all such desires choose, according to your spiritual director's advice, those you can practice and fulfill at present. Turn them to your best advantage, and this done, God will send you others that you can practice in due time. In this way you will never waste time in useless desires. I don't say that you must give up any of these good desires but say that you must bring them all forth in good order. Those that cannot be immediately put into effect should be stored away in some corner of your heart until their time comes, and meanwhile you can put into effect the ones that are mature and in season. I give this advice not only to the spiritual minded but also to worldly people. Without it we will live only in anxiety and confusion.

38. INSTRUCTIONS FOR MARRIED PERSONS

"Marriage is a great sacrament, but I speak in Christ and in the Church."[1] It is "honorable to all"[2] persons, in all persons, and in all things, that is, in all its parts. It is honorable to all persons because even virgins must honor it with humility, in all persons because it is equally holy in the rich and in the poor, in all things because its origin, purpose, advantages, forms, and matter are holy. It is the nursery of Christianity, which supplies the earth with faithful souls to fill up the number of the elect in heaven. Hence the preservation of holy marriage is of the highest importance for the state since it is the origin and source of all that flows from the state.

Would to God that his well-beloved Son were invited to every marriage, as he was to the marriage at Cana, for then the wine of his consolation and blessing would never be lacking to it. The supreme reason why there is little of that wine at the beginning of married life is because Adonis is invited instead of our Lord and Venus instead of our Lady. The man who would have fair, mottled lambs, like Jacob's, must like him place fair rods of various colors before the sheep when they meet to couple.[3] The man who wishes to have a happy married life must reflect on his wedding day on the sanctity and dignity of this sacrament. Instead of this there are countless unseemly things done in play, feasting, and speech. It is not surprising that its effects are so disordered.

Above all else I exhort married people to have that mutual love which the Holy Spirit in Scripture so highly recommends to them. O you who are married, it means nothing to say, "Love one another with a natural love"—two turtle doves make such love. Nor does it mean anything to say, "Love one another with a human love"—the pagans have duly practiced such love. With the great apostle I say to you, "Husbands, love your wives as Christ also loved the Church,"[4] and you wives, love your husbands as the Church loves her Savior. God brought Eve to Adam, our first father, and gave her to him in marriage. It was God too, my friends, who with an unseen hand tied your holy marriage bond and gave you to one another. Why then do you not cherish each other with a completely holy, completely sacred, and completely divine love?

The first effect of this love is an indissoluble union of your hearts. If the adhesive is good, two pieces of fir wood glued together will stick so fast to one another that it is easier to break them in any other place than where they have been joined together. God joins husband to wife with his own Blood and for this reason the union is so strong that the soul must sooner break away from the body of one of them than the husband from the wife. This union must be understood principally not of the body but of the heart, affections, and love.

The second effect of this love must be the inviolable fidelity of each party to the other. In ancient times seals were engraved on finger rings, as Scripture testifies.[5] Consider the inner meaning of this ceremony in marriage. By the priest's hand the Church blesses a ring. By giving it first to the man the Church testifies that in this sacrament she puts a seal and sign on his heart so that henceforward neither the name nor the love of any other woman may enter his heart as long as she who has been given to him is alive. Afterward, the bridegroom puts the ring on the bride's hand so that on her part she will understand that her heart must never admit affection for any other man as long as he whom our Lord here gives to her shall live on earth.

The third fruit of marriage is the birth and lawful rearing of children. It is a great honor to you who are married that in God's design to multiply souls who can bless and praise him for all eternity he empowers you to co-operate with him in so noble a work. This is done by your production of the bodies into which he infuses souls like drops of heaven. Thus God infuses souls by creating them just as he creates them by infusing them.

Husbands, preserve a tender, constant, heartfelt love for your wives. The woman was taken from the first man on the side nearest his heart so that she might be heartily and tenderly loved by him. Your wives' frailty and infirmity, whether of body or of mind, should never make you disdainful of them. God has created them such as they are. Hence since they are dependent on you, you will receive greater honor and respect and you will be companions to them while still remaining their heads and superiors. Wives, love the husbands God has given you with a love that is tender and heartfelt and yet filled with respect and reverence. God has created man as the more vigorous and dominant sex. He has willed that woman should depend on man, since she is bone of his bone and flesh of his flesh,[6] and that she should be made of a rib taken from beneath his arm to show that she must be under her husband's hand and guidance. All Holy Scripture explicitly enjoins such submission, but the Scriptures make it an agreeable submission for they not only prescribe that you should adapt yourselves to it with love but also command husbands to exercise it over you with great charity, tenderness, and mildness. "Husbands, in like manner, dwell with your wives considerately, paying honor to the woman as to the weaker vessel,"[7] says St. Peter. While I exhort you to advance more and more in the mutual love you owe to one another, take care that it does not degenerate into jealousy of any kind. It often happens that just as a worm is bred in the ripest, tenderest apple, so also jealousy grows in the most ardent and compelling love of man and wife. It spoils and corrupts the very substance of such love for little by little it breeds quarrels, dissension, and divorce. In fact, jealousy never gets in where friendship is based on true virtue in both persons, and its presence is therefore an infallible mark that love is in some degree gross and sensual and that its object presents only imperfect, inconstant, and untrustworthy virtue. It is a foolish boast on the part of friendship to try to exalt itself by jealousy, for jealousy is a sign of a friendship's height and bulk but not of its goodness, purity, and perfection. Perfection of friendship presupposes sure trust in the virtue of those we love, while jealousy presupposes doubt of it.

If you married men wish your wives to be faithful to you, teach them by your example. "How can you expect purity in your wives when you yourselves live in impurity? How can you demand of them what you don't give them?" asks St. Gregory Nazianzen.[8] Do you want them to be chaste? Then conduct yourselves chastely toward them and, as St. Paul says, let "everyone of you learn how to possess his vessel in holiness."[9] On the contrary, if you teach them evil ways it is no wonder that you suffer disgrace by their fall.

Wives, your honor is inseparably joined to modesty and purity. Be zealous therefore to preserve your glory and do not permit loose conduct of any sort to tarnish your spotless reputation. Be fearful of every form of improper approach, no matter how slight it may be, and never permit any impure advances to be made to you. If anyone comes praising your beauty and grace, he must be looked at with suspicion for usually anyone who praises goods he can't buy is strongly tempted to steal them. If he adds dispraise of your husband to praise of you, he does you a grievous wrong. It is obvious that he not only wants to ruin you but considers you half lost already, for when one is disgusted with the first merchant a bargain is half made with the second. In ancient times, according to Pliny,[10] ladies—like those of today—were accustomed to wear pearls in their ears because they liked to hear them jingle together. For my part, I know that Isaac, a great friend of God, sent earrings as the first pledge of his love for the chaste Rebecca.[11] I think that this mystical ornament signifies that his wife's ear is the first part a husband should take possession of, and that the wife must faithfully keep it for him so that no other sound or language should enter it but the sweet and loving music of pure, chaste words. Such words are the oriental pearls mentioned in the gospel. We must always remember that poison enters the soul through the ear, just as it enters the body through the mouth.

Love and fidelity joined together always produce familiarity and mutual trust, and hence in their married life the saints, both men and women, have used many reciprocal caresses, truly affectionate but chaste, tender, sincere caresses. Thus Isaac and Rebecca, the most chaste married couple of antiquity, were watched through a window as they caressed one another in such manner that although there was no immodesty Abimelech was convinced that they were man and wife.[12] The great St. Louis was equally rigorous to his body and tender in his love for his wife, yet he was almost blamed for being too generous with his caresses. Actually he deserved praise for being able to curb his courageous, martial spirit and subdue it to these little duties so needful to preserve conjugal love. Although such demonstrations of pure, frank affection do not bind hearts together, they tend to unite them and serve as an agreeable help to their life in common.

When St. Monica was about to give birth to the great St. Augustine, she dedicated him by repeated acts of oblation to the Christian religion and the service of God's glory. He testifies to this and says that "he had already tasted God's salt within his mother's womb."[13] The story contains a great lesson, for it tells Christian women to offer up to God's Majesty the fruit of their wombs even before it comes into the world. At such times God, who accepts the offerings of a humble and willing heart, is wont to inspire a mother's affections. Samuel,[14] St. Thomas Aquinas,[15] St. Andrew of Fiesole,[16] and many others bear witness to this. St. Bernard's mother[17]—a mother worthy of such a son—took her children as soon as they were born into her arms and offered them to Jesus Christ. From that moment she loved them with a holy respect as things consecrated to God and entrusted by him to her care. This act had such happy results that all seven became very saintly.

When children grow up and begin to have the use of reason both their fathers and their mothers must most carefully impress the fear of God on their hearts. The devout Queen Blanche performed this duty most fervently in the case of her son, St. Louis the king, and often said to him: "My dear child, I would much rather see you dead before my eyes than see you commit a single mortal sin."[18] This caution remained so deeply stamped on his soul that not a day of his life passed without his remembering it and taking all possible care to keep faithfully this divine teaching. In our language families and generations are called houses, the Hebrews themselves called the generation of children building up a house. In this sense it is said that God built up houses for the Egyptian midwives[19] to show that raising a house, that is, a family, does not consist in building a splendid residence and storing up vast worldly possessions but in training children well in the fear of God and in virtue. No trouble or labor should be spared to do this, for children are their father's and mother's crown.[20] Hence St. Monica fought so fervently and constantly against the evil inclinations of St. Augustine that after following him by sea and land she made him more happily the child of her tears, by his soul's conversion, than he had been the child of her blood by his bodily generation.[21]

St. Paul leaves to wives care of the household as their portion.[22] For this reason many truly believe that their devotion is more fruitful for the family than that of husbands who do not spend so much time at home and consequently cannot so easily form the family in virtue. In view of this fact Solomon in his Proverbs makes the whole household's happiness depend on the care and industry of the valiant woman he describes.[23]

In the book of Genesis[24] it is said that when Isaac saw that his wife Rebecca was barren he prayed to the Lord for her. Or, according to the Hebrew, he prayed to the Lord opposite to her because the husband prayed on one side of the oratory and the wife on the other and the prayer of the husband offered in this fashion was heard. The union of husband and wife in holy devotion such as this is the best and most fruitful of all and they should mutually encourage one another in it. There are certain kinds of fruit, the quince, for instance, which because of their bitter juice are agreeable only when preserved in sugar, while because of their tenderness certain others, such as cherries and apricots, cannot be kept long unless preserved in the same way. Wives should desire that their husbands be kept with the sugar of devotion. Without devotion a man is a severe, harsh, rough creature and without devotion a woman is very frail and apt to decline in virtue or lose it. St. Paul says that "the unbelieving husband is sanctified by the believing wife, and the unbelieving wife is sanctified by the believing husband,"[25] because in the close alliance of marriage the one can more easily lead the other to a virtuous life. What a blessing it is when believing husband and believing wife sanctify each other in true fear of the Lord!

As to other things, then, mutual support must be so great that they will never be angry with each other at the same time, and hence quarrels or disputes will never be seen between them. Honeybees cannot remain in a place where there are echoes, loud noises, and resounding voices, nor can the Holy Spirit remain in a home where there are quarrels, recriminations, and the echoing sounds of scolding and strife.

St. Gregory Nazianzen tells us that in his time married people kept their wedding anniversary as a festival day.[26] For my part, I approve of reviving this custom, provided that it is not attended by worldly and sensual amusements. On that day husband and wife should go to confession and receive Holy Communion and with more than ordinary fervor commend to God the success and happiness of their marriage. They should renew their good intention to sanctify it still more by mutual love and fidelity and, so to speak, they should recover breath in our Lord to support the burdens of their vocation.

39. THE SANCTITY OF THE MARRIAGE BED

The marriage bed must be kept undefiled, as the apostle says,[1] that is, it must be kept free from impurity and other profane, filthy uses. Holy wedlock was first instituted in the earthly paradise, where as yet there had been no disorder caused by concupiscence nor immodesty of any kind.

There is a certain resemblance between sexual pleasures and those taken in eating. Both of them are related to the flesh but because of their animal vehemence the first are called carnal pleasures without qualification. I will try to explain what I cannot say about sexual pleasures by what I say of the other.

1. Eating is ordained for the preservation of individual lives, and just as eating solely to nourish and maintain one's life is good, holy, and a duty, so also the act requisite in marriage for producing children and increasing the human race is a good and most holy thing for it is the principal end of marriage.

2. Just as eating not merely for the preservation of life but to maintain the mutual association and consideration we owe one another is an extremely just and virtuous act, so also mutual, lawful satisfaction of both parties in holy matrimony is called a debt by St. Paul.[2] It is a debt so great that he grants neither party exemption from its payment without the free, voluntary consent of the other.[3] This holds even in refer-

ence to exercises of devotion, as I pointed out in the chapter on Holy Communion. How much less can there be self-exemption on the score of some fanciful pretext of virtue or out of anger or disdain?

3. Those who eat in order to maintain friendly association with others must eat freely and not as if compelled to do so and must show an appetite for their food. So also the marriage debt should always be paid as faithfully and freely as if done in hope of having children, although on some occasions there may be no such expectation.

4. To eat for neither of the reasons given but merely to satisfy our appetite may be tolerated but not commended. Mere pleasure in satisfying a sensual appetite cannot be a sufficient reason to make an action praiseworthy but it is sufficient if the action is permissible.

5. To eat not merely to gratify our appetite but in an excessive and inordinate way is something more or less worthy of censure according as the excess is great or small.

6. Excess in eating does not consist only in eating too much but also in the time and manner of eating. It is a surprising fact, dear Philothea, that honey, which is proper and wholesome food for bees, may still become so harmful to them as to make them ill at times, for instance, when they eat too much of it in the spring. It disturbs their stomachs and sometimes even causes death, as when they get too much of it on the front of their head or wings.

In fact, marital intercourse, which is so holy, virtuous, and praiseworthy in itself and so profitable to society, is nevertheless in certain cases a source of danger to those who exercise it. Sometimes it causes their souls to become seriously ill with venial sins, as in cases of simple excess. Sometimes it effectively kills the soul by mortal sin, as when the order appointed for the procreation of children is violated and perverted. In the latter instance, according as one departs more or less from the appointed order, the sins are abominable in greater or less degrees but they are always mortal. Procreation of children is the first and principal end of marriage. Hence no one can ever lawfully depart from the due order that this end requires. This holds true even at times when conception cannot take place because of some condition or circumstance, as when sterility or pregnancy prevents it. In such cases sexual intercourse does not cease to be a virtuous and holy act, provided the rule of generation is followed. No accidental condition whatsoever can change the law that the principal end of marriage has imposed. Certainly the infamous and execrable act committed by Onan within his marriage was detestable in God's sight, as the holy text of Genesis, chapter 38, testifies. Certain heretics in our own times, a hundred times more deserving of condemnation than the Cynics St. Jerome speaks about in his commentary of the epistle to the Ephesians,[4] have been pleased to say that merely the perverse intention of that wicked man offended God. Scripture positively asserts the contrary and assures us that the act he committed was itself detestable and abominable in God's sight.

7. It is an infallible mark of a wayward, infamous, base, abject, and degraded mind to think about food and drink before mealtime, much more so to delight ourselves later with the pleasure we had in eating, keeping it alive in words and imagination and taking delight in recalling the sensual satisfaction had in swallowing those bits of food. Men who have their minds fixed before dinner on the oven and after dinner on the dishes served do this and such men are fit to be scullions in the kitchen. As St. Paul says, "They make a god of their bellies."[5] People of honor never think of eating except when they sit down at the table. After dinner they wash their hands and mouth so as not to retain the taste or odor of what they have eaten. The elephant is a huge beast but of all animals living here on earth it is the most decorous and intelligent. I give you an example of his chastity. He never changes his mate, has a tender love for the one chosen, and couples with her only every three years. This is only during periods of five days and so privately that he is never seen in the act. When he appears again on the sixth day the first thing he does is to go immediately to a river where he washes

his entire body, as he does not want to return to the herd until completely cleansed.[6] Good, modest habits in an animal of this kind give us an example for married people. They should not keep their affections fixed on the sensual pleasures they have indulged in as part of their vocation in life. When they are over, they ought to wash their hearts and affections and purify themselves from them as soon as possible so that afterwards they can with calm minds practice purer and higher actions.

In this counsel is found the perfect practice of the lofty doctrine St. Paul gave to the Corinthians. "The time is short . . . it remains that those who have wives should be as though they had none."[7] According to St. Gregory,[8] a man has a wife as if he had none if he takes bodily consolation with her in such wise as not to be diverted from spiritual demands. What is said of the husband holds also for the wife. "Let those who use this world be as though not using it,"[9] says the same apostle. Let everyone use the world according to his vocation, but in such manner that he does not fix his affections on it and remains as free and ready to serve God as if he did not use it. St. Augustine states, "It is man's great evil to desire and enjoy things he should merely use, and to desire to use things he should only enjoy."[10] We should enjoy spiritual things but only use corporeal things. When their use is turned into enjoyment our rational soul is also changed into a brutish and beastly soul.

I think I have said all I need to say to make myself understood without saying anything I did not wish to say.

40. INSTRUCTIONS FOR WIDOWS

St. Paul instructs all prelates, taking his disciple Timothy as their representative, when he says to him: "Honor widows who are truly widowed."[1] To be truly a widow the following conditions are required:

1. A widow must not only be a widow in body but also in mind, that is, she must have an unshakeable resolution to remain in the state of chaste widowhood. Those who remain widows only until they have a chance to marry again are separated from men only as to bodily pleasures but already joined to them in will and affection. For the true widow to establish herself firmly in the state of widowhood, she must offer God her body and chastity by means of a vow. She will thus add a great ornament to her widowhood and give great security to her resolution. After making her vow she no longer has the power to give up chastity without giving up her title to heaven. Hence she will watch over her vow so jealously that not for a single moment will she let the least thought of marriage enter her heart. In this way her holy vow will serve as a strong barrier between her soul and every project contrary to her resolution.

St. Augustine[2] very strongly recommends such a vow to Christian widows. In ancient times Origen,[3] a very learned man, went much further. He exhorts married women to vow and dedicate themselves to chaste widowhood in case their husbands die before them, so that amid the sensual pleasures of marriage by means of this anticipated promise they may enjoy also the merit of chaste widowhood. A vow not only makes good works done as a result of it more acceptable to God but it also encourages us to put them into practice. It gives God not only the good works that are the fruits of our good will but likewise dedicates to him the will itself, the tree on which all our actions grow. By simple chastity we lend our body to God while still retaining the liberty to use it for sensual pleasure at some other time. By the vow of chastity we make him an absolute and irrevocable gift of our body without reserving to ourselves any power of recall. In this way we happily make ourselves slaves of him whose service is better than all royal power.[4] Since I highly approve the advice of these two great men, I wish that souls who are so happy as to desire to follow it should do so prudently, devoutly, and firmly, having first examined their resolutions, invoked

God's divine inspiration, and taken counsel of a wise and devout director. In this way everything will be done with greater benefit.

2. Moreover, this renunciation of a second marriage must be made purely and simply with the single intention of turning all the affection of one's soul toward God and uniting one's heart wholly with that of his Divine Majesty. If a widow remains in her state of widowhood because she wishes to provide wealth for her children or for any other worldly purpose, she may earn some praise for it but certainly not before God.[5] In God's eyes nothing can truly merit praise except what is done for his sake.

3. Moreover, the widow who would be truly a widow must voluntarily remove and keep herself from worldly comforts. "For she who gives herself up to pleasures is dead while she is still alive," says St. Paul.[6] To desire to be a widow and yet to be delighted at being courted, flattered, and caressed, to be fond of balls, dancing, and banquetting, to be perfumed, splendidly dressed, and bedizened is to be a widow who lives as to the body but is dead as to the soul. I ask you, what does it matter whether the sign of Adonis and profane love consists of white feathers arranged as a plume or of black crepe spread like a veil over one's face? Often the black is put over the white out of vanity, so as to heighten the color. A widow who tries out the fashions by which women can please men casts the most dangerous bait before their minds. A widow who lives in such fond delights is dead while she lives and properly speaking she is only an image of widowhood.

"The time of pruning is come, the voice of the turtle is heard in our land," says the Canticle of Canticles.[7] All who wish to love devoutly must prune and cut away all worldly superfluities. This is especially necessary for the true widow who like a chaste turtle comes from weeping, bewailing, and lamenting the loss of her husband. When Naomi returned from Moab to Bethlehem, the women of the town who had known her when she was newly married said to one another, "This is that same Naomi." But she answered, "Do not call me Naomi, I beg of you, for Naomi means comely and beautiful, but call me Mara, for the Lord has filled my soul with bitterness,"[8] saying this because she had lost her husband. Thus the devout widow never desires to be considered either beautiful or comely but is content to be such as God wants her to be, that is, humble and abject in her own eyes.

Lamps in which aromatic oil has been burnt emit a sweeter odor after their flame has been put out, and so also widows whose married love was pure send forth a sweeter perfume of virtue and chastity after their light, that is, their husband, has been extinguished by death. To love a husband as long as he is alive is a little thing among women, but to love him so well that after his death she wants no other husband is a degree of love belonging only to true widows. To trust in God while a husband serves as her support is not unusual, but to trust in God when one is destitute of such support is worthy of great praise. Hence it is easier to recognize the presence of perfect virtue in widowhood than in marriage.

A widow with children having need of her guidance and support— this is chiefly in their spiritual concerns and in their establishment in life—should by no means desert them. St. Paul the apostle clearly sees that widows are obliged to take care of their children in order to make a just recompense to their own fathers and mothers. He says still more, that "if a man does not care for his own, and especially of his household, he is worse than an unbeliever."[9] If a widow's children have no need for her guidance, she should gather up all her affections and thoughts and use them solely for her own advancement in God's love.

Unless absolute necessity obliges in conscience the true widow to engage in external troubles, such as lawsuits, I counsel her to avoid them altogether and follow the way of conducting her affairs that appears most peaceable and quiet, although it may not seem the most advantageous. The advantages reaped from worldly troubles must be very great to bear any comparison with the happiness brought by holy tranquillity. This is aside from the fact that disputes and lawsuits distract the mind and often open a gate to the enemies of chastity. To please those whose favor they need, people adopt ways that are indevout and offensive to God.

Let a widow be constant in the practice of prayer. Since she must love no one but God, she must speak to almost no one but God. If a diamond is near a piece of iron the iron is kept from following a magnet's attractive power but springs toward it as soon as the diamond is removed. It is the same with a widow's heart, which could not very well give itself completely to God or follow the attractions of his love during her husband's life. Immediately after his death her heart should ardently run after the sweet odor of heavenly perfumes, and say in imitation of the sacred Spouse, "O Lord, now that I am all my own, take me so that I may be all yours. 'Draw me, we will run after you to the odor of your ointments.' "[10]

For a holy widow the proper virtues are perfect modesty, renunciation of honors, rank, assemblies, titles, and all such empty things, serving the sick and poor, comforting the afflicted, instructing young girls in a devout life, and making themselves perfect patterns of every virtue to young women. Cleanliness and simplicity must be the ornaments of their dress, humility and charity the ornaments of their conduct, courtesy and mildness the ornaments of their speech, modesty and purity the ornaments of their eyes, and Jesus Christ crucified their hearts' sole love.

In brief, the true widow is a little March violet within the Church. By the odor of her devotion she sends forth incomparable sweetness and almost always keeps herself hidden under the leaves of her abjection. By her subdued colors she testifies to her mortification. She grows in cool, uncultivated places, and does not wish to be importuned by the conversation of worldly people so that she may better preserve the cool depths within her heart from all the heat that desire for wealth, honors, or even fond love might bring to her. "She shall be blessed if she shall so remain,"[11] says the holy apostle.

I could say much more on this subject but it will suffice to advise the widow who is solicitous for the honor of her state to read carefully the excellent letters that the great St. Jerome wrote to Furia and Salvia[12] and all the other ladies who were fortunate in being spiritual children of so great a father. Nothing can be added to his instructions except this admonition. The true widow ought never to blame or censure those who enter into a second or even a third or fourth marriage. In some cases God so arranges things for his own greater glory. It is necessary always that she keep before her eyes the doctrine of the ancients that neither widowhood nor virginity has any place or rank in heaven but that brought to them by humility.

41. A WORD TO VIRGINS

Virgins, if you hope to enter into a temporal marriage, guard jealously your first love for your first husband. In my opinion it is very deceitful to present him with a heart quite worn out, spoiled, and weary with love instead of a whole and sincere heart. If it is your good fortune to be called to a chaste, virginal, spiritual marriage, and if you wish to preserve your virginity forever, I pray God that with all possible care you keep your love for this divine Spouse. He is purity itself and loves nothing as much as purity.[1] To him we owe the first fruits of all things and above all those of our love. St. Jerome's letters will furnish you with all needed advice. Since your condition obliges you to obedience, choose a guide under whose direction you can dedicate in a more holy manner your body and soul to his Divine Majesty.

THE FOURTH PART OF THE INTRODUCTION

Necessary Counsels Against the
Most Frequent Temptations

1. WE MUST DISREGARD THE CRITICISMS OF THIS WORLD'S CHILDREN

As soon as worldly people see that you wish to follow a devout life they aim a thousand darts of mockery and even detraction at you. The most malicious of them will slander your conversion as hypocrisy, bigotry, and trickery. They will say that the world has turned against you and being rebuffed by it you have turned to God. Your friends will raise a host of objections which they consider very prudent and charitable. They will tell you that you will become depressed, lose your reputation in the world, be unbearable, and grow old before your time, and that your affairs at home will suffer. You must live in the world like one in the world. They will say that you can save your soul without going to such extremes, and a thousand similar trivialities.

Philothea, all this is mere foolish, empty babbling. These people aren't interested in your health or welfare. "If you were of the world, the world would love what is its own but because you are not of the world, therefore the world hates you,"[1] says the Savior. We have seen gentlemen and ladies spend the whole night, even many nights one after another, playing chess or cards. Is there any concentration more absurd, gloomy, or depressing than this last? Yet worldly people don't say a word and the players' friends don't bother their heads about it. If we spend an hour in meditation or get up a little earlier than usual in the morning to prepare for Holy Communion, everyone runs for a doctor to cure us of hypochondria and jaundice. People can pass thirty nights in dancing and no one complains about it, but if they watch through a single Christmas night they cough and claim their stomach is upset the next morning. Does anyone fail to see that the world is an unjust judge, gracious and well disposed to its own children but harsh and rigorous towards the children of God?

We can never please the world unless we lose ourselves together with it. It is so demanding that it can't be satisfied. "John came neither eating nor drinking," says the Savior, and you say, "He has a devil." "The Son of man came eating and drinking" and you say that he is "a Samaritan."[2] It is true Philothea, that if we are ready to laugh, play cards, or dance with the world in order to please it, it will be scandalized at us, and if we don't, it will accuse us of hypocrisy or melancholy. If we dress well, it will attribute it to some plan we have, and if we neglect our dress, it will accuse of us of being cheap and stingy. Good humor will be called frivolity and mortification sullenness. Thus the world looks at us with an evil eye and we can never please it. It exaggerates our imperfections and claims they are sins, turns our venial sins into mortal sins and changes our sins of weakness into sins of malice.

"Charity is kind," says St. Paul,[3] but the world on the contrary is evil.[4] "Charity thinks no evil," but the world always thinks evil and when it can't condemn our acts it will condemn our intentions. Whether the sheep have horns or not and whether they are white or black, the wolf doesn't hesitate to eat them if he can. Whatever we do, the world will wage war on us. If we stay a long time in the confessional, it will wonder how we can have so much to say; if we stay only a short time, it will say we haven't told everything. It will watch all our actions and at a single little angry word it will protest that we can't get along with anyone. To take care of our own interests will look like avarice, while meekness will look like folly. As for the children of the world, their anger is called being blunt, their avarice economy, their intimate conversations lawful discussions. Spiders always spoil the good work of the bees.

Let us give up this blind world, Philothea. Let it cry out at us as long as it pleases, like a cat that cries out to frighten birds in the daytime. Let us be firm in our purposes and unswerving in our resolutions. Perseverance will prove whether we have sincerely sacrificed ourselves to God and dedicated ourselves to a devout life. Comets and planets seem to have just about the same light, but comets are merely fiery masses that pass by and after a while disappear, while planets remain perpetually bright. So also hypocrisy and true virtue have a close resemblance in outward appearance but they can be easily distinguished from one another. Hypocrisy cannot last long but is quickly dissipated like rising smoke, whereas true virtue is always firm and constant. It is no little assistance for a sure start in devotion if we first suffer criticism and calumny because of it. In this way we escape the danger of pride and vanity, which are comparable to the Egyptian midwives whom a cruel Pharaoh had ordered to kill the Israelites' male children on the very day of their birth.[5] We are crucified to the world and the world must be crucified to us.[6] The world holds us to be fools; let us hold it to be mad.

2. WE MUST HAVE FIRM COURAGE

Although light is beautiful and pleasing to our eyes, it nevertheless dazzles them after we have been in the dark for a long time. Until we become familiar with a country's inhabitants we find that we are lost among them no matter how courteous and gracious they may be. Philothea, it may well turn out that this change in your way of life will cause you many problems. You have bid a great, general farewell to the world's follies and vanities and this may bring on a feeling of sadness and discouragement. If this should be the case, have a little patience, I beg of you, for it will come to nothing. Things will seem a little strange because they are new, but when such feelings pass you will receive countless blessings. Perhaps at first it will be hard for you to give up the glory that fools and scoffers brought you in the midst of your vain pursuits. In God's name, would you forfeit the eternal glory that God will certainly give you? The worthless amusements on which you have hitherto wasted your time will again come to lure your heart away and ask it to return to them. Can you resolve to reject eternal happiness for such deceitful and trivial things? You may take my word, if you persevere it will not be long before you obtain consolations so delicious and pleasing that you will acknowledge that the world is mere gall compared to such honey and that a single day of devotion is better than a thousand years[1] of worldly life.

You see that the mountain of Christian perfection is very lofty and you say "O God, how shall I be able to climb it!" Courage, Philothea! When young bees begin to take form they are called nymphs and they cannot yet fly out among the flowers, mountains, or nearby hills to gather honey. Little by little, by continuing to eat honey the older bees have prepared, the little nymphs take on wings and grow strong so that later they fly all over the country in search of food. It is true that in devotion we are still only little bees and cannot fly up high according to our plan, which is nothing less than to reach the peak of Christian perfection. But as our desires and resolutions begin to take form and our wings start to grow, we hope that some day we shall become spiritual bees and be able to fly aloft. In the meantime let us feed on honey found in works of instruction that devout persons of ancient days have left us. Let us pray to God to give us "wings like a dove"[2] not only to fly upward during the time of our present life but also to find repose in the eternity that is to come.

3. THE NATURE OF TEMPTATION AND THE DIFFERENCE BETWEEN FEELING TEMPTATION AND CONSENTING TO IT

Imagine to yourself, Philothea, that a young princess is deeply loved by her spouse and a depraved man wishes to debauch her marriage bed and sends a foul messenger of love to discuss his abominable plans with her. First, the messenger states his master's intention to the princess; secondly, the princess is either pleased or displeased with the message and the proposal; thirdly, she either consents or refuses. In exactly the same manner when Satan, the world, and the flesh see a soul espoused to the Son of God, they send temptations to it. By these temptations (1) sin is proposed to the soul; (2) it is either pleased or displeased by this proposal; (3) finally, either it gives consent or it refuses. These are the three steps in the descent into iniquity: temptation, delight, and consent. Although these three acts are not always clearly evident in all kinds of sin, they may be clearly seen in great, enormous sins.

Temptation to a certain sin, to any sin whatsoever, might last throughout our whole life, yet it can never make us displeasing to God's Majesty provided we do not take pleasure in it and give consent to it. The reason is that when we are tempted we are not active but passive and inasmuch as we do not take pleasure in it we cannot incur any guilt. St. Paul long suffered temptations of the flesh,[1] yet he was far from being displeasing to God on that account; on the contrary God was glorified by them. The Blessed Angela of Foligno suffered such cruel temptations of the flesh that when she describes them she moves us to compassion.[2] So great were the temptations suffered by St. Francis and St. Benedict that to overcome them one threw himself naked on thorns and the other into the snow. For all that, they lost nothing of God's grace but increased greatly in it.

You must have great courage in the midst of temptation, Philothea. Never think yourself overcome as long as they are displeasing to you, keeping clearly in mind the difference between feeling temptation and consenting to it. That is, we may feel temptations even though they displease us but we can never consent to them unless they please us, since to be pleased by them usually is a step toward consent to them. Let the enemies of our salvation put as many baits and enticements in our path as they please. Let them stand continually at our heart's door in order to gain entrance. Let them make all the proposals they wish. As long as we remain steadfast in our resolutions not to take pleasure in the temptation, it is utterly impossible for us to offend God, any more than the prince married to the princess I referred to could take offense at his spouse because of the message if she took no pleasure whatever in it. There is the difference, however, between her and our soul. When she hears that evil proposal she may, if she likes, drive away the messenger and never let him show himself again in her presence. On the other hand, our soul does not always have power not to feel the temptation but it can always refuse consent to it. Therefore, no matter how long a temptation lasts it cannot harm us so long as it displeases us.

As to the delight that may follow a temptation, it must be noted that there are two parts in the soul, the inferior and the superior. The inferior part does not always follow the superior part but acts apart by itself. Hence it often happens that the inferior part takes delight in the temptation without actually giving consent and does so even against the will of the superior part. This is the warfare the apostle describes when he says that "the flesh lusts against the spirit,"[3] and that there is a law of the members and a law of the spirit.[4]

Have you ever seen a large fire covered over with ashes, Philothea? Ten or twelve hours later when someone comes looking for fire, he finds a little in the center of the hearth and even that little is found with difficulty. Yet there it was, since it is found there, and from it he can again light up the other coals which had died out. It is the same with charity, our spiritual life, in the midst of great, violent temptations. Temptation drives the delight accompanying it deep into the interior part of the soul, covers the entire soul with ashes, and reduces the love of God to a narrow space. It appears nowhere except in the very center of the heart and the interior of the soul, and even there it seems scarcely perceptible and is found only with great difficulty. Yet in spite of all the trouble and disorder we feel in both soul and body it is really there. We still keep our resolution never to consent to either the sin or the temptation. Moreover, delight that pleases the outward man displeases the inward man. Hence even though it surrounds the will, it is not inside it. By this we see that such delight is involuntary and as such it cannot be sinful.

4. TWO GOOD ILLUSTRATIONS OF THE SUBJECT

Since it is important to have a thorough understanding of this matter, I do not hesitate to explain it at greater length. St. Jerome speaks[1] of a young man who was skillfully tied by silk cords to a soft bed and was there aroused by every kind of vile touch and enticement by a depraved woman lying with him for the express purpose of breaking his resolution. It was impossible for him not to experience improper sensations. His senses must have been seized with delight and his imagination completely filled with those voluptuous images. It must have been so, yet under such attacks, amid so terrible a storm of temptations, and among such pleasures on every side of him, he proved that his heart was not vanquished and that his will did not give any consent. Since his mind saw all that was in rebellion against him and that he had no bodily part under control except his tongue, he bit it off with his teeth and spat it into the face of the vile woman who tormented his soul more cruelly by her lust than executioners could have done with their worst torments. The tyrant who had despaired of conquering him by torture had thought he could overcome him by such pleasures.

There is a striking story about St. Catherine of Siena's struggle on a similar occasion.[2] The evil spirit was permitted by God to assail this holy virgin's purity with the greatest possible fury and since he was not allowed to touch her he made every kind of impure suggestion to her heart. To move her more effectively, he and his companions came in the form of men and women and before her committed thousands and thousands of lascivious carnal acts, adding to them the filthiest words and solicitations. Although all these were done outside her yet they penetrated through her senses deep into her virginal heart. As she herself confessed, her heart was filled with them to the very brim so that except for the pure higher will there remained nothing within her unshaken by this storm of filth and carnal pleasure. This temptation continued for a long time until our Lord one day appeared to her and she said to him, "Where were you, my sweet Lord, when my heart was filled with such great darkness and filth?" He answered, "My daughter, I was within your heart." "But how could you dwell within my heart where there was so much impurity?" she asked, "Is it possible that you could dwell in so foul a place?" Our Lord replied to her, "Tell me, did the filthy thoughts within your heart bring you pleasure or gloom, grief or delight?" and she said, "The very greatest grief and gloom." He replied, "Who placed this great grief and gloom in your heart but me who remained hidden in the very center of your soul? My daughter, believe me, if I had not been present there those thoughts which beset your will and which you could not drive away would certainly have conquered and entered into it. Once accepted with pleasure by your free will, they would have brought death to your soul. Since I was present within you, I put that displeasure and resistance in your heart and thus enabled it to reject the temptation as far as it could. When unable to do as much as it wanted to it felt still greater displeasure and dislike for both the temptation and for itself. Thus these trials have been a great source of merit and profit for you and have greatly increased your strength and virtue."

See how the fire was covered over with ashes and how temptation and pleasure had even entered her heart and surrounded her will. By our Savior's help, her will alone resisted, showed grief, displeasure, and detestation of the evil proposed to her, and steadfastly refused to give consent to sins on every side. O God, how distressful it must be for a soul that loves God not even to know whether he is within it or not or whether the divine love for which it fights is completely extinct within it or not! It is the finest flower of perfect heavenly love to make the lover suffer and fight for love without knowing whether he possesses the love for which and by which he fights.

5. ENCOURAGEMENT FOR A SOUL UNDER TEMPTATION

God permits violent assaults and strong temptations such as these, Philothea, only in souls whom he desires to raise up to his own pure and surpassing love, but it does not follow that they shall later attain it. It has often happened that those who have remained steadfast during such violent attacks have afterwards been overcome by very slight temptations because they have not faithfully responded to God's grace. I tell you this so that if you ever happen to be attacked by strong temptations you can know that God confers an extraordinary favor on you. By it he declares that he wants to make you great in his sight but that you must always be humble and self-fearful. Your only assurance that you will be able to overcome little temptations even after you have prevailed over great ones is by constant fidelity to his Majesty. No matter what temptations may come to you and no matter what pleasure accompanies them, as long as your will refuses consent not only to the temptation but also to the pleasure, they should not disturb you since God is not offended by them.

When a man has suffered an apoplectic stroke so severe that he shows no sign of life the doctor lays his hand on his heart. If he feels even the least movement he concludes that he is alive and that by using some restorative or poultice he can restore the man's strength and consciousness. In like manner it sometimes happens that before violent temptations our soul seems to have suffered complete loss of strength and is so stricken that it no longer has any spiritual life or movement. If we want to know how it is with ourselves let us lay our hand on our heart. Let us see whether heart and will still retain their spiritual movement, that is, let us see whether they have done their duty by refusing to consent and to yield to temptation and pleasure. As long as this act of refusal remains within our heart we may rest assured that charity, the life of the soul, remains within us, and that Jesus Christ our Savior, although hidden and covered over, is present in our soul. Hence by means of the continued practice of prayer, the sacraments, and confidence in God, our strength will return and we will live a healthful and happy life.

6. HOW TEMPTATION AND PLEASURE MAY BECOME SINFUL

The princess we spoke of could not stop that vile proposal being made to her because, as was presupposed, it was made against her will. On the contrary, if she had given it the least encouragement or shown herself willing to give her love to the suitor, she certainly would have been guilty with regard to his solicitation. No matter how she might cover it over, she would deserve both condemnation and punishment. Similarly, it sometimes happens that the temptation itself involves us in sin because we are ourselves its cause. For example, I know that whenever I gamble I voluntarily give way to anger and blasphemy and that gambling offers me temptation to this. I commit sin as often as I gamble and am responsible for all the temptations that assail me while gambling. In the same way, if I know that certain associations will expose me to temptation and to giving way and yet willingly go there, I am undoubtedly guilty of all the temptations I encounter there.

At times the pleasure proceeding from the temptation can be avoided. Hence it is always a greater or less sin to permit the temptation in proportion as the pleasure taken or the consent given is great or small or long or short in duration. The young princess before alluded to would be culpable if after hearing the foul, indecent proposal made to her she took pleasure in it and entertained her heart with satisfaction in so improper a subject. Although she does not consent to the actual deed proposed to her, still by taking pleasure in it she consents to give her heart in a spiritual way to the evil act. It is always sinful to turn either your heart or your body to anything immodest, although the sin depends so much on the heart's consent that without it even giving the body could not be a sin. Hence, whenever tempted to any sin, consider whether you have voluntarily given occasion to the temptation. In that case the temptation itself puts you in a state of sin on account of the danger you have exposed yourself to. This must be understood of times when you could have conveniently avoided the occasion of the temptation. If you have in no way given occasion to the temptation it can in no way be charged against you as a sin.

When pleasure follows the temptation and could have been avoided but was not, there is always some kind of sin according to the amount of time it is dwelt on and the pleasure taken in it. A woman who has not given occasion to a flirtation but still enjoys it must be censured if the pleasure issues solely from the flirtation and not from some other source. But for example, if the ladies' man who seeks her love is an accomplished lute player and she takes pleasure not in his attempt to win her but in the harmony and sweetness of the music, there would be no sin. However, she should not indulge for long in such pleasure for fear that she should pass from it to pleasure in his suit. Similarly, suppose that someone proposes to me a clever way of taking revenge on an enemy of mine and I neither delight in it nor consent in any way to the proposed revenge but am pleased only with the subtlety of this artful plan. Although this would not be a sin, it would not be well to amuse myself long with such pleasure for fear that little by little I might be led to take some delight in the revenge itself.

Sometimes we are caught off guard by certain symptoms of pleasure immediately following a temptation. At most this can be only a very slight venial sin. However, it becomes greater if after we perceived the evil that has befallen us we carelessly delay for some time and dally with the pleasure to decide whether we ought to allow or reject it. The sin becomes still greater if after becoming aware of the pleasure we dwell on it for some time through downright negligence and without any determination to reject it. When we voluntarily and with full deliberation resolve to take pleasure in such delights, this deliberate purpose is of itself a great sin if the object in which we take delight is also very evil. It is a serious vice for a woman to desire to entertain illicit advances although she never plans actually to yield herself to a lover.

7. REMEDIES AGAINST GREAT TEMPTATIONS

As soon as you are conscious of being tempted, follow the example of children when they see a wolf or bear out in the country. They immediately run to the arms of their father or mother or at least call to them for help and protection. Turn in the same way to God and implore his mercy and help. This is the remedy our Lord himself has taught us: "Pray that you do not enter into temptation."[1]

If you find that the temptation still continues or even increases, run in spirit to embrace the Holy Cross as if you saw Christ Jesus crucified before you. Insist that you will never consent to the temptation, implore his assistance against it, and continue steadfastly to protest that you will refuse consent as long as the temptation continues. When you make such protestations and refusals of consent, do not look the temptation in the face but look solely at our Lord. If you look at the temptation, especially when it is strong, it may shake your courage.

Turn your thoughts to some good, commendable activity. When such thoughts enter and find place in your heart, they will drive away temptations and evil thoughts.

The sovereign remedy against all temptation, whether great or small, is to open your heart and express its suggestions, feelings, and affections to your director. Note well that the first condition the evil one makes with a soul he desires to seduce is for it to keep silence, just as those who want to seduce girls or women from the very first forbid them to say anything about their proposals to father or husband. On the other hand, in his inspirations God requires that we make the temptations known to our superiors and directors.

If temptation continues to harass and persecute us after all this, there is nothing further to do on our part but to remain steadfast in our protestations never to consent to it. Just as girls can never be married as long as they say no, so too a soul though tempted can never sin as long as it says no.

Never argue with your enemy or answer him with any words but those of our Savior when he put him to rout: "Begone, Satan, 'the Lord your God shall you adore and him only shall you serve!' "[2] A chaste wife must never answer a single word to the base wretch that makes her a dishonorable proposal, nor should she look him in the face. Without any discussion she must leave him abruptly and at the same instant turn her heart toward her husband and renew the fidelity she has promised him. So also when a devout soul sees itself attacked by temptation, it must not lose time in argument or discussion but with all simplicity turn toward Jesus Christ, its spouse, and affirm again its fidelity to him and its desire to be solely and entirely his forever.

8. WE MUST RESIST SMALL TEMPTATIONS

While we must resist great temptations with unconquerable courage and while the victory we gain over them is in the highest degree helpful to us, it may be that we will profit more by resisting small temptations. Although great temptations exceed in quality, small ones immeasurably exceed in number so that victory over them may be comparable to that gained over greater temptations. Wolves and bears are certainly more dangerous than flies but don't give us as much trouble or try our patience as much. It is easy enough to refrain from murder but it is extremely difficult to restrain all the little angry feelings for which occasions are offered at every moment. It is easy enough for a man or woman to refrain from adultery, but it is not so easy to guard one's glances, refrain from giving or taking signs of love, procuring gifts or little favors, or speaking or listening to flattering words. It is easy enough not to admit a rival of husband or wife as to the body, but not so easy not to admit one as to the heart. It is easy enough to refrain from defiling the marriage bed, but it is difficult to refrain from everything that may be harmful to conjugal affection. It is easy enough not to steal our neighbor's property, but it is difficult not to desire and covet it. It is easy enough not to bear false witness in court, but it is difficult not to lie in conversation. It is easy enough to refrain from drunkenness, but it is difficult to maintain sobriety. It is easy enough not to desire another man's death, but it is difficult not to desire something harmful to him. It is easy enough to abstain from slandering a man, but it is difficult not to despise him.

In a word, these little temptations to anger, suspicion, jealousy, envy, fond love, frivolity, vanity, affection, craftiness, and evil thoughts continually attack even the most devout and resolute. For this reason,

my dear Philothea, we must carefully prepare ourselves for such combat. Let us rest assured that for as many victories as we gain over these
trifling enemies so many precious stones will be added to the crown of
glory that God prepares for us in paradise. Therefore I say that while
being always ready to fight well and valiantly against great temptations
if they come, we must in the meantime diligently defend ourselves
against attacks that seem small and weak.

9. REMEDIES TO BE TAKEN AGAINST SMALL TEMPTATIONS

Now then as to these smaller temptations to vanity, suspicion, impatience, jealousy, envy, foolish love, and such like deceptive things
which like flies and gnats continually hover before our eyes and sometimes sting our cheeks or nose, since it is impossible to be completely
free from being plagued by them our best defense is not to disturb ourselves too much over them. They may annoy us, but they can never
harm us as long as we remain firmly resolved to serve God.

Despise these petty assaults and do not deign even to think of what
they propose. Let them buzz about your ears as much as they like and flit
around you on every side like flies. When they try to sting you and you
see that they somehow light on your heart, be content with quietly removing them. Don't do this by struggling or disputing with the temptations but by performing some actions of a contrary character, especially
acts of love of God. If you follow my advice, you will not persist in op-
posing the temptation with the contrary virtue—this would be to dispute
with it—but after performing an act of that directly contrary virtue, then
if you have time to observe the nature of the temptation, turn your heart
gently toward Jesus Christ crucified and lovingly kiss his sacred feet.

This is the best way to overcome the enemy in small as well as in great
temptations. As the love of God contains within itself every perfection of

every virtue and more excellently than the virtues themselves, so also it is the sovereign antidote against vice of every kind. By accustoming your mind at such times to turn to this remedy, you do not need even to consider and examine the kind of temptation by which it has been disturbed. At the bare perception of trouble this great remedy will set your mind at rest. Moreover, this is so terrifying to the evil spirit that as soon as he sees that his temptations urge us on to God's love he ceases to tempt us.

Let this suffice with respect to these little ordinary temptations. The man who would strive against them one by one would give himself great trouble and accomplish nothing.

10. HOW TO STRENGTHEN OUR HEART AGAINST TEMPTATION

Consider from time to time which passions are most predominant in your soul. When you have discovered them adopt a way of life that will be completely opposed to them in thought, word, and action. For example, if you find that you are inclined to the passion of vanity, reflect often on the miseries of human life. Think of the dismay that these vain deeds will raise in your conscience on the day of your death, of how unworthy they are of a generous heart, how they are nothing more than the toys and games of little children, and similar things. Speak out often against vanity and no matter what repugnance you feel do not cease to despise it. By such means you will stake your reputation on the opposite side. If we denounce a thing we bring ourselves to hate it, although previously we may have had great affection for it. Perform as many works of abjection and humility as possible, even though they may be done very reluctantly. By this means you accustom yourself to humility and wear down vanity, so that when temptation comes, you will be less inclined to consent and have greater strength to resist it.

If you are inclined to avarice, think often about how foolish a sin is that makes us slaves of what was only made to serve us. Remember that at death we must give it all up and leave it in the hands of someone who may squander it or to whom it may be a cause of ruin and damnation, and have similar thoughts. Speak clearly against avarice, have great praise for contempt of this world, force yourself to give alms generously and to perform acts of charity, and pass up chances to make profits.

If you are inclined to give or accept fond love, think often about how dangerous such amusement is both to yourself and to others, about what a degrading thing it is to profane and use as an idle pastime the noblest affection our souls can have, and about how greatly such extreme frivolity of mind deserves to be condemned. Speak often in praise of purity and simplicity of heart, and as far as possible by avoiding all affectations and flirtations always make your deeds conform to your words.

In short, in time of peace, that is, when not bothered by temptations to a sin you are prone to, perform many acts of the contrary virtue and if occasions to do so do not present themselves seek them out. By such means you will strengthen your heart against future temptations.

11. ANXIETY

Anxiety is not a simple temptation but a source from which and by which many temptations arise and for this reason I will say something concerning it. Sadness is merely the grief of mind we have because of an evil experienced contrary to our will. The evil may be external, like poverty, sickness, or contempt, or internal, like ignorance, aridity, discontent, or temptation. When the soul perceives that it has suffered a certain evil, it is displeased at having it and hence sadness follows. The soul immediately desires to be free of it and to have some means of getting rid of it. Thus far the soul is right, for everyone naturally desires to embrace good and flies from what he thinks to be evil.

If it is out of love for God that the soul seeks escape from its troubles, it will do so patiently, meekly, humbly, and calmly and look for deliverance rather by God's providence than its own efforts, industry, or diligence. If it seeks deliverance because of self-love then, as if success depended on itself rather than on God, it will excite and wear itself out in its search for means of escape. I do not say that the soul thinks so but that it acts as if it thought so. Now if it does not immediately succeed in the way it wants it grows very anxious and impatient. Instead of removing the evil, it increases it and this involves the soul in great anguish and distress together with such loss of strength and courage that it imagines the evil to be incurable. You see, then, that sadness, which is justified in the beginning, produces anxiety, and anxiety in turn produces increase of sadness. All this is extremely dangerous.

With the single exception of sin, anxiety is the greatest evil that can happen to a soul. Just as sedition and internal disorders bring total ruin on a state and leave it helpless to resist a foreign invader, so also if our heart is inwardly troubled and disturbed it loses both the strength necessary to maintain the virtues it had acquired and the means to resist the temptations of the enemy. He then uses his utmost efforts to fish in troubled waters, as they say.

Anxiety proceeds from an inordinate desire to be freed from a present evil or to acquire a hoped for good. Yet there is nothing that tends more to increase evil and prevent enjoyment of good than to be disturbed and anxious. Birds stay caught in nets and traps because when they find themselves ensnared they flutter about wildly trying to escape and in so doing entangle themselves all the more. Whenever you urgently desire to escape from a certain evil or to obtain a certain good you must be especially careful both to put your mind at rest and in peace and to have a calm judgment and will. Then try gently and meekly to accomplish your desire, taking in regular order the most convenient means. When I say gently I do not mean carelessly but without hurry, trouble, or anxiety. Otherwise, instead of obtaining the effect you desire you will spoil everything and cause yourself all the more trouble.

"My soul is constantly in my hands, O Lord, yet I do not forget your law,"[1] said David often during the day or at least at morning and evening. See if you have your soul "in your hands" or if some passion or fit of anxiety has robbed you of it. Consider whether you have command over your heart or if it has slipped out of your hands and into some disorderly passion of love, hatred, envy, covetousness, fear, uneasiness, or joy. If it has gone astray, look for it before doing anything else and bring it quietly back into God's presence, subjecting all your affections and desires to the obedience and direction of his divine will. Just as men who are afraid of losing some valuable object hold it firmly in their hands, so also in imitation of this great king, we must always say, "O my God, my soul is in danger. Hence I always carry it in my hands, and in this way I have not forgotten your holy law."

No matter how small or trivial your desires may be, do not let them disturb you. After little desires greater and more important ones may find your heart still more involved in trouble and disorder. When you perceive that anxiety begins to affect your mind, recommend yourself to God. Resolve to do nothing that your desire insists on until your mind has regained peace, unless it is something that cannot be put off. In that case you must meekly and calmly try to check the current of your desires and restrain and moderate them as much as possible. This done, perform the action, not according to your desire but according to reason.

If you can reveal the cause of your anxiety to your spiritual director, or at least to some faithful and devout friend, you may be sure that you will speedily find relief. To share your heart's grief with others produces the same effect in the soul as bleeding does in the body of a man in a constant fever. It is the remedy of remedies. St. Louis the king gave this counsel to his son: "If your heart is disturbed in any way tell it immediately to your confessor or to some reliable person. In this way you will be enabled to endure the evil very easily because of the relief he will bring you."[2]

12. SORROW

"Sorrow that is according to God produces penance that surely tends to salvation, whereas the sorrow that is according to the world produces death,"[1] says St. Paul. Sorrow, then, can be either good or evil according to its different ways of affecting us. True enough, it produces more bad effects than good for it has only two good effects, namely, compassion and repentance, whereas it has six evil effects, namely, anxiety, sloth, wrath, jealousy, envy, and impatience. This caused the Wise Man to say that "sorrow has brought death to many and there is no profit in it."[2] For two good streams flowing from sorrow as their source, there are six that are very evil.

The enemy uses sorrow to set temptations before good men. Just as he tries to make the wicked rejoice in their sins, so also he tries to make the good grieve over their virtues and good works, and just as he cannot bring men to do evil except by making it look attractive, so also he cannot turn us away from good except by making it look disagreeable. The evil one is pleased with sadness and melancholy because he himself is sad and melancholy and will be so for all eternity. Hence he desires that everyone should be like himself.

Evil sorrow disturbs and upsets the soul, arouses inordinate fears, creates disgust for prayer, stupefies and oppresses the brain, deprives the mind of prudence, resolution, judgment, and courage, and destroys its strength. In a word, it is like a severe winter which spoils all the beauty of the country and weakens all the animals. It takes away all sweetness from the soul and renders it disabled and impotent in all its faculties.

If you are ever caught by this evil kind of sorrow, Philothea, apply the following remedies. "Is any one of you sad?" asks St. James, "Let him pray."[3] Prayer is a sovereign remedy for it lifts up the soul to God who is our only joy and consolation. In your prayers make use of words and affections, whether interior or exterior, that tend to confidence in

God and to his love, such as, "O God of mercy!" "My most good God!" "My sweet Savior!" "O God of my heart, my joy and my hope!" "My cherished Spouse!" "Well-beloved of my soul!" and the like.

Oppose vigorously any tendency to sadness. Although it may seem that everything you do at this time is done coldly, sadly, and sluggishly, you must persevere. By means of sorrow the enemy tries to make us weary of good works, but if he sees that we don't give them up and that being done in spite of his opposition they have become very meritorious, he will stop troubling us. Sing spiritual canticles for the evil one has often ceased work because of them. When an evil spirit besieged or even possessed Saul its violence was checked by the singing of psalms.[4]

It is also good to occupy ourselves in exterior works and to vary them as much as possible. This is done to divert the soul from depressing subjects and to purify and warm our spirits, for sorrow is a passion found in cold, dry dispositions.

Perform fervent external actions even though it may be without relish, such as embracing the crucifix, clasping it to your breast, kissing the feet and hands, lifting up your eyes and hands to heaven, and raising your voice to God in words of love and confidence like these: "My beloved to me, and I to him."[5] "A bundle of myrrh is my Beloved to me: he shall abide between my breasts."[6] "My eyes strain after you, O my God, saying, 'When will you comfort me?' "[7] "O Jesus, be a Jesus to me." "Live, Jesus, and my soul shall live!" "Who shall ever separate me from the love of God,"[8] and the like.

Moderate use of the discipline is also good against sadness because such voluntary affliction is a prayer for interior consolation and when the soul feels pain from without it turns away from pains within it. To receive Holy Communion frequently is excellent, for this heavenly bread strengthens the heart[9] and brings joy to one's spirit.

Humbly and sincerely reveal to your confessor all the feelings, affections, and suggestions that proceed from your sadness. Try to talk to spiritual persons and be with them as much as you can during this period. Last of all, resign yourself into God's hands and be ready to suffer patiently this distressing sadness as a just punishment of your vain joys. Do not doubt that after God has put you on trial he will deliver you from this evil.

13. CONCERNING SPIRITUAL AND SENSIBLE CONSOLATIONS AND HOW WE MUST CONDUCT OURSELVES IN THEM

God conserves this great world in existence amid constant change wherein day unceasingly turns into night, spring into summer, summer into autumn, autumn into winter, and winter into spring. One day is never perfectly like another: some are cloudy, some rainy, some dry, and some windy. Such variety gives great beauty to the universe. It is the same with man, who, according to a saying of the ancients, is an epitome of the world.[1] He never remains in the same state. His life on earth flows away like waters that float and undulate in a perpetual diversity of movement. Sometimes they buoy him up in hope and sometimes they cast him down in fear. Sometimes they carry him to the right hand by consolation, sometimes to the left by affliction. Not one of his days, not even one of his hours, is completely like another.

For us there is a great lesson in all this. We must try to keep our heart steadily, unshakeably equable during such great inequality of events. Even though everything turns and changes around us, we must always remain unchanging and ever looking, striving, and aspiring toward God. No matter what course the ship may take, no matter whether it sails to the east, west, north, or south, no matter what wind drives it on, the mariner's needle never points in any direction except toward the fair polar star. Everything may be in confusion not only around us, I say, but within us as well. Our soul may be overwhelmed with sorrow or joy, with sweetness or bitterness, with peace or trouble, with light or darkness, with temptation or repose, with pleasure or disgust, with aridity or tenderness, it may be scorched by the sun or refreshed by the dew—for all that, ever and always our heart's point, our spirit, our higher will, which is our compass, must unceasingly look and tend toward the love of God, its Creator, its Savior, its sole and sovereign good. "Whether we live or whether we die," says the apostle, "if we are of God, who shall separate us from the love and charity of God?"[2] No, nothing shall ever separate us from this love. Neither tribulation, nor anguish, nor death, nor life, nor present sorrow, nor fear of future troubles, nor the wiles of evil spirits, nor the height of consolation, nor the depth of affliction, nor tenderness, nor aridity must ever separate us from that holy charity which is founded on Jesus Christ.[3]

This absolute resolution never to forsake God and never to abandon his merciful love serves our soul as a counterweight to keep it in a holy equilibrium amid all the inequality of the various changes brought to it by the conditions of this life. When caught out in the fields by a storm little bees pick up small stones so that they can keep their balance in the air and not be easily carried away by the wind. So also when our soul has made its resolution and firmly embraced God's precious love, it keeps steady amid the inconstancy and change that come from consolations and afflictions, whether spiritual or temporal and whether exterior or interior. In addition to this general doctrine, we need certain particular instructions.

1. I hold that devotion does not consist in the sweetness, delight, consolation, and sensible tendeness of heart that move us to tears and sighs and bring us a certain pleasant, relishful satisfaction when we perform various spiritual exercises. No, dear Philothea, devotion is not identical with such things. Many souls experience these tender, consoling feelings but still remain very vicious. Consequently, they do not have true love of God, much less true devotion. When Saul was in deadly pursuit of poor David, who had fled from him into the wilderness of Engaddi, he went alone into a cave where David and his men lay

hidden. At that time David had many opportunities to kill Saul but he spared his life and did not even want to frighten him. After he let Saul leave in safety, he called out to prove his innocence and show Saul that he had been at his mercy. Did Saul then refrain from showing that his heart had softened toward David? He called him his child, wept aloud, praised him, admitted his mercy, and commended him to his posterity. What greater display of sweetness and tenderness of heart could he make? For all that, Saul's heart had not changed and he did not stop persecuting David just as cruelly as before.[4]

In like manner, some men think about God's goodness and our savior's passion, feel great tenderness of heart, and are thus aroused to utter sighs, tears, and prayers, and acts of thanksgiving so ardently that we say their hearts have been filled with intense devotion. But when a test comes, we see how different it is. Just as in the hot summer passing showers send down great drops that fall on the earth but do not sink into it and serve only to produce mushrooms, so also these tender tears fall on a vicious heart but do not penetrate inside and are completely useless to it. In spite of all this show of devotion such unfortunate people will not part with a single penny of their ill-gotten riches; they will not give up one of their perverse affections; they will not endure the least temporal inconvenience for the service of that Savior over whose sufferings they have just been weeping. The good feelings they experience are no better than spiritual mushrooms. Not only are they not true devotion but very often they are tricks played by the enemy. He charms such souls with these trifling consolations to make them content and satisfied with such things, and keep them from further search for true, solid devotion. True devotion consists in a constant, resolute, prompt, and active will to do whatever we know is pleasing to God.

A child will weep tenderly when it sees its mother bled by the lancet, yet if the very mother for whom he is weeping asks for the apple or piece of candy he holds in his hand, he won't part with it. Such for the most part are our own tender devotions. When we meditate on the stroke of the lance that pierced the heart of Jesus Christ crucified we shed tender tears. Alas, Philothea, it is a good thing to lament the sorrowful death and passion of our Father and Redeemer. Why then do we not give him in earnest the apple that we hold in our hands and that he so urgently asks of us? Why do we not give him our heart, the sole apple of love that this dear Savior asks from us? Why don't we turn over to him all those petty affections, delights, and pleasures he wants to pluck out of our hands but cannot because they are our sweets and we love them more than his heavenly grace? Ah! this is the friendship of little children, tender indeed, but weak, wilful, and useless. Devotion does not consist in sensible affections, for sometimes they issue from a soft nature susceptible to any impression we wish to stamp on it and sometimes from our enemy who, to lure us on, excites our imagination to conceive such effects.

2. Still these tender, delightful affections are sometimes very good and useful. They arouse the affections of our soul, strengthen our spirit, and add holy joy and cheerfulness to active devotion. All this makes our actions lovely and pleasing even in their outward appearance. The relish found in the things of God caused David to cry out, "O Lord, how sweet are your words to my palate! more than honey to my mouth!"[5] Surely, the least consolation we receive from devotion is in every way preferable to the world's most delightful amusements! The breasts and milk, that is, the favors of our divine Spouse are sweeter to the soul than the most precious wine[6] of earthly pleasures. The man who has once tasted such sweetness holds all other consolation to be mere gall and wormwood. One who eats the herb called scitic finds that it has so sweet a taste that he does not feel hungry or thirsty.[7] So also a man who to whom God has given the heavenly manna of interior delight and consolation can neither desire nor accept this world's consolations, at least so far as to set his desires upon them and solace his affections with them. They are small foretastes of the immortal delights God gives to souls that seek him. They are little delicacies that he gives

to his children to lure them to himself. They are cordials that he gives to comfort them and sometimes too they are an earnest of eternal rewards. It is said that Alexander the Great while sailing the high seas discovered Arabia Felix because he smelled the fragrant odors the wind blew from there and this aroused both his spirits and the hearts of all his companions.[8] So too on the sea that is our mortal life we often sense these sacred consolations and they undoubtedly give us a foretaste of the delights of the heavenly fatherland to which we strive and aspire.

3. You may object that certain sensible consolations are good and come from God, while others are useless, dangerous, and even pernicious and come either from nature or from the enemy himself. How shall I distinguish the one from the other or know the evil or useless from the good? With regard to the affections and passions of the soul, dearest Philothea, the general teaching is that we must know them by their fruits.[9] Our hearts are trees, affections and passions are branches, and works or actions are fruits. A heart with good affections is good and those affections and passions are good which produce in us good effects and holy actions. If these delights, tender feelings, and consolations make us more humble, patient, adaptable, charitable, and sympathetic towards our neighbor, more fervent in mortifying our desires and evil inclinations, more faithful to our exercises, more cooperative and submissive to those we are bound to obey, more sincere in our lives, then, Philothea, they certainly come from God. If they are sweet only to ourselves and make us selfish, harsh, quarrelsome, impatient, obstinate, haughty, presumptuous, and severe to our neighbors while we think that we are little saints and resent being subject to direction or correction, then beyond doubt such consolations are false and pernicious. A good tree does not bear anything but good fruit.[10]

4. Whenever we experience these delights and consolations we must (1) humble ourselves deeply before God and be strictly on guard against saying because of them, "Oh, how good I am." No, Philothea, such goods cannot make us better for, as I have said, devotion does not

consist in them. Let us say, "Oh, how good God is to those who hope in him, to the soul that seeks him."[11] A person having sugar in his mouth cannot say that his mouth is sweet but only that the sugar is sweet. So also although this spiritual sweetness is very good and God who gives it to us is supremely good, it does not follow that the one receiving it is also good. (2) Let us acknowledge that we are still little children who need milk and that we are given these bits of sugar because our minds are still tender and delicate and must have some bait and allurement to entice us to love God. (3) Speaking in general and as to usual conditions, let us later humbly accept these graces and favors and esteem them to be very great not so much because they are such in themselves but because God's hand puts them in our hearts. God is like a mother who to please her child puts pieces of candy one by one into his mouth. If the child has reached the use of reason, he prizes his mother's tender caresses and fondling more than the delicious candy. Thus we see, Philothea, that it is important to taste these delights but it is the delight of all delights to know that it is God's hand, as loving as a mother's, that puts them into our mouths, hearts, souls, and spirit. (4) When we have thus humbly received them, let us use them carefully according to the intention of the giver. What is God's purpose in giving us these sweet consolations? It is to make us sweet toward everyone and loving toward him. The mother gives a piece of candy to her child to induce him to kiss her. Let us then kiss the Savior who grants us these delights. To kiss him is to obey him, keep his commandments, do his will, and follow his desires, in brief, to embrace him with tender obedience and fidelity. Therefore whenever we receive any spiritual consolation, on that very day we must be more diligent in doing good and humbling ourselves. (5) Besides all this we must from time to time renounce such delights, tender feelings, and consolations by withdrawing our heart from them and protesting that although we humbly accept them and love them because God sends them and they arouse us to his love, yet it is not such things that we seek but God and his holy love. It is not the consolations we seek but the Consoler, not their sweetness but the sweet Savior, not their tenderness but him who is the delight of heaven and earth. In this spirit we must resolve to stand fast in a holy love of God even though we may never find any consolation throughout our whole life. We must be ready, as ready on Mt. Calvary as on Mount Tabor,[12] to say, "Lord, it is good for me to be with you, whether you are on the Cross or in your glory." (6) To conclude, I admonish you that if you experience any great abundance of such consolations, tender feelings, tears, delights, or other such extraordinary things, you must confer faithfully with your spiritual director so that you may learn how to moderate and conduct yourself in their regard. It is written, "You have found honey, eat what is sufficient for you."[13]

14. SPIRITUAL DRYNESS AND STERILITY

As long as consolations continue, do as I have just now directed you to do, dearest Philothea. This fine, pleasant weather will not always last. Sometimes you will find yourself deprived and destitute of all feelings of devotion and your soul will seem like barren, sterile desert where there is no path or road leading to God, nor any water[1] of grace to refresh you because of the aridity that now seems to threaten it with complete and absolute desolation. Alas, how greatly does a soul in this state deserve compassion, especially when the evil is violent! Thus in imitation of David it feeds upon tears day and night.[2] At the same time in an attempt to drive the soul to despair the enemy mocks it with countless suggestions to despair and says: "Ah, poor wretch, where is your God? By what path can you find him? Who can ever restore to you the joy of his holy grace?"

What will you do at such a time, Philothea? Look for the source from which this evil has come upon you. It is ourselves who are often the cause of our own sterile, arid state.

1. Just as a mother refuses to give sugar to a child subject to worms, so God holds back consolations from us when we have a foolish complacence in them and are subject to the worms or presumption. "It is good for me that you have humbled me." Yes, O my God, for "before I was humbled I offended you."[3]

2. When we neglect to gather the dear delights of God's love at the proper season, he takes them from us in punishment for our sloth. An Israelite who neglected to gather manna early in the morning could gather none after sunrise for by then it had all melted away.[4]

3. Sometimes we lie on a bed of sensual pleasures and fleeting consolations, as did the sacred Spouse in the Canticles.[5] The Spouse of our soul comes and knocks at our heart's door and inspires us to return to our spiritual exercises. We put him off because we do not want to cast aside those vain amusements and give up those false satisfactions. For this reason he departs and leaves us to wallow in idleness. Later on when we wish to seek him, it is only with great difficulty that we find him. We have justly deserved this since we have been so unfaithful and disloyal to his love as to refuse to share in it in order to seek the things of this world. Ah, if you still retain the flour of Egypt you shall not have the manna from heaven. Bees detest artificial odors and the sweetness of the Holy Spirit is incompatible with the counterfeit delights of the world.

4. The duplicity and subtlety that we use in our confessions and spiritual communications with our director may also produce spiritual aridity and sterility. Since you lie to the Holy Spirit, it is no wonder that he should refuse his consolations. If you will not be sincere and plain as a little child, you will not have the sugar plums that are given to little children.

5. You have glutted yourself with worldly pleasures and it is no wonder that spiritual delights disgust you. There is an old saying that when doves are stuffed with food, they find cherries bitter. "He has filled the hungry with good things, and the rich he has sent away

empty,"[6] says our Lady. Those who are rich with the world's pleasures are incapable of spiritual delights.

6. Have you been careful to preserve the fruits of the consolations you have received? If you have, you shall receive new ones. To him who has more shall be given, but from him who has not kept what was given to him but lost it through his own fault even things he does not yet possess shall be taken away.[7] That is, he will be deprived of graces prepared for him. Rain enlivens plants with leaves but from leafless plants it takes away even the life they might have had since it rots them completely.

For various such reasons we lose the consolations of devotion and fall into a state of spiritual aridity and sterility. We must examine our conscience to see if similar defects are found within ourselves. Philothea, note that this examination is not to be made with anxiety or in too much detail. If we carefully consider our conduct in this regard and find the cause of the evil in ourselves, let us thank God for this discovery. An evil is half cured when its cause is known. On the contrary, if you can find nothing in particular that may seem to have occasioned this aridity, do not be concerned or pry into it but with all simplicity and without further detailed examination, do as I shall now advise.

1. Humble yourself greatly before God in recognition of your own nothingness and misery. Alas, O Lord, what am I when left to myself but parched soil covered with cracks and showing its thirst for his heavenly rain while the wind scatters it and turns it to dust?

2. Call on God and beg him for comfort. "Restore to me the joy of your salvation."[8] "My Father, if it is possible, let this chalice pass from me."[9] "Away, thou barren north wind, who witherest my soul, and come, gentle gale of consolation and blow upon my garden and its good affections will send forth the odor of sweetness."[10]

3. Go to your confessor, open your heart to him, reveal to him all the recesses of your soul, and accept the advice he gives you with the utmost humility and simplicity. God has infinite love for obedience. He

often makes profitable the counsels we take from others, especially those who guide our souls, when otherwise there might appear to be little show of success. Thus he made the waters of the Jordan beneficial to Naaman, after Eliseus without any sign of human reason had ordered Naaman to use them.[11]

4. After all this there is nothing so profitable and fruitful in such states of aridity and sterility as not to have too much longing and desire for release from them. I do not say that we must even wish for release. What I say is that we should not set our heart on it. In this way we give ourselves up to God's pure mercy and special providence so that he may use us to serve him among such thorny and deserted places as long as he wishes to do so. At such times let us say to God, "Father, if it is possible, let this chalice pass from me," but let us courageously add, "But not my will, but yours be done."[12] Let us remain in this state as calmly as we can, for when God sees such holy indifference he will comfort us with many graces and blessings. Thus when God saw that Abraham was resolved to give up his son Isaac, it was sufficient merely to see him in this state of pure resignation. God comforted him with a most pleasing vision and with his sweetest blessings.[13] In all kinds of affliction, whether bodily or spiritual, and in all the distractions or subtractions of sensible devotion we may endure, we must say from the bottom of our hearts and with deep submission, "The Lord has given me these consolations, the Lord has taken them away from me; blessed be his holy name."[14] If we continue in such humility, he will restore to us his delightful favors as he did to Job, who constantly used similar words in his time of desolation.

5. Finally, Philothea, let us never lose courage in time of spiritual aridity and sterility, but patiently wait for the return of consolation, always continuing on our accustomed way. We must not omit any exercises of devotion but if possible multiply our good works. Unable to present liquid sweets to our dear Spouse, let us offer him some that are dry. It is all one to him, provided the heart offering them is perfectly

firm in its resolution to love him. When there is a fine spring, bees make more honey but produce fewer young ones, for when fine weather favors them they are so busy at their harvest out among the flowers that they forget to produce their young. On the other hand, in a cold, stormy spring they produce more young and less honey, for when they cannot go about their business and gather honey they set themselves to work at home at increasing and multiplying their kind. So also it often happens, Philothea, that a soul finds itself in the bright springtime of spiritual consolations and so busily gathers and enjoys them that amid all these sweet delights it produces very few good works. On the contrary, in the midst of the asperity and sterility of spiritual dryness the more it lacks of the consolations of devotion, the more it multiplies good works and abounds in the interior generation of true virtues—patience, humility, self-contempt, resignation, and renunciation of self-love.

Among many persons, especially women, the great mistake is made of believing that the services we perform for God without relish, tenderness of heart, or sensible satisfaction are less agreeable to his divine Majesty. On the contrary, our actions are like roses—they are more beautiful when fresh but stronger and sweeter when dry. In like manner, works performed with tenderness of heart are more pleasant to us—to us, I say, who are concerned only with our own satisfaction. When performed in times of aridity they are sweeter and become more precious in God's sight. Yes, dear Philothea, in arid times our will forces us to serve God as it were by violence; consequently it must be more vigorous and steadfast than in times of consolation. It is no great merit to serve one's king in the piping days of peace and amid the delights of court life. To serve him during the hardships of war and amid troubles and persecutions is a true mark of constancy and fidelity.

Blessed Angela of Foligno says that the prayer most acceptable to God is that which we force and constrain ourselves to say.[15] Such is the prayer we turn to not for the pleasure found in it or because of our own inclination but purely to please God. Against our wishes our will brings us to do this, thus forcing and driving away all aridity and distaste opposed to it. I repeat this as to good deeds of every kind, whether interior or exterior. The greater our repugnance in doing them, the more God esteems and prizes them. In pursuit of virtue the less we consult our own interests, the more the purity of divine love shines forth from them. A child readily kisses his mother when she gives him a lump of sugar, but it is a sign of great love if he kisses her after she has given him wormwood or aloes.

15. CONFIRMATION AND CLARIFICATION OF WHAT HAS BEEN SAID BY A REMARKABLE EXAMPLE

To clarify this entire instruction I will relate an excellent passage from the life of St. Bernard, as I found it stated by a learned and judicious writer.[1] He writes thus:

With almost all those beginning to serve God but not yet experienced in the loss of special graces and in spiritual vicissitudes it is a common thing that when deprived of the sweet taste of sensible devotion and the pleasant light that invites them to hasten forward in the path to God, they soon get out of breath and become weak of soul and sad of heart. Men of good judgment explain this by saying that our rational nature cannot long remain without food and some kind of delight, either heavenly or earthly. Souls lifted up above themselves by the enjoyment of spiritual pleasures easily give up visible objects. So also, when God orders spiritual joy to be taken away from them and they are thus both deprived of corporeal consolations and not yet accustomed to wait patiently for the return of their true sun, they think they are neither in heaven nor on earth and that they shall remain buried in everlasting night. Like babes weaned from the breast, they languish and cry and grow fretful and troublesome to everyone, especially themselves.

The following incident is described in St. Bernard's biography as happening to one of a group making a journey, a certain Geoffrey of Peronne, who had recently dedicated himself to God's service. Suddenly left in a state of aridity, deprived of all consolation, and plunged into interior darkness, he began to think again about his friends, relations, and the wealth he had just given up. For this reason he was assailed by so violent a temptation that he could not conceal it by his external appearance. One of his closest friends saw this, took occasion to speak mildly to him, and said privately, "Geoffrey, what does this mean? How is it that, contrary to your usual manner, you are so worried and dejected?" Geoffrey answered with a deep sigh, "Ah, my brother, never again will I have any joy in life." The other was so moved to pity at these words that he immediately went to St. Bernard, their common father, who perceived the danger and went to the nearest church to pray to God in Geoffrey's behalf. In the meantime Geoffrey was overwhelmed with grief and fell asleep with his head resting on a stone. Shortly afterwards both men arose, the one from prayer after obtaining the favor he had asked for and the other from sleep. But Geoffrey's face was so pleasant and serene that his dear friend was surprised to see this great and sudden a change and could not help reproaching him in a friendly way for what he had said only a little while before. Geoffrey replied, "If I told you before that I would never again be happy, I now assure you that I shall never again be sad."

That was how the temptation assailing this devout person turned out, dear Philothea, and in the story you can note the following things. (1) God generally grants some foretaste of heavenly delight to those who enter his service in order to draw them away from earthly pleasures and encourage them in the pursuit of his love. He is like a mother who puts honey on her breasts to entice her child to them. (2) It is this same God who according to his wise decision sometimes keeps from us the milk and honey of consolation, so that being weaned in this manner we may learn to feed on the dryer, firmer bread of vigorous devotion, tested and proved by distaste and temptation. (3) Sometimes great storms arise during periods of aridity and sterility and we must fight steadily against such temptations since they are not sent by God. Nevertheless, we must patiently suffer the aridity itself, since God has ordained it for the development of our interior virtue. (4) We must never lose courage during these interior troubles. Nor should we say like the good Geoffrey, "I shall never again have any joy in life." During the night we must wait for the light. On the other hand, during the very finest spiritual weather we must not say, "I shall never again be sad." No, as the Wise Man says, "In the day of good things do not be unmindful of evils."[2] In the midst of afflictions we must have hope and in the midst of prosperity we must fear. Moreover we must remain just as humble during one of these periods as in the other. (5) It is a sovereign remedy to reveal our trouble to a spiritual friend who may be able to comfort us.

Finally, as a conclusion to this indispensable piece of advice, I note that here as in all other things God and our enemy have contrary designs. God seeks to lead us to great purity of heart, renunciation of all self-interest in what relates to his service, and perfect self-denial. On the other hand, the evil one uses such trials to cause us to lose courage, entice us back to sensual pleasures, and finally make us such a burden to ourselves and to others so as to run down and defame holy devotion. Still, if you follow the instructions I have given you you will greatly perfect yourself by the exercises you perform during these interior afflictions. However, I cannot dismiss this important subject without adding a few additional words.

It sometimes happens that distaste, aridity, and sterility come from some bodily indisposition, as when we are overcome by fatigue, drowsiness, indifference, and the like because of protracted vigils, work, or fasting. Although they affect our body, they are such that they also affect our mind because of the close connection between the two. At such times we must not forget to perform various acts of virtue with all the power of our spirit and with our highest will. Although our whole soul seems to be asleep and overcome by drowsiness and fatigue, yet the actions of the superior part do not cease to be most acceptable to God. At the same time we may say with the sacred Spouse, "I was sleeping but my heart kept vigil."[3] As I have observed before, there is less satisfaction in such activity, but there is greater merit and virtue in it. At such times the remedy is to build up strength and vigor by some kind of lawful relief and recreation. Thus St. Francis ordered that his religious should use moderation in their work so as not to weigh down their spiritual fervor.[4]

The glorious father of whom we speak was himself once assailed and disturbed by such deep spiritual melancholy that he could not help showing it in his conduct. If he wanted to talk with his religious he could not do so; if he withdrew from their company it was worse. Abstinence and bodily mortification weighed him down and prayer gave him no relief. He went on in this way for two years, so that he seemed completely abandoned by God. Finally, after he had humbly endured this violent storm, the Savior in a single instant restored him to a happy calm.[5] This means that God's greatest servants are subject to such attacks and that the least of them must not be astonished if they too have to suffer some of them.

THE FIFTH PART OF THE
INTRODUCTION

*Exercises and Instructions for
Renewing the Soul and
Confirming It in Devotion*

1. EACH YEAR WE MUST RENEW OUR GOOD RESOLUTIONS BY THE FOLLOWING EXERCISES

The first point of these exercises consists in becoming thoroughly aware of their importance. Because of the frailty and evil inclinations of the flesh, our nature as men easily forgets its good dispositions. The flesh rests heavily on the soul and constantly drags it downward unless the soul frequently lifts itself up by fervent resolutions, just as birds soon fall to the ground unless they beat their wings again and again to keep themselves in the air. For this reason, dear Philothea, you must often renew and repeat your good resolutions to serve God, so that you don't neglect them and slip back into your former state or rather into one far worse.[1] Spiritual falls have this peculiarity: they always cast us down to a lower state than the one from which we rose up to devotion.

There is no clock, no matter how good it may be, that doesn't need resetting and rewinding twice a day, once in the morning and once in the evening. In addition, at least once a year it must be taken apart to remove the dirt clogging it, straighten out bent parts, and repair those worn out. In like manner, every morning and evening a man who really takes care of his heart must rewind it for God's service by means of the foregoing exercises. Moreover, he must often reflect on his condition in order to reform and improve it. Finally, at least once a year he must take it apart and examine every piece in detail, that is, every affection and passion, in order to repair whatever defects there may be. Again, a watchmaker oils his watch's wheels, springs, and works with delicate oil so that the wheels can move more easily and the whole watch be less subject to rust. So also with a devout person. After he has re-examined his heart in order to renovate it, he must anoint it with the sacraments of confession and Holy Eucharist. Such an exercise will restore your strength, which has been impaired by time, warm up your heart, bring new life to your good resolutions, and make your soul's virtues flourish with fresh vigor. The first Christians were careful to practice this devotion on the anniversary day of our Lord's baptism. On that day, as St. Gregory, bishop of Nazianzus, relates,[2] they renewed the professions and protestations made in that sacrament. Let us also, my dear Philothea, willingly dispose and carefully employ ourselves to follow their example.

After consulting your spiritual director, choosing a convenient time and withdrawing a little more into both spiritual and actual solitude than usual, make one, two, or three meditations on the following points according to the method I have prescribed in the second part.

2. CONSIDERATION OF HOW GOD BENEFITS US BY CALLING US INTO HIS SERVICE ACCORDING TO THE PROTESTATION ALREADY SET DOWN

1. Consider various parts of your protestation.[1] The first is that you have given up, cast away, detested, and renounced forever all mortal sin; the second, that you have dedicated and consecrated your soul, heart, body, and all their faculties to God's love and service; the third, that if you happen to fall into any evil deed, you will immediately rise up again by the help of God's grace. Are not these noble, just, and worthy resolutions? Reflect carefully within your soul on how holy, reasonable, and desirable this protestation is.

2. Think of the one to whom you have made this protestation, for it is to God. If words given to men under reasonable conditions impose strict obligations on us, how much more those which we have given to God! Ah, Lord, said David, "My heart has said it to you. My heart has uttered this good word. No I shall never forget it."[2]

3. Remember in whose presence you have made it, for it is in the sight of the whole heavenly court. Yes, the Holy Virgin, St. Joseph, your guardian angel, St. Louis, and that whole blessed company saw you and upon your words they breathed sighs of joy and approval. With eyes filled with ineffable love they saw your heart as it lay prostrate at the Savior's feet and consecrated itself to his service. Then there was particular joy in the heavenly Jerusalem and now there will be a commemoration of it if you renew your resolutions with a sincere heart.

4. Remember by what means you were led to make your protestation. How sweet and gracious God was to you at that time! Tell me sincerely, were you not summoned by the sweet attractions of the Holy Spirit? Were not the cords by which God drew your little boat to this blessed haven woven out of love and charity?[3] How earnestly God sought to allure you to it by his divine mercy—by the sacraments, spiritual reading, and prayer! Ah, dear Philothea, you were asleep and God

watched over you and over your heart. He thought "thoughts of peace"[4] and meditated for you meditations filled with love.

5. Reflect upon when it was that God inspired you with these holy resolutions, for it was in the flower of your youth. How fortunate it is to learn early that which we can know only too late in life! When called at the age of thirty years, St. Augustine cried out, "O ancient Beauty, why is it that I have known you so late?"[5] Alas! I saw you before but I paid no heed to you. You too may well say, "O ancient Sweetness! why did I not relish you before?" Alas! you did not then deserve it. However, acknowledge the grace God gave you when he drew you to himself in your youth and say with David, "You have taught me, O God, and touched me from my youth; and till the present I will proclaim your wondrous deeds."[6] And if this has happened in your old age, ah, Philothea, what a grace it is that after you had thus misspent all your earlier years, God calls you before your death and now puts an end to your life of misery! If it had continued you would have been in misery for eternity!

6. Consider the effects of this calling. Compare what you now are with what you were. I think you will find a great change for the better. Do you not esteem it fortunate that you can converse with God in prayer, that you have the desire and will to love him, that the great passions that troubled you are now appeased and pacified, that you have avoided innumerable sins and troubles of conscience, and finally that you have received Communion so much oftener than you would have done, thus uniting yourself to that sovereign source of everlasting grace? How great are these favors! Philothea, we must weigh them in the scales of the sanctuary. It is God's right hand that has done all this. "The right hand of the Lord has struck with power," says David. "His right hand has raised me up . . . Ah, I shall not die, but live, and I shall declare"[7] with mouth, and deeds the wonderful works of his bounty!

After all these considerations, which, as you see, furnish you with abundance of devout affections, you should end simply with an act of thanksgiving and a fervent prayer that you may make good use of them.

Retire with the humility and great confidence in God, but do not attempt to form your resolutions until after the second point of this exercise.

3. EXAMINATION OF OUR SOUL ON ITS PROGRESS IN THE DEVOUT LIFE

This second part of the exercise is rather long. I point out that to practice it you do not need to do it all at once but at different times. You may consider your duties toward God at one time, what relates to yourself at another, things relating to your neighbor at a third, and your passions at the fourth. It is neither necessary nor expedient to perform it on your knees, except the beginning and the end, which concern the affections. The other points of the examination you may profitably make while walking outside or still more profitably in bed, provided that you can keep yourself for some time from dozing off and stay wide awake. To do this you must read them carefully beforehand. However, it is necessary to go through the whole of the second point in three days and two nights at most, dedicating as much time to it on each day and night as you conveniently can. If this exercise should be put off to times far apart from one another, it would lose its force and have only a weak effect. After each point of the examination you should note things in which you find that you have failed, in what you are still deficient, and what are the principal disorders that you have discovered. This is in order that you can speak of them so as to obtain advice, resolution, and spiritual direction.

On days when you perform this and the other exercises it is not absolutely necessary to withdraw from all company, but there should be some period of retirement, especially towards the evening, so you can go earlier to bed and get the bodily and mental rest necessary for reflection. During the day you must make frequent aspirations to God, our Lady, the angels, and the whole heavenly Jerusalem. Moreover, all this must be done with a heart that loves God and your soul's perfection.

To begin this examination in the proper manner: (1) Place yourself in the presence of God. (2) Invoke the Holy Spirit. Ask him for light and sight that you may attain a perfect knowledge of yourself. With St. Augustine cry out to God in the spirit of humility, "Lord, let me know you and let me know myself!"[1] and with St. Francis, who asked God, "Lord! who are you and who am I?"[2] Protest that you do not wish to learn of your progress in order to rejoice in yourself but solely to rejoice in God and not to glorify yourself but only to glorify God and give him thanks. (3) Protest likewise that if you find, as you fear you shall, that you made only a little progress, or none at all, or even that you have fallen backward, you will not on that account be depressed or made cold by discouragement or despondency of any sort. On the contrary, protest that you wish to encourage and animate yourself all the more, humble yourself, and correct your faults by the assistance of God's grace.

This done, meekly and calmly consider how you have conducted yourself up to the present hour toward God, your neighbor, and yourself.

4. EXAMINATION OF OUR STATE OF SOUL IN RELATION TO GOD

1. What is your state of soul with respect to mortal sin? Are you firmly resolved never to commit it for any reason whatsoever? Has this resolution continued from the time of your protestation up to the present moment? In this resolution consists the foundation of the spiritual life.

2. How is your heart with regard to God's commandments? Do you find them good, sweet, and pleasant? My child, if a man's sense of taste is in good condition and his stomach is sound he loves good food and rejects bad.

3. How is your heart with regard to venial sin? We cannot keep ourselves so pure as not to fall now and then into such sins, but is there any

of them to which you have a particular inclination? Or what would be still worse, is there any for which you have affection and love?

4. How is your heart with regard to spiritual exercises? Do you like them? Do you esteem them or do they make you ill at ease? Are you repelled by them? Which of them do you prefer—to hear the word of God, read it, or speak about it, to meditate, to aspire to God, to go to confession, receive spiritual counsel, prepare for Communion, receive Holy Communion, to restrain your affections? Is there anything in all this that you find repugnant? If you note anything to which your heart has less inclination, look for the source of such dislike and discover its cause.

5. How is your heart toward God himself. Do you take delight in thinking about him? Does such remembrance leave an agreeable sweetness behind it? "I remembered God, and I was delighted,"[1] said David. Does your heart feel an inclination to love God and a particular satisfaction in dwelling on this love? Does your heart love to reflect on God's immensity, goodness, and sweetness? If remembrance of God comes to you amid worldly affairs and vanities, do you willingly receive it and does it take possession of your heart? Does it seem to you that your heart turns that way and, as it were, runs out to meet God? Certainly there are such souls. When a woman's husband returns home from a distant country, as soon as she knows of his return or hears his voice, even though she is burdened with duties or forcibly detained from him by some urgent need, her heart does not hold back from him but puts away every other thought in order to think of the husband who has returned to her. It is the same with souls that really love God. No matter how busy they are, when remembrance of God comes to them they lose almost the very thought of all other things because of joy that this dear remembrance has returned. This is a very good sign.

6. How is your heart toward Jesus Christ, God and man? Do you place your happiness in him? Honey bees find pleasure in their honey and wasps in decayed things. Similarly, good souls seek happiness in

thinking on Jesus Christ and feel a tender affection toward him, while the wicked take pleasure in vanities.

7. How is your heart toward our Lady, the saints, and your guardian angel? Do you love them firmly? Have you special trust in their patronage? Are their pictures, accounts of their lives, and things said in praise of them dear to you?

8. With regard to language how do you speak of God? Do you find pleasure in speaking well of him according to your state in life and ability? Do you love to sing his praises?

9. As to works: Consider whether you sincerely seek God's external glory and wish to accomplish something in his honor. For those who love God love together with God the adornment of his house.[2]

10. Can you discover that you have sacrificed any affection or given up anything for the sake of God? It is a true sign of love to deprive ourselves of something for the sake of the one we love. What have you given up out of love of God?

5. EXAMINATION OF OUR STATE WITH REGARD TO OURSELVES

1. What kind of love do you have for yourself? Do you love yourself too much for the sake of this world? If so, you will desire to live always here and you will have great care to establish yourself on this earth of ours. If you love yourself for the sake of heaven, you will desire or at least be ready to depart from here below at whatever hour it may please our Lord.

2. Do you observe due order in such self-love? It is only inordinate love of self that ruins us. A well-ordered love requires that we love the soul more than the body, be more solicitous to acquire virtue than anything else, and set a higher value on heavenly than on base and perishable honor. A well-ordered heart will more often ask itself,

"What will the angels say if I think of such a thing?" than "What will men say?"

3. What kind of love have you for your own heart? Isn't it true that you like to cater to its weaknesses? Alas! whenever passions torment it you ought to help it and obtain help for it and for this purpose leave all other things aside.

4. What do you think of yourself in God's sight? Doubtless nothing. For a fly it is no great act of humility to esteem itself nothing in comparison with a mountain, or for a drop of water to hold itself nothing in comparison with the sea, or for a spark or flash of fire to hold itself nothing in respect to the sun. Humility consists in not esteeming ourselves above others and in not desiring to be esteemed by others. Where do you rank in this respect?

5. As to your language: Isn't it true that you sometimes boast of yourself in one way or another? Don't you flatter yourself when you speak about yourself?

6. As to deeds: Don't you take pleasure contrary to good health? I mean vain, useless pleasure, such as staying up too late without reason and the like.

6. EXAMINATION OF OUR STATE OF SOUL WITH REFERENCE TO OUR NEIGHBOR

The love of husband and wife must be sweet, peaceful, firm, and steady and it must be so principally because God orders and wills it. I say the same about love for our children, near relatives, and friends, each according to rank.

But to speak in a general way, how is your heart disposed toward your neighbor? Do you love him with your whole heart and out of love of God? To determine this correctly, you must picture to yourself troublesome and disagreeable persons. It is among them that we exercise love of God toward our neighbor and much more so among those who injure us by deeds or words. Carefully examine your heart to see whether it is well disposed toward them, or whether you find it very disagreeable to love them.

Isn't it true that you are apt to speak ill of your neighbors, especially those who dislike you? Have you done any wrong to your neighbors either directly or indirectly? If you use even a little reason, you will easily judge yourself in this regard.

7. EXAMINATION OF THE AFFECTIONS OF OUR SOUL

I have developed these points in this way because knowledge of our spiritual progress depends on an examination of this kind. An examination of conscience merely as to sins is for the confessions of those who have no thought of advancement in devotion. However, we must not delay too long on any of these points but very calmly consider our state of heart with regard to them since making our resolution and any notable faults we have committed against them.

To shorten the whole matter, we must reduce the examination to an investigation into our passions. If it is inconvenient to consider every particular point, as has been said, we may examine in general what our dispositions have been and how we have conducted ourselves:

In love of God, our neighbor, and ourselves.

In hatred of sins found in ourselves and those found in others, for we must desire the destruction of both.

In desires in relation to riches, pleasures, and honors.

In fear of the danger of sin and of the loss of worldly goods. We fear the second too much and the first too little.

In our hopes, perhaps putting them too much on the world and creatures and too little on God and things eternal.

In sadness, if it is too excessive over useless things.

In joy, if it is excessive and over unworthy things.

Finally, what affections have entangled our heart? What passions possess it? How has it especially gone astray? When we examine the passions of the soul one by one, we pass judgment on its condition. The lute player touches all the strings to find which are out of tune and tunes them either by tightening or loosening them. So also if we examine the passions of love, hatred, desire, hope, sadness, and joy in our soul and find them out of tune for the melody we wish to raise to God's glory, we put them in tune by means of his grace and the counsel of our spiritual father.

8. AFFECTIONS TO BE FORMED AFTER THIS EXAMINATION

After you have calmly considered each point in the examination and have seen the state you are in, you must then proceed to the affections in this manner.

Return thanks to God for whatever small improvement found in your life since making your resolution and acknowledge that it has been his mercy alone that has brought it about in you and for you.

Humble yourself exceedingly before God. Acknowledge that if you are not much improved it has been your own fault, since you have not faithfully, courageously, and constantly corresponded with the inspiration, light, and help he has given you in prayer and at other times.

Promise that you will eternally praise him for the graces he has bestowed on you to draw you away from your own inclinations and make this slight improvement.

Ask his pardon for the infidelity and the disloyalty you have shown him.

Offer him your heart so that he may make himself its sole master.

Beseech him to make you forever faithful to him.

Invoke the saints, the Blessed Virgin, your guardian angel, your patron saint, St. Joseph, and other saints.

9. CONSIDERATIONS PROPER FOR RENEWING OUR GOOD RESOLUTIONS

After you have finished your examination of conscience and conferred with a suitable director concerning your defects and the remedies for them, turn to the following considerations, using one of them each day by way of meditation and spending the time for your mental prayer on it. Always keep to the same method for the preparation and the affections as you did in the meditations of the first part. That is, immediately place yourself in God's presence and then implore his grace to establish you in his holy love and service.

10. FIRST CONSIDERATION: THE EXCELLENCE OF OUR SOUL

Consider the nobility and excellence of your soul. It is endowed with understanding, which knows not only this visible world but also that there are angels and a paradise. It knows that there is a God, most sovereign, most good, and most ineffable. It knows that there is an eternity and knows also what manner is best designed for living well in this visible world so that our soul may be joined with the angels in paradise and enjoy God for all eternity. Moreover, your soul has a most noble will and that will can love God and cannot hate him in himself.

Look into your heart and behold how generous it is. As bees can never remain upon anything decayed but only among flowers, so also our heart finds rest solely in God and no creature can ever satisfy it. Think deeply on the dearest and strongest affections that have filled your heart up to now and judge truthfully whether they were not full of worry and unrest, tormenting thoughts and demanding cares in the midst of which your poor heart was wretched.

Our heart, alas! runs after creatures. It eagerly seeks them, thinking that they will satisfy its desires. As soon as it has obtained them, it sees that it is all to do over again and that nothing can satisfy it. God does not will that our heart should find a place of rest, any more than did the dove that went out from Noah's ark,[1] so that it may return to himself from whom it came. Ah! what natural beauty is there in our heart! Why then do we detain it against its will in the service of creatures?

"O beauteous soul!" you must exclaim, "Since you can know and will God, why do you beguile yourself with any lesser thing? Since you can advance your claim to eternity, why should you beguile yourself with passing things? One of the prodigal son's regrets was that he might have lived in plenty at his father's table whereas he had eaten filth among beasts.[2] O my soul, you are made for God! Woe to you if you are satisfied with anything less than God!" Raise your soul aloft on this consideration. Remind it that it is eternal and worthy of eternity. Fill it with courage for this project.

11. SECOND CONSIDERATION: THE EXCELLENCE OF VIRTUE

Reflect that in this world nothing but virtue and devotion can satisfy your soul. See how beautiful they are. Compare the virtues and their contrary vices. How sweet is patience when compared with revenge! Meekness, compared with anger and vexation! Humility, compared with arrogance and ambition! Liberality, compared with avarice! Charity, compared with envy! Sobriety, compared with dissipation! Virtues have the wonderful quality of delighting our soul with incomparable sweetness and fragrance after we have practiced them, whereas vices leave the soul infinitely weary and distraught. Courage, then! Why do we not strive to gain such delights?

With regard to vices, one who has only a few of them is not contented and one who has too many of them is discontented. But as for virtues, even one who has only a little has some contentment, and this increases as the virtues themselves increase. O devout life! how beautiful, lovely, sweet, and delightful you are! You lighten our tribulations and add sweetness to our consolations. Without you, good is evil and pleasures are filled with unrest, trouble, and deceit! Ah, a man who knew you well could cry out with the Samaritan woman, "*Domine, da mihi hanc aquam*: Lord, give me this water!"[1]—an aspiration frequently made by the holy Mother Teresa and St. Catherine of Siena although upon different occasions.

12. THIRD CONSIDERATION: THE EXAMPLE OF THE SAINTS

Look at the example given by saints in every walk of life. There is nothing that they have not done in order to love God and be his devoted followers. See the martyrs, unconquerable in determination! What torments they suffered to keep their resolutions! Above all, behold those fair and flower-like women, whiter than lilies in purity, redder than the rose in charity, some of whom at twelve, others at thirteen, fifteen, twenty, and twenty-five years of age endured a thousand kinds of martyrdom rather than break their resolution both in their profession of faith and in their protestation of devotion. Some died rather than give up their virginity, others rather than cease from serving the afflicted, consoling the tormented, and burying the dead. O God, what constancy has been shown by this fragile sex in doing such deeds!

Consider the throng of holy confessors. What strength they showed in their contempt of the world! How invincible they proved themselves in their resolutions! Nothing led them to break those vows in any way. They embraced them without reserve and practiced them unswervingly. My God! how wonderful are the things St. Augustine tells about his mother, Monica, and how steadfast was her resolution to serve God in both marriage and widowhood![1] How well St. Jerome speaks of his dear daughter Paula amid so many reverses and so many changing events![2] What might we not do if we look at such excellent patrons? They were what we are. They did this for the same God and for the same virtues. Why then should we not do as much according to our position and vocation in life to keep the cherished resolution and holy protestation that we have made?

13. FOURTH CONSIDERATION: THE LOVE THAT JESUS CHRIST HAS FOR US

Consider the love with which Jesus Christ our Lord has suffered so much in this world, especially in the Garden of Olives and on Mount Calvary. That love was for you and by all his pains and sufferings he won from God the Father those good resolutions and protestations for your heart. By the same means he also obtained whatever you need to keep, nourish, strengthen, and fulfill your resolutions. How precious that resolution is, for it is the daughter of such a mother, my Savior's passion! Oh, how tenderly must my soul cherish you, since you have been so dear to my Jesus! Alas! O Savior of my soul, you died to purchase these resolutions for me! Grant me the grace to die rather than lose them.

See, my Philothea, it is certain that on the tree of the Cross the Heart of Jesus, our beloved, beheld your heart and loved it. By the love he bore it he obtained every good that you shall ever have, among others our resolutions. Yes, dear Philothea, we may all say with the prophet Jeremias, "O Lord, before I was you beheld me and called me by my name."[1] For in his love and mercy God's goodness prepared for us all the general and particular means of salvation, including our good resolutions. Yes, this is certain. Just as an expectant mother prepares cradle, linen, swaddling clothes, and even a nurse for the child she hopes to bring forth, although it is not yet in the world, so also since our Lord's bounty is fruitful and heavy with you and he plans to bring you forth to salvation and make you his child, he prepared on the tree of the cross whatever was necessary for you—a spiritual cradle, linen, swaddling clothes, nurse, and all else needed to make you happy. Such are all those means, all those attractions, all those graces by which he leads your soul and seeks to bring it to perfection.

Ah, my God, how deeply must we imprint this upon our memory! Is it possible that I could have been loved, so tenderly loved, by my Savior that he should think of me in particular even in all these little events by which he has drawn me to himself? How much then must we love and cherish them and turn them all to our own profit! How sweet this is! God's loving heart has thought of Philothea, loved her, and brought her countless means of salvation, so many that it would seem there had been no other soul in the world for him to think of. The sun shines upon a certain spot on the earth and gives it no less light than if it shone nowhere else and shone only for that place. In the very same manner our Lord thinks about all his beloved children and gives them his care. He thinks of each of them as though he did not think of all the others. "He loved me," says St. Paul, "and delivered himself for me."[2] He says "for me alone," as if he had done nothing for the rest. Philothea, these words should be engraved upon your soul so that you may rightly cherish and nourish a resolution that has been so precious to the Savior's heart.

14. FIFTH CONSIDERATION: GOD'S ETERNAL LOVE FOR US

Reflect upon the everlasting love God has had for you. Before our Lord Jesus Christ as man suffered on the Cross for you his Divine Majesty by his sovereign goodness already foresaw your existence and loved and favored you. When did his love for you begin? It began even when he began to be God. When did he begin to be God? Never, for he has been forever, without beginning and without end. So also he has always loved you from all eternity and for this reason he has prepared for you all these graces and favors. Hence he speaks to you as well as to others when he says by the prophet, "I have loved you with an everlasting love, therefore have I drawn you, taking pity on you."[1] Among other things, he has thought of enabling you to make your resolution to serve him.

O God, what resolutions are these which you have thought of and meditated upon and projected from all eternity! How dear and precious should they be to us! What should we not suffer rather than forget the least of them! Rather let the whole world perish! For all the world together is not worth one single soul and a soul is worth nothing without these resolutions.

15. GENERAL AFFECTIONS ON THE PRECEDING CONSIDERATIONS AND CONCLUSION OF THE EXERCISE

Beloved resolutions, you are the fair tree of life that God with his own hand has planted within my heart, the tree my Savior desires to water with his Blood and thus make fruitful! I would rather suffer a thousand deaths than permit any storm to uproot you. No, neither vanity nor delights nor riches nor tribulations shall ever lead me from my purpose. Lord, you yourself have planted and eternally preserved in your paternal breast this fair tree for my garden. Alas! how many souls are there who have not been favored in this manner! How then can I ever sufficiently humble myself beneath your mercy? O fair and holy resolutions, if I keep you, you will keep me; if you live in my soul, my soul will live in you. Live then forever, O resolutions, which are everlasting in the mercy of my God! Live eternally in me, and let me never forsake you!

After such affective acts you must consider the particular means necessary to maintain these cherished resolutions and determine to be faithful in making good use of them. Such means are frequency in prayer, the sacraments, and good works, amendment of faults discovered in the second point, avoiding occasions of evil, and following counsels that will be given you for this purpose. Afterward, by way of regaining your breath and strength, make a thousand protestations that you will presevere in your resolutions. As if holding your heart, soul, and will in your own hands, dedicate, consecrate, sacrifice, and immolate them to God. Affirm that you will never take them back again but leave them in the hand of his Divine Majesty in order to follow everywhere and always his holy ordinances. Beseech God in prayer. Pray to God to make you entirely new and to bless and strengthen your repeated protestations. Invoke the Virgin Mary, your guardian angel, St. Louis, and other saints.

In this state of heart go to your spiritual father and accuse yourself of the principal faults that you find you have committed since your general confession. Receive absolution in the same manner as the first time and pronounce and sign your protestation in his presence. In conclusion, unite your renewed heart to its first principle and Savior in the most holy sacrament of the Eucharist.

16. OUR SENTIMENTS AFTER THIS EXERCISE

On the day you make this renewal and on the following days you must often repeat with all your heart the ardent words of St. Paul, St. Augustine, St. Catherine of Genoa, and others: "No, I am no longer my own. Whether I live or die, I am my Savior's. I no longer have anything in me or of me; my very self is Jesus and my being is his being. O world, you are always yourself and hitherto I have been always myself, but henceforth I will be myself no more." No, we shall no longer be ourselves for we shall have a changed heart and the world, which has so often deceived us, shall be deceived in us. Because it will perceive our change only little by little, it will think that we are like Esau but we shall find ourselves to be like Jacob.

All these exercises must remain embedded in our heart. When we have finished our consideration and meditation we must turn quietly back to our ordinary concerns and associations so that the precious liquor of our resolutions may not be suddenly spilled. It must penetrate throughout every part of the soul but without any mental or bodily effort.

17. ANSWER TO TWO OBJECTIONS THAT MAY BE MADE TO THIS INTRODUCTION

The world will tell you, my Philothea, that these exercises and counsels are so numerous that anyone who wants to practice them must do nothing else. Alas! dear Philothea, should we do nothing else we would do enough for we would do all that we ought to do in this world. But do you not perceive their error? If they were all performed every day without fail, they would then indeed constitute our whole occupation. However, it is not necessary to perform them except at the proper time and place, each one according to the opportunity for it. There are many civil laws in the digests and code and all of them must be observed. However, it is understood that they are to be executed on proper occasions and that not all of them must be observed every day. After all, David, a king charged with the most difficult duties, performed many more exercises than I have prescribed for you. St. Louis, a king who was admirable in both war and peace and administered justice and managed his affairs with unrivalled care, heard two Masses every day, said vespers and compline with his chaplain, made his meditation, visited hospitals, confessed and took the discipline every Friday, heard many sermons, and held many spiritual conferences. With all this, he never let pass a single occasion of promoting the public good without improving it and diligently putting it into effect. Moreover, under him the court was more splendid and flourishing than it had ever been in the time of his predecessors. Perform these exercises confidently, as I have marked them out for you, and God will give you sufficient leisure and strength to perform all your other duties. Yes, even though he should have to make the sun stand still for you, as he did for Joshua.[1] We always do enough when God works with us.

The world will say that I assume throughout almost the whole work that Philothea has the gift of mental prayer, whereas everyone does not have that gift and therefore this *Introduction* will not serve for all. It is certainly true that I have made this assumption and it is also true that not everyone has this gift. It is likewise true that almost all men, even the most ignorant, can have it, provided they have good guides and are willing to take as many pains to obtain it as it deserves. Should there be some who do not have this gift in any degree whatever, which I think will rarely happen, a prudent spiritual director will easily supply this defect. He will instruct them to be sure to read or to have others read to them the considerations included in the meditations.

18. THE THREE LAST AND PRINCIPAL COUNSELS FOR THIS INTRODUCTION

On the first day of every month repeat after your meditation the protestation inserted in the first part. At all times protest that you are determined to observe it, and say with David, "No, my God, your justifications I will never forget."[1] When you feel any disorder in your soul, take up your protestation and, humbly prostrate in spirit, recite it with your whole heart. You will thus find great relief.

State openly that you desire to be devout. I do not say that you should assert that you are devout but that you desire to be devout. Don't be ashamed to practice the ordinary, necessary actions that bring us to the love of God. Acknowledge frankly that you are trying to meditate, that you would rather die than commit a mortal sin, that you are resolved to frequent the sacraments and to follow your director's advice, although sometimes for various reasons it may not be necessary to give his name. This candid confession of our desire to serve God and to consecrate ourselves entirely to his love is most acceptable to his Divine Majesty. He does not want us to be ashamed either of him or of his Cross. Besides, it prevents many arguments the world would offer for the contrary way and binds us in honor to act in keeping with what we profess. The philosophers openly called themselves philosophers so that they might be allowed to live devoutly. If anyone tells you that you may live devoutly without following this advice and these exercises, do not deny it but answer mildly that you are so weak that you need more help and assistance than others do.

In conclusion, my dearest Philothea, I entreat you by all that is sacred in heaven and on earth, by the baptism you have received, by the breasts with which Jesus Christ was nourished, by that loving Heart with which he loved you, and by the bowels of that mercy in which you hope, continue and persevere in this blessed enterprise of the devout life. Our days glide away; death is at the gate. "The trumpet sounds retreat," says St. Gregory Nazianzen, "let every man be ready, for judgment is near."[2] When St. Symphorian's mother saw her son led away to martyrdom, she cried after him, "My son, my son, remember eternal life! Look up to heaven, and think of him who reigns there! Your approaching end will quickly close the brief course of this life."[3] My Philothea, I too say to you, look up to heaven, and do not forfeit it for earth. Look down into hell, and do not cast yourself into it for the sake of fleeting things. Look upon Jesus Christ, and do not renounce him for all the world. And when the labors of a devout life seem hard to you, sing with St. Francis of Assisi:

> *Such are the joys that lure my sight,*
> *All pains grow sweet, all labors light.*[4]

Live, Jesus! to whom, with the Father and the Holy Spirit, be all honor and glory, now and throughout the endless ages of eternity. Amen.

BIBLIOGRAPHY

I

Oeuvres de saint François de Sales, évêque de Genève et docteur de l'église. Editions complète. 26 vols. Annecy: J. Niérat, 1892–1932.

St. Francis de Sales. *On the Love of God.* Translated with an Introduction and Notes by John K. Ryan. 2 vols. Garden City, N.Y.: Doubleday & Company, 1963.

St. Francis de Sales. *On the Preacher and Preaching.* Translated with an Introduction and Notes by John K. Ryan. Chicago: Henry Regnery Company, 1962.

II

Barberis, Giulio. *Vita di san Francesco di Sales.* 3d. ed.; 2 vols. Torino: Società editrice internazionale, 1927.

Brasier, V., Morganti, E., St. Durica, M. *Opere e scritti riguardenti san Francesco di Sales. Repertorio bibliografico 1623–1953.* Torino: Società editrice internazionale, 1956.

Bremond, Henri. *Histoire littéraire du sentiment religieux en France depuis la fin des guerres de religion jusqu'd nos jours*. 11 vols. Paris: Bloud et Gay, 1916–1933.

Bremond, Henri. *Devout Humanism*. Translated by K. L. Montgomery. London: Society for Promoting Christian Knowledge, 1928.

Butler, Alban. *Butler's Lives of the Saints*. Complete edition, edited, revised, and supplemented by Herbert Thurston, S. J., and Donald Attwater. 4 vols. New York: P. J. Kenedy & Sons, 1962.

Camus, Jean Pierre. *The Spirit of Saint François de Sales*. Translated by C. F. Kelley. New York: Harper and Brothers, 1952.

Carney, Edward J. *The Mariology of St. Francis de Sales*. Eichstatt-Wien: Franz-Sales Verlag; Westminster, Maryland: Newman Press, 1963.

Migne, J. P. *Patrologiae cursus completus*. Paris: 1844–1928. St. Francis de Sales' references to the Greek and Latin Fathers of the Church—e.g., St. Gregory Nazianzen, St. Basil, St. Jerome, St. Augustine (with the exception of the *Confessions*) and of certain later writers (such as St. Bernard of Clairvaux)—are in the Migne *patrologia graeca* and *patrologia latina*.

Pourrat, P. *Christian Spirituality*. Translated by W. H. Mitchell, S. P. Jacque, and Donald Attwater. 4 vols. Westminster, Maryland: Newman Press, 1952–1955.

III

Biblia sacra vulgatae editionis . . . critice descripsit . . . P. Michael Hetzenauer . . . editio altera emendatior. Ratisbonae: Sumptibus et typis Friderici Pustet, 1922.

The Holy Bible. New York: Benziger Brothers, 1961. The Old Testament is the new Confraternity of Christian Doctrine translation for Genesis to Ruth, Job to Sirach, and the prophetical books; the remaining books are the Douay version. The New Testament is the new CCD translation. This translation has been used as far as possible throughout the text.

La sainte bible, traduite en français sous la direction de l'Ecole Biblique de Jerusalem. Paris: Les Editions du Cerf, 1956.

NOTES TO THE TEXT

TRANSLATOR'S INTRODUCTION

1. For St. Francis de Sales' account of his efforts, finally successful, to speak privately with Théodore de Bèze (Beza) whom he describes in a letter to Pope Clement VIII dated April 21, 1597 as having "a heart of stone," cf. *Oeuvres*, XI, 268–74.

2. Cf. Proverbs 5:15.

3. *On the Love of God*. Translated, with an Introduction and Notes, by John K. Ryan. 2 vols. (Garden City, N.Y.: Doubleday & Co., 1963).

4. St. Francis de Sales wrote countless letters, many of which have been preserved. Cf. *Oeuvres*, XI–XXI. Some of the letters are of considerable length, as for instance that addressed to André Frémyot, archbishop of Bourges, translated by the writer as *On the Preacher and Preaching*.

5. John Milton, *Paradise Lost*, VII, 364–65.

6. Quoted by Dom Mackey in *Oeuvres*, III, xiv.

7. *Ibid.*, xvi.

8. "Sins crying to heaven for vengeance" are (1) wilful murder, cf. Gen. 4:10; (2) sodomy, cf. Gen. 17:20–21; (3) oppression of the poor, cf. Exod. 2:13; and (4) defrauding workmen of their wages, cf. Jas. 5:4.

9. Cf. Joseph Rickaby, *Waters that Go Softly* (London: 1934) pp. 43–44: "It was the remark of an acute theologian: 'In mortal sin the whole man sins.'" Rickaby develops this thought with his customary perception and effective style.

10. Job 7:1.

11. In the intellectual order Socrates advances something very like the three ways of the ascetic life. He begins with a catharsis: A man must first recognize his own ignorance and error; having cleared it away, he can begin to acquire true knowledge. Yet the purgation of ignorance and error is a continuing process and we can never attain to total knowledge, that is, to complete enlightenment, and to total union with the truth.

12. I Th. 4:3.

13. Rom. 11:33.

14. Dom Mackey writes: "Plusieurs autres traductions anglicanes parurent dans la suite" (cf. *Oeuvres*, III, xxix, n. 2). Only one such translation is known to the writer, viz., that of Thomas Barnes.

DEDICATORY PRAYER

1. St. Francis uses the title of God as king in various ways, especially as "your Majesty," "his Divine Majesty," and the like. Having its basis in Scripture, the title has been used throughout the history of the Church, in earlier centuries, during the Middle Ages and later, and in recent times. The feast of Christ the King, instituted by Pope Pius XI and kept on the last Sunday of October, was first celebrated in 1926.

2. Cf. 1 Cor. 9:27.

3. "Vive, Jésus!"—"Live, Jesus!" may be taken as the motto and theme of St. Francis de Sales' writings and life work.

THE AUTHOR'S PREFACE

1. Pliny, *Natural History*, with an English translation by H. Rackham, W. H. S. Jones, and D. E. Eichholz (10 vols., Cambridge, Mass.: Harvard

University Press, 1938–1965), XXI, iii, 4. The *Historia naturalis* of Pliny (A.D. 23–79) was a favorite with St. Francis and is quoted frequently in the *Introduction* and elsewhere in his writings. It is hereafter referred to as Pliny.

2. The castor oil plant. The Latin name has been anglicized as palmacrist.

3. Cf. Pliny, IX, liv–lvii, 106–16, and Pietro Andrea Mattioli, *Commentarii in libros sex Pedacii Dioscoridis de Materia medica* (Venice: 1554) II, iv. Dioscorides, a Greek physician and naturalist, lived in the first century of the Christian era. His principal work, in the Greek and in Latin translation, became a standard work in both East and West.

4. Pliny, II, cvi, 226.

5. Aristotle, *Historia Animalium*. Translated by D'Arch Wentworth Thompson (Oxford: Clarendon Press, 1910) V, 19, 552b 10–15. This work, a favorite with St. Francis, is hereafter referred to as *History of Animals*.

6. Mme de Charmoisy. Cf. Translator's introduction, p. 9ff.

7. Père Jean Forier, S. J., then rector of the College de Chambéry. The term religious in this and similar contexts means a member of a religious community.

8. Dionysius the Pseudo-Areopagite, *The Ecclesiastical Hierarchy*, V, 6, 7. The author of this work and of certain letters and three other treatises—*The Celestial Hierarchy, Mystical Theology*, and *On the Divine Names*—is an obscure fifth-century figure who was later erroneously identified (1) with the judge of the Areopagus in Athens converted by St. Paul (cf. Acts 17:16–34) and (2) with St. Dionysius, i.e., Denis, the third-century martyr and bishop of Paris. St. Francis accepted both identifications, which Renaissance and later scholarship dispelled as unfounded.

9. Caesar Baronius, *Annales ecclesiastici* (Rome: 1593), for the year A.D. 69.

10. Antonio Galonius, *Historia delle sante vergini* (Rome: 1591), I.

11. 2 John 1:1.

12. Pliny, VIII, xxv, 66.

13. The great man of letters may be Erasmus, to whom St. Francis attributes this thought in his letter on preaching addressed to André Frémyot, archbishop of Bourges and brother of St. Jeanne Françoise Frémyot de Chantal. Cf. St.

Francis de Sales, *On the Preacher and Preaching*. Translated, with an Introduction and Notes, by John K. Ryan (Chicago: Henry Regnery Co., 1964), pp. 24 and 82.

14. St. Augustine, *Epistle* 266, 1.

15. Pliny, XXXV, xxxvi, 86, 87.

16. Gen. 24:20–22.

THE FIRST PART
§1

1. Cf. Aristotle, *On the Heavens*. With an English translation by W. K. C. Guthrie (London: William Heinemann, 1939), A 271b, 8–13; St. Thomas Aquinas, *Concerning Being and Essence*. Translated by George C. Leckie (New York: Appleton-Century, 1937), *in initio*, p. 3.

2. Cf. Pliny, XXXV, xxxvi, 86, 87.

3. Cf. 1 Kings 19:11–16.

4. Cf. Ps. 118:32.

5. St. Thomas Aquinas states that a good deed should be done "expedite, firmiter, et delectabiliter," that is, promptly, thoroughly, and joyfully. Cf. *De virtutibus in commune*, I, ad 13. Note the parallel to Vitruvius' requirements for a good building: it should have firmness and utility and afford delight. Cf. Vitruvius, *On Architecture*, translated by Frank Granger (London: William Heinemann, 1955), I, iii, 2.

§2

1. Num. 13:33, 34.

2. Num. 14:7, 8.

3. Mt. 11:28–30.

4. Gen. 28:12.

§3

1. Gen. 1:11.

2. Cf. John 15:5: "I am the vine, you are the branches."

3. Cf. Aristotle, *History of Animals*, V, 22. The quotation is not found in Aristotle.

4. St. Joseph, a carpenter by trade, spouse of the Virgin Mary and foster-father of Jesus. Cf. Mt. 1:18–25; 2:13–22 and Luke 1:29, 27; 2:4, 39–52. His feast day is March 19. In recent centuries devotion to St. Joseph has spread greatly and St. Francis de Sales contributed to this spread. St. Joseph has the title of Patron of the Universal Church. On the various saints mentioned in the text abundant material will be found in Butler's *Lives of the Saints* (cf. bibliography), hereafter referred to as Butler.

5. Lydia, "a seller of purple, of the city of Thyatira." Cf. Acts 16:14–15, 40.

6. St. Crispin, a shoemaker. According to tradition, Saints Crispin and Crispinian were third-century missionaries and martyrs in Britain. Their feast day is October 25.

7. St. Anne, the name traditionally given to the mother of the Blessed Virgin Mary. Her feast day is July 26.

8. Martha, sister of Mary and Lazarus, all of whom were close friends of Jesus Christ. Cf. Luke 10:38–41 and John 11:1–39; 12:2.

9. St. Monica (332–387), mother of St. Augustine. Cf. his *Confessions*. Translated, with introduction and notes, by John K. Ryan (Garden City, N.Y.: Doubleday & Co., 1960), especially Book 3, chs. 11, 12; Book 5, ch. 8; Book 6, ch. 1; Book 8, ch. 12; Book 9, chs. 8–13. Her feast day is May 4.

10. Aquila and Priscilla. According to Acts 18:1–3, Aquila, a Jew originally from Pontus and like St. Paul a tentmaker by trade, had gone from Rome to Corinth where Paul resided with Aquila and Priscilla (or Prisca), his wife. Their feast day is July 8.

11. Cornelius, a centurion of "the Italian band" stationed in Caesarea. His conversion is described in Acts 10:1–31.

12. St. Sebastian, a third-century martyr. According to legends that grew up about him, he was an officer of the pretorian guard and a devout Christian whose martyrdom was ordered by Diocletian. He is represented in art as pierced by arrows and is patron of archers. His feast day is January 20.

13. St. Maurice, an officer in the Theban legion made up of Christian sol-

diers who refused to sacrifice to pagan gods. He was martyred in the third century in Gaul. His feast day is September 22.

14. Constantine (272–337), considered the first Christian emperor.

15. St. Helena (c. 250–c. 330), Constantine's mother. Her feast day is August 18. Cf. Evelyn Waugh, *Helena* (Boston: Little, Brown, 1950).

16. St. Louis IX (1215–1270), king of France and one of the saints to whom St. Francis de Sales had a special devotion. His feast day is August 25.

17. Blessed Amadeus IX, Duke of Savoy (1435–1472), born at Thonon, later the center of St. Francis de Sales' missionary activities in Chablais.

18. St. Edward the Confessor, born 1002, king of England from 1042 to 1066.

19. St. Gregory the Great, *Homily on Ezechiel*, I, 1, Homily IX, §52.

§ 4

1. Tob. 5:2–4.

2. Blessed John of Avila, *Commentary on the Verse, Audi, filia*, LV, 1; also the brief work, *Advice for a Christian Life*. John of Avila (1500–1569), a Spanish priest known as the apostle of Andalusia, was an early friend and adviser of St. Francis Borgia.

3. Cf. St. Teresa of Avila, *Libro de las relaciones*, III. St. Teresa (1515–1582) was canonized a saint in 1622.

4. St. Catherine of Siena, *Dialogues*, Tract. IV.

5. Cf. Jean Sire de Joinville, *The History of St. Louis*, tr. Joan Evans (London: Oxford University Press, 1938), Book II, ch. cxlv, 224.

6. Sirach (Ecclesiasticus), 6:14, 16.

7. Sir. 6:16.

8. Cf. Blessed John of Avila, *Advice for a Christian Life*.

§ 5

1. Cant. 2:12.

2. Deut. 21:12–13.

3. Eph. 4:22, 24.

4. Cf. Acts 9:1–9.

5. St. Catherine of Genoa (1447–1510), widow, mystic, author of treatises *On Purgatory* and *On the Pure Love of God*. Cf. Butler, III, 557–60; F. von Hügel, *The Mystical Element in Religion* (2 vols.; London: 1908), I, 371–466.

6. St. Pelagia the Penitent was a legendary figure sometimes confused with St. Pelagia of Antioch, a fourth-century virgin and martyr. Cf. Butler, IV, 59–61.

7. Prov. 4:18.

8. Ps. 126:2.

9. Ps. 50:3.

10. Cf. Ps. 54:9.

§6

1. Louis of Granada (1504–1588), a Spanish Dominican. His most famous work is *Memorial of a Christian Life*. Cf. *Summa of the Christian Life:* Selected texts from his writings translated and edited by Jordan Aumann (2 vols.; St. Louis: B. Herder, 1954–55) and *Obras de Fray Luis de Granada de la orden de santo Domingo*. Edicion critica y completa por Fr. Justo Cuervo (14 vols. Madrid: 1906).

2. Vincenzo Bruno (1532–1594), author of *Trattato del sacramento della penitenza, con l'esame della confessions generale* (Venice: 1585).

3. Francisco Arias (1533–1605), a Spanish Jesuit, author of *L'usance de la confession . . . translatée par un père de la mesme Société* (Antwerp: 1601).

4. Emond Auger (1530–1591), a French Jesuit, author of *La Maniere d'ouyr la Messe . . . Item, un formulaire de bien confesser ses pechez* (Tyons: 1571).

§7

1. Num. 11:4, 5.

2. Gen. 19:26.

§8

1. Ps. 118:104, 128.

2. Cf. Ps. 102:5.

§9

1. St. Francis adapts words from Ps. 38:7 and Ps. 8:5. The CCD version reads: "A phantom only, man goes his way," and "What is man that you are mindful of him?"

2. Ps. 99:3.

3. Ps. 137:8.

4. Sir. 10:9.

5. Ps. 102:1.

§11

1. Cf. Ps. 85:5.

2. Ps. 8:5.

3. Cf. Ps. 61:1.

§12

1. Cf. Ps. 39:13.

§14

1. Luke 21:26.

2. Cf. Joel 3:2.

3. Mt. 25:41.

4. Mt. 25:34.

5. Job 26:11.

6. Cf. 1 Cor. 11:31.

§15

1. Cf. 2 Kgs. 14:32.

2. Cf. Is. 33:14.

§18

1. 1 Cant. 4:8.

§19

1. Cf. Mattioli, *op. cit.*, VI, 8.
2. Luke 7:34–48.
3. 1 Kgs. 3:9.
4. Luke 10:16.

§20

1. In this chapter St. Francis de Sales clearly shows his training as a lawyer.
2. Ps. 15:1.
3. Ps. 72:25.

§21

1. Cf. Cant. 8:6.

§22

1. Cf. Sir. 10:11.

§23

1. Cf. Num. 6:3.
2. Must—the word is from the Latin "mustum" (new, fresh) as in "mustum vinum" (new wine)—is grape juice as yet unfermented or in the process of fermentation.

§24

1. St. Jerome, *Epistle* 108, 20.
2. Pliny, XVII, xliii, 252.

THE SECOND PART

§1

1. John 8:12.

2. Cf. Cant. 2:3.

3. Cf. John 4:6.

4. Cf. John 14:6.

5. John 6:1.

6. St. Bonaventure (1221–1274), Franciscan theologian and philosopher; cardinal and bishop of Albano. One of the greatest of medieval thinkers, he is known as the Seraphic Doctor.

7. Matthia Bellintani da Solo (1534–1611), Italian Capuchin, author of *Practica dell'oration mentale* (Venice: 1592).

8. Vincenzo Bruno, cf. n. 2, pt. I, chap. 6. The work here referred to is *Meditationes sur les mysteres de la passion . . . traduites d'italien en françoys par Philibert du Sault* (Douai: 1596).

9. Andrea Capiglia or Capilia, a Jesuit who became a Carthusian and bishop of Urgel (1530–1609). He was the author of *Meditations sur les Evangiles . . . nouvement traduictes en françoys par* R. G. A. G. (Paris: 1601).

10. Granada, cf. n. 1, pt. I, chap. 6. The work here referred to is probably *Devotes contemplations et spirituelles instructions sur la vie, passion, mort, resurrection et ascension de* N.S.J.C. *Traduict de l'espagnol de R.P. Louis de Grenade par F. de Belleforest* (Paris: 1572).

11. Luis de la Puente (1545–1624), a Spanish Jesuit, author of *Meditations des Mysteres de nostre saincte foy, avec la pratique de l'oraison mentale . . . traduictes par René Gaultier* (Douai: 1611).

12. The Divine Office is the set of prayers of daily obligation for priests and certain others. It includes matins, lauds, prime, tierce, sext, nones, vespers, and compline. It is said either by a group, in choir or privately by individuals.

§2

1. Ps. 138:8.

2. Gen. 28:17.

3. Ps. 72:26.

4. Cf. Acts 17:28.

5. Acts 7:54–60.

6. Cant. 2:9.

7. The defined Catholic doctrine of the Eucharist to which St. Francis alludes may be stated briefly as follows: At the consecration of the bread and wine in the Mass there is a real change of the entire substance of the bread and wine into the Body and Blood, soul and divinity of Jesus Christ, while there is no change in the appearances—accidents or phenomena in philosophical language—of the bread and wine. That is, the taste, color, shape, weight, odor, and other accidental determinations of the bread and wine remain unchanged. As long as the consecrated bread and wine remain in being Christ is there substantially and personally present in a real and true although mysterious manner. On September 3, 1965 Pope Paul VI issued an encyclical letter entitled *Mysterium Fidei* on the Eucharist which was in part occasioned by certain questionable doctrines advanced by present-day theologians.

§3

1. Ps. 50:13.

2. Ps. 30:17; 118:135.

3. Ps. 118:18.

4. *Ibid.* 34.

5. *Ibid.* 125.

§6

1. Cf. Part 2, ch. 1, n. 9.

2. Cf. Part 1, ch. 6, n. 3.

§9

1. Gen. 32:26.

2. Mt. 15:27.

§12

1. Cf. Ps. 30:3 and Sir. 34:19.

2. Ps. 72:23.

3. Ps. 15:8.

4. Ps. 122:1.

5. Ps. 24:15.

6. Ps. 101:7, 8.

7. Cf. *Vita B. Elzeari*, c. XXX. Cf. *De probatis sanctorum vitis quas tam ex Mss. codicibus quam ex editis authoribus* R. A. Fr. Laurentius Surius Carthusiae Coloniensis Professus primum edidit (Cologne: 1617). St. Elzear of Sabran (1285–1323) was a great French nobleman who exemplifies what St. Francis teaches about practice of the devout life at court and in the management of estates and fulfillment of public duties. His nephew and godson became Pope Urban V and in 1369 canonized Elzear. His feast day is September 27, the day of his death; that of Blessed Delphina is December 9. Cf. Butler, III, 661–62.

§13

1. St. Augustine, *Ep.* 130, cix.

2. St. Augustine, *Enarratio* 11 *in Ps.* 26, et alibi; *Confessions*, Book 10, ch. 6.

3. St. Gregory Nazianzen, *Oratio* 26, nn. 8, 9.

4. Ps. 68:1, 15, 3.

5. Anon. *Life of St. Fulgentius*, ch. XIII. St. Fabius Claudius Gordanianus Fulgentius (468–533), a descendent of a noble family of senatorial rank of Carthage, became procurator of Byzacena. Entering the monastic life, he suffered cruel persecution from the Arians. In 508 he was consecrated bishop of Ruspe, the present Kudiat in Tunisia. His feast day is on January 1. Cf. Butler, I, 6–9.

6. St. Anselm, Archbishop of Canterbury (1033–1109), was born at Aosta in the Italian Alps. One of the most important of medieval thinkers, he is famous for the *ratio Anselmi*, i.e., Anselmian argument, for the existence of God, generally but improperly called the ontological argument. For the incident of the hare, see Eadmer, *Vita Anselmi*, c. 189.

7. St. Athanasius, *The Life of Saint Antony*. Newly translated and annotated by Robert T. Meyer (Westminster, Maryland: Newman Press, 1950), n. 81.

8. Thomas de Celano, *Legenda antiqua S. Francisci*, L. 1, c. ix.

9. St. Bonaventure, *Vita S. Francisci*, c. VIII.

10. Cf. Ribadeneira, *Vida del P. Francisco de Borgia* (1598); I, v. St. Francis Borgia (1510–1572), Duke of Gandia. After the death of his wife he became a member of the Society of Jesus and was ordained a priest in 1550 and in 1565 was named St. Ignatius Loyola's second successor as General of the Society. A man of high sanctity and great administrative ability, his renunciation of estates and position to become a Jesuit created a great sensation. Early lives, such as that of P. de Ribadeneira, which St. Francis uses, are extravagantly eulogistic. Cf. Butler, IV, 74–78.

11. St. Basil, *Oratio de Paradiso*, appendix.

12. Andrea Valladierus, *Speculum sapientiae matronalis ex vita Sanctae Franciscae Romanae. Fundatricis Sororum Turris Speculorum panegyricus*, VIII. St. Frances of Rome, a widow (1384–1440) canonized in 1608, was foundress of the Oblates of Mary, a community of women dedicated to serve the poor while living in the world. Cf. Butler, I, 529–33.

13. Ps. 16:8.

14. Cf. n. 3.

15. Cf. 1, 24.

§14

1. Cant. 7:5.

2. Cant. 3:6.

3. St. John Chrysostom, *On the Priesthood*, Book VI, 4.

§15

1. Hours, i.e., of the Divine Office, prime, tierce, sext, and none, as recited publicly in church.

2. Cf. St. Augustine, *Confessions*, Book 9, chs. 6 and 7.

§16

1. Mt. 22:30.

2. Ps. 137:2.

3. St. Peter Faber (Favre) (1506–1596), a native of Savoy. His feast day is August 11. Cf. Butler, III, 306–8.

4. St. Ignatius Loyola was canonized in 1622.

5. The reference is to Guillelmine d'Arenthon d'Alex, wife of Humbert Critan, both members of noble families and the parents of the Rev. Pierre Critan of Thonon, a close friend of St. Francis de Sales.

§17

1. Luke 2:19.

2. Cf. Part 2, ch. 1, n. 6. Certain of St. Bonaventure's works, especially his *Itinerarium mentis in Deum*, have been translated into English.

3. John Gerson (1362–1429), the great chancellor of the University of Paris, long thought to be the author of *The Imitation of Christ*, which St. Francis probably had in mind here.

4. Denis the Carthusian (1402–1471), called the Ecstatic Doctor, was born at Ryckel in Belgian Limburg. His collected works fill 45 large volumes.

5. Blosius, i.e., Louis de Blois, a Flemish Benedictine, author of the *Institutio Spiritualis* and other works.

6. Diego Stella (1524–1598), a Portuguese Franciscan.

7. Luca Pinelli, an Italian Jesuit, who died in 1607, author of *Gersone della perfezione christiana*, i.e., *Gerson on Christian Perfection*.

8. Cf. pt. 1, ch. 2, n. 11.

9. *The Spiritual Combat* by Luigi Scupoli (1530–1610) is still a popular spiritual book.

10. For the saints mentioned in this passage consult Butler under their names.

§18

1. Cf. Ps. 20:4.

2. Scriptural references in this sentence are to Is. 40:2; Osee 2:14; Cant. 5:2; 2:10, 13; 5:1; 6:1; 2:14.

3. Ps. 94:10, 11.

4. Cant. 5:6.

5. Cant. 5:5, 6.

§19

1. Pliny, VIII, xvii, 43.

§20

1. Aulus Gellius, *The Attic Nights*. With an English translation by John C. Rolfe (3 vols., London: William Heinemann, 1927–28), XVII, xvi; III, 261–63.

2. John 6:50, 59.

3. Pseudo-Augustine, *De ecclesiasticis dogmatibus*, XXXIII, 1. This passage is probably taken from the *Corpus juris canonici* (Decreti Illa pars, tit. II. c. xiii), where the book is attributed to St. Augustine, an opinion commonly held up to the seventeenth century. Modern criticism ascribes the book to Gennadius of Marseilles, who died about 497.

4. Raimondo da Capua, O.P., *Vita miracolosa della serafica 8. Catherina da Siena tradotta in lingua volgare dal R. P. Frate Ambrosio Catarino da Siena . . .* (Venezia: Pietro Marinelli, 1587) II, 17. Cf. also Raymundus de Vineis, O.P., *The Life of St. Catherine of Siena*. Translated by George Lamb (New York: P. J. Kenedy, 1960).

5. Deut. 15:1–3.

6. St. Francis wrote over 350 years ago when the custom of daily Communion had not yet been established. The practice of St. Pius V (1504–1572) of saying Mass every day was instanced as part of his great sanctity. The most important name in the spread of frequent and even daily Communion is that of St. Pius X (1835–1914).

§21

1. Mt. 8:8.

2. Pliny, VIII, lxxxi, 217.

THE THIRD PART

§1

1. Ps. 1:3.

2. Cf. Sir. 22:6.

3. Rom. 12:15.

4. 1 Cor. 13:4.

5. St. Jerome, Epistle 108, *Ad Eustochium in Epitaphium Paulae*, XX.

6. Acts 6:2.

7. Butler, I, 153–55. For contemporary lives of St. John the Almoner cf. the translation by N. H. Baynes and Elizabeth Dawes, *Three Byzantine Saints* (Oxford: Blackwell, 1948). His feast day is January 23.

8. Cf. *Vitae patrum*, VII, 19; VIII, 14.

9. John Cassian, *Collationes patrum*, XVIII, 14.

10. Cf. Ps. 44:10, 14, 15.

11. St. Gregory Nazianzen, *Oratio* XIV, 2.

12. Cf. Jos. 6; Heb. 11:31; Jas. 2:25.

§2

1. St. Augustine, Sermon XX in psalmum 118, I. P.L.

2. Cf. William of St. Thierry, *Vita et tres gestae sancti Bernardi*, I, 4, 6.

3. 1 Cor. 9:22.

4. St. Jerome, *Epistle* 108, 20.

5. Prov. 3:5.

6. 1 Kgs. 9:1–17.

7. Cf. Gen. 24:10–67.

8. Cf. Ruth 2:2–9; 3:7–14; 4:5–13.

§3

1. Heb. 10:36.
2. Lk. 21:19.
3. Cf. St. Gregory the Great, *Moralia in Job, XXII*, 30–34.
4. Rom. 4:2.
5. John 16:21.

§4

1. 4 Kgs. 4:3, 4.
2. Pliny, X, lvii, 109.
3. *Ibid.*, IX, xxxv. V. Mattioli, *op. cit.*, II, iv.

§5

1. St. Thomas Aquinas, *Summa theologiae*, 2–2, 82, 3.
2. Cf. 1 Cor. 4:7.
3. Luke 1:46, 49.
4. Is. 7:11, 12.
5. Mt. 5:48.
6. Pliny, XII, xxiii, 40.
7. 2 Kgs. 6:14–22.

§6

1. Luke 1:48.
2. Ps. 83:11.
3. Ps. 21:7.

§7

1. Sir. 41:15.
2. Ps. 51:4.
3. 2 Cor. 6:8.
4. Ps. 68:8.

§8

1. Mt. 11:29.

2. Cf. Part III, ch. IV.

3. St. Bernard, *Tractatus de caritate*, c. V.

4. Cf. Mattioli, *op. cit.*, VI, 40.

5. Gen. 45:24.

6. Jas. 1:20.

7. St. Augustine, *The City of God*, Book, 14, 19.

8. St. Augustine, Ep. 38, 2.

9. Eph. 4:26.

10. Ps. 30:10.

11. St. Augustine, Ep. 250, 3.

12. Mt. 8:24–26.

13. Cant. 4:11.

§9

1. Ps. 42:5, 6.

§10

1. Luke 10:41.

2. Prov. 19:2.

§11

1. "State of perfection" is a technical term in theology analogous to various terms in common use such as "civil status" and "state in society." A man who has taken vows to observe the evangelical counsels of poverty, chastity, and obedience has dedicated himself to a life of perfection. Thus Christ says "If you would be perfect, go, sell what you have and give to the poor" (Mt. 19:21). It is evident that a person can take vows to lead a perfect life and yet fail to observe them perfectly. As St. Francis says, although bishops and religious "are in the state of perfection"—and therefore have all the strict obligations of

that high state—"yet not all of them have arrived at perfection itself." On the other hand, it is possible with God's grace to live a life of perfection without being in the state of perfection.

2. Phil. 2:8.

3. St. Bernard, *Tractatus de moribus et officio episcopi*, IX.

§12

1. As in the phrase "an honest woman."

2. Pliny, IX, liv–lvii, 106–16.

3. St. Augustine, *Confessions*, Book 6, ch. 12.

4. St. Jerome, Ep. 117, *Ad Matrem et filiam*, 6.

5. Ps. 4:5.

6. Bl. Raymond of Capua, *op. cit.*, II, 6.

7. Heb. 12:14.

8. St. Jerome, *Commentary on Hebrews*, 12:14.

9. St. John Chrysostom, *Homilia* XV *in Matthaeum*, IV.

10. Cf. Ps. 14:1.

11. Cf. Ps. 23:4.

12. Cf. Apoc. 22:15.

13. Mt. 5:8.

§13

1. Eph. 5:3.

2. Cant. 5:5; 4:3, 1; 1:10; 7:4.

3. Cassian, *Institutiones*, VI, xix.

4. Tertullian, *On Chastity*, IV.

5. Pliny, XVII, xxxviii, 234.

6. Pliny, VIII, xxxii and xxxiii, 78.

7. Cf. Ps. 11:7.

8. Cf. Ps. 118:127.

9. Vincent of Beauvais, *Speculum naturae*, VIII, 106.

10. Pliny, XXIV, xxxviii, 59.

§14

1. Mt. 5:3.
2. Pliny, X, xlvii, 89.
3. Ex. 3:2.
4. 3 Kgs. 21:2, 3.
5. Cf. Mt. 5:3.

§15

1. Pliny, XXIV, xxxvi, 69.
2. Cf. Osee, 9:10.
3. A Pythagorean maxim, also used elsewhere by St. Francis. Cf. *On the Preacher and Preaching*, p. 9.
4. 2 Cor. 11:29.
5. Mt. 5:3.
6. Cf. Mt. 25:34–36.
7. Gen. 27.

§17

1. Osee, 9:10.
2. Pliny, XXI, xxv, 77, 78. Mattioli, *op. cit.*, VI, 8.

§18

1. St. Gregory Nazianzen, *Carmina*, 1, 2.
2. Pliny, XXIV, ci, 158.
3. Sir. 12:13.
4. The French has a play on words here: "le jouet des cours, mais la peste des coeurs."

§19

1. The four cardinal virtues of Greek philosophy. Cf. Wis. 3:7, 8; Prov. 8:14.
2. Ps. 132:1.

3. Ps. 132:4.

4. John 13:23.

5. St. Gregory Nazianzen, *Oratio* XLII, 20.

6. St. Augustine, *Confessions*, Book 6, Chs. 1, 2.

7. Rom. 1:31.

8. St. Thomas Aquinas, *Summa theologiae*, 2–2, 23, 3, ad 1; *In X libros Ethicorum Aristotelis*, IX; *Quaestiones disputatae De malo*, VII, 2, ad 12.

§20

1. Pliny, XXI, xlv, 77, 78. Mattioli, *op. cit.*, VI, 8.

2. St. Gregory Nazianzen, *Carmina*, I, 2.

3. Ps. 57:5.

§21

1. Cf. Cant. 2:15.

2. Aristotle, *History of animals*, I, 11, 492a, 14.

3. Pliny, XXVIII, vi, 31.

4. St. Ambrose, *De poenitentia*, II, 10.

5. St. Augustine, *Confessions*, Book 4, ch. 7.

6. Cf. Part 2, ch. 12.

7. Cf. Ps. 115:16, 17.

§22

1. "Be good bankers." These words are not found in Scripture but are reported by Origen, Clement of Alexandria, St. Jerome, and others.

2. Jer. 15:19.

3. St. Gregory Nazianzen, *Oratio* 43, 77.

4. Pliny, X, lxxxvi, 188.

5. Sir. 6:17.

6. Jas. 4:4.

§23

1. Palladius, *Opus agriculturae*. J. C. Schmitt, ed. (Leipzig: Teubner, 1898) II, 15.

2. Joel 2:12.

3. Prov. 23:26.

4. Cant. 8:6.

5. Gal. 2:20.

6. St. Jerome, *Epistle* 107, 10.

7. Luke 10:8.

8. Cf. Zach. 3:8; 6:12.

9. Cant. 6:9.

10. Num. 22:21–24.

11. 2 Kings, 12:16.

12. Cf. Joel 2:13.

§24

1. Mt. 22:39.

2. St. Bernard, *De consideratione*, I, 3.

3. Rom. 12:15.

4. Phil. 4:4, 5.

5. St. Gregory Nazianzen, *Oratio* 26, 8, 9.

6. St. Augustine, *Confessions*, VI, 3.

7. Mk. 6:31.

§25

1. Tim. 2:9, 10.

2. Is. 52:11.

3. 1 Pet. 3:3.

4. Cf. Part 3, ch. 27.

5. Joinville, *op. cit.*, I, 6; pp. 10–11.

§26

1. Mt. 12:37.

2. Ps. 36:30.

3. St. Bonaventure, *Life of St. Francis*, Ch. X.

4. Cant. 4:11.

§27

1. Jas. 3:2.

2. Mt. 12:34.

3. Eph. 5:3.

4. 1 Cor. 15:33. St. Paul here uses a line from Menander, the Greek comic dramatist, but it had probably become a proverb.

5. Cf. St. Thomas Aquinas, *Summa Theologiae*, 2–2, 23, 3, ad 1.

6. Joinville, *op. cit.*, II, 135; p. 204.

§28

1. Luke 6:37.

2. 1 Cor. 4:5.

3. 1 Cor. 11:31.

4. Amos 6:13.

5. Luke 18:11.

6. Pliny, XXIV, cil, 163.

7. St. Francis writes: "Toutes choses paroissement jaunes aux yeux icteriques et qui ont la grande jaunisse." The quotation used by the translator is from Pope's *Essay on Criticism*, II, 358–59.

8. Mattioli, *op. cit.*, II, 176.

9. Gen. 26:7–9.

10. Mt. 1:19.

11. Luke 23:34.

12. John 3:18.

13. Gen. 29:11.

14. Gen. 24:22.

§29

1. Cf. Is. 6:6–7.

2. St. Bernard, *On the Canticle of Canticles*, Sermon XXIV, 3.

3. Ps. 139:13.

4. Aristotle, *History of animals*, 11, 17, 508a 24.

5. Pliny, XXV, xcv.

6. Ps. 13:3; 139:4.

7. Jos. 10:13.,

8. Lk. 23:45.

9. Gen. 9:21.

10. Cf. Gen. 19:30–38.

11. John 18:10–11.

12. Mt. 26:69–75; Lk. 22:54–62.

13. Lk. 7:39.

14. Lk. 18:11–14.

15. Cf. Rochefoucauld's well-known observation: "In the misfortune of our best friends we find something not displeasing to us."

16. "Beware of false prophets who come to you in sheep's clothing but inwardly are ravenous wolves." Mt. 7:5.

17. When St. Francis wrote this he may have been thinking of the lines: Le mutin Anglois, et le bravache Escossois, Le bougre Italien, et le fol Francois, Le poultron Romain, le larron de Gasconge, L'Espagnol superbe, et l'Aleman yvronge. The verses are quoted by Sir Thomas Browne, *Religio Medici*, II, 4.

§30

1. Ps. 30:6.

2. Wis. 1:5.

3. Prov. 10:9.

4. St. Augustine, *Confessions*, Book 4, ch. 6.

5. St. Augustine, *Retractationes*, 11, 6.

6. Pss. 38:1; 140:3.

7. Joinville, *op. cit.*, Book I, ch. III, p. 3.

8. *Ibid.*, Book I, ch. V, p. 8.

§31

1. Cassian, *Collationes patrum*, XXIV, xxi.

§32

1. Joinville, *op. cit.*, Book II, ch. LXXIX, p. 121.

2. Tob. 3:16–17.

§33

1. Pliny, XXII, xlvi, 92–95.

§34

1. Pliny, II, cvi.

§35

1. Cf. Cant. 4:9: "You have ravished my heart, my sister, my bride; you have ravished my heart with one glance of your eyes, with one bead of your necklace."

2. Mt. 10:42.

3. Raymond of Capua, *op. cit.*, I, ii.

4. Cf. Prov. 31:19.

5. Mt. 25:21.

6. Cf. Col. 3:17.

7. 1 Cor. 10:31.

§36

1. Cant. 2:15.

2. Pliny, XI, lxx, 184.

3. Ps. 11:2.

4. Ps. 11, 1; 20:10, 23; Deut. 25:13.

5. Eutropius, *Breviarium historiae romanae.* Ed. F. Ruehl (Leipzig: Teubner, 1897), VIII, 5.

§38

1. Eph. 5:32.

2. Heb. 13:4.

3. Cf. Gen. 30:38, 39.

4. Eph. 5:25.

5. Cf. Est. 8:8; Dan. 6:17; 14:10.

6. Cf. Gen. 2:23.

7. 1 Pet. 3:7.

8. St. Gregory Nazianzen, *Oratio*, xxxvii, §7.

9. 1 Thess. 4:4.

10. Pliny, IX, lvi, 114.

11. Gen. 29:22.

12. Gen. 26:8, 9.

13. St. Augustine, *Confessions*, Book 1, ch. 11.

14. Cf. 1 Kgs. 1:1–28.

15. St. Thomas Aquinas. Cf. Angelus Walz, *Saint Thomas Aquinas, a Biographical Study* (Westminster, Maryland: Newman Press, 1951), pp. 1–7.

16. St. Andrew of Fiesole, a ninth-century (?) saint of whom very little is known with certainty. Cf. Butler, II, 226–28.

17. St. Bernard's mother was Aleth, wife of Tescelin Sorrel, a Burgundian noble. Their children were Blessed Guy, Blessed Gerard, St. Bernard, Blessed Humbeline, Andrew, Bartholomew, and Blessed Nivard.

18. Joinville, *op. cit.*, Book II, ch. XVI, p. 22.

19. Ex. 1:21.

20. Prov. 17:6.

21. St. Augustine, *Confessions*, Book 8, ch. 12.

22. Tit. 2:5.

23. Prov. 30.

24. Gen. 25:21.

25. 1 Cor. 7:14.

26. St. Gregory Nazianzen, *Oratio* XL, 1.

§39

1. Heb. 13:4.

2. 1 Cor. 7:3.

3. 1 Cor. 7:5.

4. Eph. 5:3.

5. Phil. 3:19.

6. Pliny, VIII, v, 13.

7. 1 Cor. 7:29.

8. St. Gregory, *Homilies on the Gospel,* Book II, homily 16, 12.

9. 1 Cor. 7:31.

10. St. Augustine, De LXXXIII quaestionibus, xxx.

§40

1. 1 Tim. 5:3.

2. St. Augustine, *De bone viduitatis*, XIX.

3. Origen, *Homilia* XVII *in Lucam* at the end.

4. Various prayers in the Latin liturgy refer to God with the words "cui servire regnare est": whom to serve is to reign. This derives from Seneca's words on philosophy: "philosophiae servire libertas est": to serve philosophy is to be free. Seneca, *Ad Lucilium epistulae morales*. Translated by Richard M. Gummere (3 vols., London: Wm Heinemann, 1917), vol. 1, p. 40.

5. Rom. 4:2.

6. 1 Tim. 5:6.

7. Cant. 2:12.

8. Ruth 1:19, 20.

9. 1 Tim. 5:4, 8.

10. Cant. 1:3.

11. 1 Cor. 7:40.

12. St. Jerome, *Epistle*, 54.

§41

1. Cant. 2:16.

THE FOURTH PART
§1

1. John 15:19.

2. Mt. 11:18, 19.

3. 1 Cor. 13:4, 5.

4. 1 John 5:19.

5. Ex. 1:12, 16.

6. Gal. 6:14.

§2

1. Ps. 83:11.

2. Ps. 54:7.

§3

1. 2 Cor. 12:7–9.

2. Arnaldus, *Vita B. Angelae de Foligno*, c. xix.

3. Gal. 5:17.

4. Rom. 7:23.

§4

1. St. Jerome, *Vita S. Pauli Eremitae*, 3.

2. Raymond of Capua, *op. cit.*, ch. 11.

§ 7

1. Mt. 26:41.
2. Mt. 4:10.

§ 11

1. Ps. 118:109.
2. Joinville, *op. cit.*, II, 45.

§ 12

1. 2 Cor. 7:10.
2. Sir. 30:25.
3. Jas. 5:13.
4. 1 Kings 16:23.
5. Cant. 2:16.
6. Cant. 1:12.
7. Cf. Ps. 118:82.
8. Rom. 8:35.
9. Cf. Ps. 103:15.

§ 13

1. Democritus (c. 460–c. 362 B.C.), the founder of atomism, first said, "Man is a microcosm."
2. Rom. 14:8.
3. Cf. Rom. 8:35, 38, 39.
4. Cf. 1 Kings 24.
5. Ps. 118:103.
6. Cf. Cant. 1:1.
7. Pliny, XXV, xliii, 82.
8. *Ibid.*, XII, xlii, 86.
9. Mt. 7:16.

10. *Ibid.* 7:17.

11. Lam. 3:25.

12. Cf. Mt. 17:41–8.

13. Prov. 25:16.

§14

1. Cf. Ps. 62:3.

2. Cf. Ps. 41:3.

3. 118:71, 67.

4. Ex. 16:21.

5. Cant. 5:2–6.

6. Luke 1:53.

7. Mt. 25:29.

8. Ps. 1:14.

9. Mt. 26:39; Luke 22:42.

10. Cant. 4:16.

11. 4 Kings 5:14.

12. Mt. 20:39.

13. Gen. 22:15–18.

14. Job 1:21.

15. Arnaldus, *op. cit.*, LXII.

§15

1. *Vita prima S. Bernardi*, IV, III.

2. Sir. 11:27.

3. Cant. 5:2.

4. *Rule of St. Francis*, c. v.

5. Bartholomaeus de Pisis, *De conformitate vitae B. Francisci ad vitam Domini Jesu Christi Redemptoris Nostri*, Book 1, Conf. VII.

THE FIFTH PART

§1

1. Luke 11:26.

2. St. Gregory Nazianzen, *Oratio* XXXIX, xl.

§2

1. Cf. Part I, c. xx.

2. Pss. 26:8; 44:1; 118:6.

3. Osee 11:4.

4. Jer. 29:11.

5. Cf. St. Augustine, *Confessions*, Book 10, ch. 27: "Too late have I loved you, O Beauty so ancient and so new, too late have I loved you!"

6. Ps. 70:17.

7. Ps. 117:17.

§3

1. St. Augustine, *Soliloquy I.*

2. Cf. *Speculum vitae s. Francisci*, about the middle.

§4

1. Ps. 76:3.

2. Ps. 25:8.

§10

1. Gen. 8:9.

2. Luke 15:16–17.

§11

1. John 4:15.

§12

1. St. Augustine, *Confessions*, Book 9, ch. 9.
2. St. Jerome, *Epistle*, CVIII.

§13

1. Jer. 1:5.
2. Gal. 2:20.

§14

1. Jer. 31:3.

§17

1. Jos. 10:12–14.

§18

1. Ps. 118:93.

2. Nicetas David, *in Tetrasticha sancti Gregorii Nazianzeni*, 229.

3. Caesar Baronius, *Annales Ecclesiastici, ad annum* 273.

4. *The Little Flowers of St. Francis of Assisi.* Appendix: *First Consideration on the Stigmata.*

INDEX OF PROPER NAMES

FRANCIS DE SALES (1567–1622) was educated by his father to be a lawyer so that the young man could eventually take the elder's place as a senator from the province of Savoy in France. After receiving his doctorate, he returned home and told his parents he wished to enter the priesthood. Francis was ordained and elected provost of the Diocese of Geneva, then a center for Calvinists. Francis set out to convert them, especially in the district of Chablais. By preaching and distributing the little pamphlets he wrote to explain true Catholic doctrine, he had remarkable success. At thirty-five he became bishop of Geneva. While administering his diocese he practiced his own axiom, "A spoonful of honey attracts more flies than a barrelful of vinegar." Besides his two well-known books, *The Introduction to the Devout Life* and *A Treatise on the Love of God*, he wrote many pamphlets and carried on a vast correspondence.

IMAGE STUDY GUIDE

Introduction to the Devout Life
by St. Francis de Sales

TRANSLATED AND EDITED
by John K. Ryan

OVERVIEW

Introduction to the Devout Life was written by St. Francis de Sales between 1607 and 1609, during which time he was serving as the bishop of Geneva. In these essays detailing the benefits of religious life, St. Francis de Sales offers concrete instructions for attaining Catholic virtues. Devotion, he explains, is the highest possible virtue, providing a moral framework and a guidepost, both for contemplation of God and as a means to organize the way life is lived. Interior contemplation and external action are joined into the singular pursuit of a properly religious life. The concordance of spirit and civic engagement is a central component of de Sales's definition of devotion and is key to understanding his theology.

Introduction to the Devout Life has had lasting popularity and influence because it is the singular product of a singular personality. In its tone and method of construction, the work consistently provides evidence of the experiences, concerns, and skills of its author. Organized as a series of arguments and instructions, Introduction draws on de Sales's early work as a writer of pamphlets designed to convert Calvinists. Adapted from letters written to specific individuals—addressed collectively as Philothea—it displays his desire to continually engage in the "labor" of spiritual instruction, which "refreshes and revives the heart" (p. 24). The work is written in clear, direct language and reflects the busy schedule of a bishop who did not have much time for writing. This last point, the simplicity of the prose, also reflects de Sales's understanding of the most effective way to engage his intended audience. As a result, *Introduction to the Devout Life* is a deeply personal, earnest work, proving that to be open and giving is a joyful enterprise.

A hallmark of this book is the tone of warmth it conveys in its pages, in the construction of its arguments, and in the purpose for which it was composed. This warmth is the product of its author's personality. De Sales, whose office as bishop brought him into daily contact with spiritual seekers from all walks and stations of life, emphasizes the pleasure and benefit that comes from devoutness over the harm and punishment that result from its absence. De Sales's humaneness is apparent in his belief—which undergirds and informs *Introduction*—that it is possible for any soul to form a devout relationship with God, not only abstractly or in the solitude of religious asceticism, but practically, and in the everyday world of society. As he writes in the Author's Preface,

> Almost all those who have hitherto written about devotion have been concerned with instructing persons wholly withdrawn from the world or have at least taught a kind of devotion that leads to such complete retirement. My purpose is to instruct those who live in town, within families, or at court, and by their state of life are obliged to live an ordinary life as to outward appearances. (p. 22)

Alongside the book's welcoming tone and generosity of spirit, de Sales displays rigorous fidelity to the tenets of Catholic doctrine. Not only does the work exhort average people to pursue a devotional life, but it also prescribes the exact means by which they should do so. Fidelity to doctrine, he writes, manifests in the lessons delivered, the values espoused, and the meditations prescribed. Among the spiritual exercises are the disavowal of sin and sensual pleasures, detachment from the physical world, and observance of religious practice. Drawing on a lineage of authority that extends back to St. Augustine, through the apostles and even to the philosopher Aristotle, de Sales advocates three necessary stages of spiritual progression: the purgative, whereby a soul cleanses itself of its most egregious sins; the illuminative, in which it begins to foster virtues; and the unitive, in which the soul further strengthens its virtues and enters into a proper relationship with God.

Accordingly, *Introduction to the Devout Life* is built on these three stages, with the first section offering thoughts, advice, and meditations on the process of beginning to purge oneself of sins, from the most severe to the more trivial. The second section capitalizes on the cleansing achieved in the first, and offers further lessons on how to build upon the purgative stage. Throughout, de Sales uses the idea of energy and momentum to frame his arguments. While acknowledging that at first the way can seem very difficult, and that setbacks and relapses can always occur, he also spurs his readers to contemplate the force of spiritual momentum, and the corresponding sense of joy it creates, both of which arise from the adherence to proper religious practice and meditation.

The importance of de Sales's work lies in the way he guides his readers to continue practicing spiritual devotions even in a corporeal world where perfection is unattainable. De Sales recognizes that the three stages are continual, ongoing processes, and that by dedication souls can make progress even in the face of adversity and temptation. In encouraging the reader to become more devout, he advocates the need to valorize the reasons and intentions behind religious practice over their display. The result for the reader is a blueprint for spiritual practice that can not only withstand the pressures of secular life, but also transform them.

PASSAGES FOR REFLECTION AND CONTEMPLATION

Since devotion consists in a certain degree of eminent charity, it not only makes us prompt, active, and faithful in observance of God's commands, but in addition it arouses us to do quickly and lovingly as many good works as possible, both those commanded and those merely counseled or inspired. A man just recovered from illness walks only as afar as he must and then slowly and with difficulty; so also a sinner just healed of his iniquity walks as far as God commands him, but he walks slowly and with difficulty until such time as he has attained to devotion. Then like a man in sound health he not only walks but runs and leaps forward "on the way of God's commandments" (cf. Ps. 118:32). Furthermore, he moves and runs in the paths of his heavenly counsels and inspirations. To conclude, charity and devotion differ no more from one another than does flame from the fire. Charity is spiritual fire and when it bursts into flames, it is called devotion. Hence devotion adds nothing to the fire of charity except the flame that makes charity prompt, active, and diligent not only to observe God's commandments but also to fulfill his heavenly counsels and inspirations. (p. 29)

Contrition and confession are so beautiful and have so good an odor that they wipe away the ugliness of sin and purify its stench. Simon the leper called Magdalen a sinner but our Lord denied that she was one and spoke rather of the perfumes she poured out and of her great charity (Luke 7:34–48). (p. 61)

Always remember, then, Philothea, to retire at various times into the solitude of your own heart even while outwardly engaged in discussions or transactions with others. This mental solitude cannot be violated by the many people who surround you since they are not standing around your heart but only around your body. Your heart remains alone in the presence of God. (p. 86)

The care and diligence with which we should attend to our concerns are very different from solicitude, worry, and anxiety. The angels have care for our salvation and are diligent to procure it, yet they are not solicitous, worried, and anxious. Care and diligence may be accompanied by tranquillity and peace of mind but not by solicitude and worry, much less anxiety. (p. 140)

Ordinarily moderate cheerfulness should predominate in our associations with others. St. Romuald and St. Anthony have been highly praised because in spite of all their austerity they always had their countenance and speech adorned with joy, gaiety, and courtesy. "Rejoice with them that rejoice" (Rom. 12:15), and with the apostle I tell you, "Again I say, rejoice always, but in the Lord. Let your modesty be known to all men" (Phil. 4:4, 5). To rejoice in the Lord, the reason for your joy must be not only lawful but also suitable. I say this because there are some things that are lawful but not fitting. That your moderation may be known to all, keep free from insolence, which certainly is always reprehensible. To cause one of the party to fall down, soil another's face, tease a third, or harm a feeble-minded person in some way, all these are foolish, insolent jokes and amusements. (p. 178)

Great opportunities to serve God rarely present themselves but little ones are frequent. Whoever will be "faithful over a few things" will be placed "over many" says the Savior (Mt. 25:21). "Do all things in the name of God" (cf. Col. 3:17), and you will do all things well. Provided you know how to fulfill your duties properly, then "whether you eat or drink" (1 Cor. 10:31), whether you sleep or take recreation or turn the spit, you will profit greatly in God's sight by doing all these things because God wishes you to do them. (p. 202)

Let us be firm in our purposes and unswerving in our resolutions. Perseverance will prove whether we have sincerely sacrificed ourselves to God and dedicated ourselves to a devout life. Comets and planets seem to have just about the same light, but comets are merely fiery masses that pass by and after a while disappear, while planets remain perpetually bright. So also hypocrisy and true virtue have a close resemblance in outward appearance but they can be easily distinguished from one another. Hypocrisy cannot last long but is quickly dissipated like rising smoke, whereas true virtue is always firm and constant. It is no little assistance for a sure start in devotion if we first suffer criticism and calumny because of it. In this way we escape the danger of pride and vanity, which are comparable to the Egyptian midwives whom a cruel Pharaoh had ordered to kill the Israelites' male children on the very day of their birth (Ex. 1:12, 16). We are crucified to the world and the world must be crucified to us (Gal. 6:14). The world holds us to be fools; let us hold it to be mad. (p. 224)

Reflect that in this world nothing but virtue and devotion can satisfy your soul. See how beautiful they are. Compare the virtues and their contrary vices. How sweet is patience when compared with revenge! Meekness, compared with anger and vexation! Humility, compared with arrogance and ambition! Liberality, compared with avarice! Charity, compared with envy! Sobriety, compared with dissipation! Virtues have the wonderful quality of delighting our soul with incomparable sweetness and fragrance after we have practiced them, whereas vices leave the soul infinitely weary and distraught. Courage, then! Why do we not strive to gain such delights? (p. 270)

All these exercises must remain embedded in our heart. When we have finished our consideration and meditation we must turn quietly back to our ordinary concerns and associations so that the precious liquor of our resolutions may not be suddenly spilled. It must penetrate throughout every part of the soul but without any mental or bodily effort. (p. 276)

DISCUSSION QUESTIONS

1. When discussing his reasons for teaching and counseling, de Sales says, "How much more willingly will a fatherly heart take charge of a soul in which he finds a desire for holy perfection and carry it in his breast as a mother does her little child without being wearied by so precious a burden! But his must be truly a father's heart" (p. 25). How do you think having a spiritual counselor impacts a seeker's journey? And why do you think that de Sales believes it is so important for the teacher to "truly" have "a father's heart"?

2. De Sales claims that "devotion must be exercised in different ways by the gentleman, the worker, the servant, the prince, the widow, the young girl, and the married woman. Not only is this true, but the practice of devotion must also be adapted to the strength, activities, and duties of each particular person" (p. 32). How does this adaptable view of devotion impact your understanding of society as a whole? How do you view devotion in regards to your own position in society?

3. Among the first considerations de Sales counsels is to reflect on the fact that God created humans to serve and praise him. Why is it important for this lesson to reach individuals who are just beginning a spiritual practice?

4. At the beginning of the Second Part of the Introduction, de Sales discusses the importance of consistent prayer, because it helps one focus the mind on the Lord and on the virtues. Is prayer a part of your daily life? How does it affect your relationship with the world?

5. On page 124, de Sales discusses the importance of becoming humble. Why is humility such an important component of a proper relationship with God?

6. De Sales describes obedience, chastity, and poverty as "the three principal means to attain" charity (p. 142). How do these three qualities coalesce to foster a charitable attitude? Do you think it is important to develop all three in a balanced manner?

7. "To scoff at others is one of the worst states a mind can be in. God detests this vice and in past times inflicted strange punishments on it" (p. 183). Why do you think this attitude is one of the worst? Do you sometimes find yourself slipping into this mode of behaving, and, if so, how does it affect your interactions with others?

Image Books

A Division of Random House LLC
www.ImageCatholicBooks.com

Publishing Books of Catholic Interest Since 1954

Bible Study • Biography/Memoir • Family • Formation
Inspirational • Saints • Reference • Spirituality • Theology